LIGHTNING
BOLT
BOOKS™

The Statue of Liberty

Jill Braithwaite

Lerner Publications Company

Minneapolis

To Lauren and Kendra, two proud and free ladies

Lerner Publications Company
A division of Lerner Publishing Group, Inc.
241 First Avenue North
Minneapolis, MN 55401 U.S.A.

Website address: www.lernerbooks.com

Library of Congress Cataloging-in-Publication Data

Braithwaite, Jill.
    The Statue of Liberty / by Jill Braithwaite.
        p.   cm. — (Lightning bolt books™—Famous places)
    Includes index.
    ISBN 978-0-7613-6020-9 (lib. bdg. : alk. paper)
    1. Statue of Liberty (New York, N.Y.)—Juvenile literature. 2. New York (N.Y.)—Buildings, structures, etc.—Juvenile literature. I. Title.
    F128.64.L6B73 2011
    974.71—dc22   2009041718

Manufactured in the United States of America
1 — BP — 7/15/10

Contents

Standing Proud

Where are these people standing?

They are inside the Statue of Liberty. The Statue of Liberty towers over New York City.

The Statue of Liberty looks across the water.

The Statue of Liberty stands for freedom.

The statue is made of copper. Copper turns green when it sits outside.

The statue is of a proud woman. She wears robes and a crown.

In one hand, she holds a torch. She holds a tablet in the other hand.

8

On the tablet is the date July 4, 1776. That day, the United States of America was born.

Numbers on the tablet are written in Roman numerals. This is a way of writing numbers with letters of the alphabet.

French Friends

The British king once ruled America. Americans fought a war to be free. France helped the United States win the war.

French and American soldiers line up together at the end of the war against the British.

France and the United States became friends. Many French people wanted to give the United States a gift.

U.S. general George Washington shakes hands with the French commander.

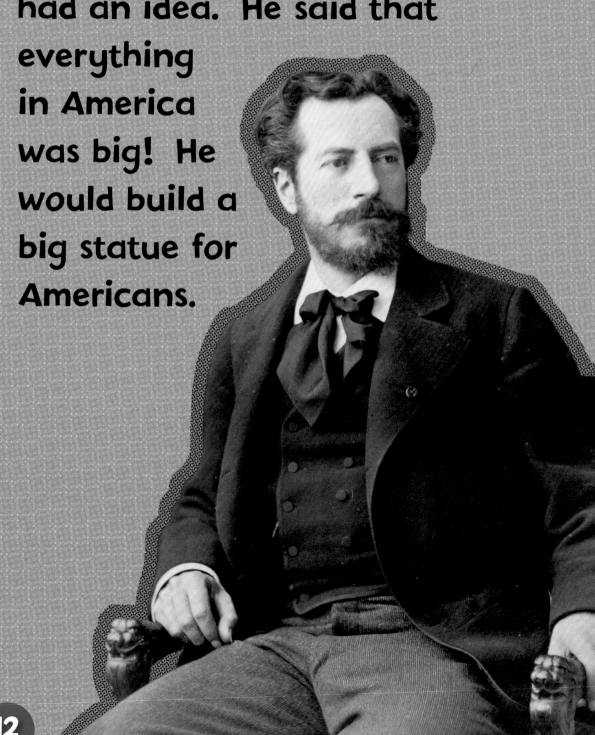

A French artist named Frédéric-Auguste Bartholdi had an idea. He said that everything in America was big! He would build a big statue for Americans.

Building the Statue

Bartholdi found the perfect spot for the statue. It was Bedloe's Island in the harbor of New York City.

Ships sail in New York Harbor. Across the water is Bedloe's Island. It was later renamed Liberty Island.

Workers began building the statue in Paris, France, in 1875.

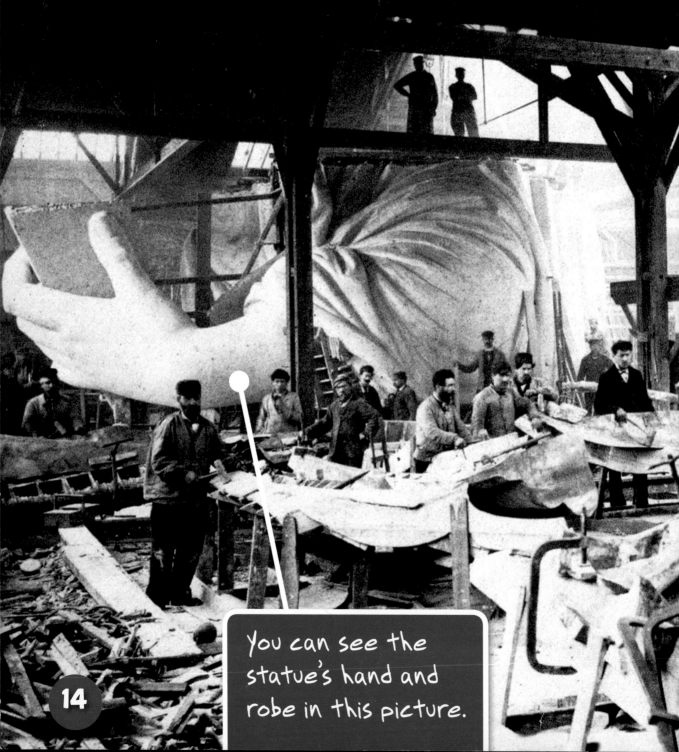

You can see the statue's hand and robe in this picture.

They hammered copper sheets
into the right shapes.

Workers get copper sheets ready for the statue.

Later, workers nailed the copper sheets to a huge iron frame.

Workers stand on wooden platforms as they attach copper sheets to the frame.

Bartholdi and his crew finished the statue in 1884. It was taken apart and sent to the United States.

Crowds in New York came out to greet the ship carrying the Statue of Liberty from France.

There the statue was put together for the second time. It was finally ready in 1886.

Workers put the statue back together.

Americans celebrated on October 28, 1886. Thousands came to see the lady of liberty.

Fireworks explode as Americans celebrate the Statue of Liberty in 1886.

Welcome to America

In the late 1800s, the Statue of Liberty stood for something new.

Many new people, called immigrants, began coming to the United States. The immigrants often arrived on ships in New York Harbor. **The Statue of Liberty stood for their hope for a better life.**

The Statue of Liberty greets immigrants.

By the 1980s, the statue needed fixing up. She got a shiny new torch. Her copper skin was cleaned. Bolts were tightened.

The finishing touches are put on the statue's gold torch.

New Yorkers celebrated the repairs in 1986, on the statue's one-hundredth birthday.

Visiting the Statue

Millions of visitors come to the Statue of Liberty every year.

They take a ferryboat across the harbor.

There's no way to drive to the statue. So visitors travel by boat.

People enjoy looking out
the windows inside the
statue's crown.

Visitors look out
the top of the
statue's crown.

The statue's torch still glows in New York Harbor.

People see its light and think of freedom.

27

New York City Area

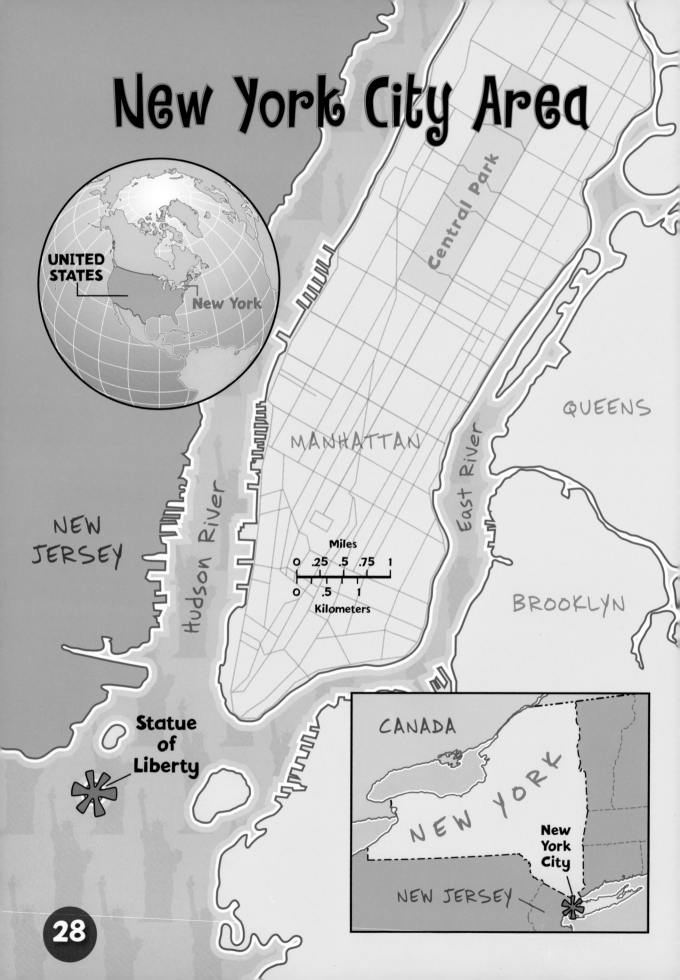

UNITED
STATES

New York

Central Park

MANHATTAN

Hudson River

East River

QUEENS

NEW
JERSEY

Miles
0   .25   .5   .75   1

0   .5   1
Kilometers

BROOKLYN

Statue
of
Liberty

CANADA

NEW YORK

New
York
City

NEW JERSEY

was nothing mean about the appearance of the dwellings; they were miners' dwellings, and it irked Mrs Morel to go there. The back door looked down to the ash-pit, at the end of the back garden. And outside, beyond the rows, which backed inwards, the alley ran between a rather disgusting avenue of ash-pits. In this alley the women gossiped, the children played, and the men not at work sat on their heels, their backs to the ash-pits, smoking.

It was some consolation to Mrs Lawrence that she had an end house, a bit larger with a bit more garden, for which she had to pay sixpence a week more rent. She was respected, but not much liked, and the only person she could really talk to was the congregational minister. But she did not really respect the minister. He was not, in her sense, a success. The sort of man she really admired, and taught her children to look up to, was Henry Saxton who owned the grocery shop next door to the Victoria Street house. He was an uneducated bully and loudmouth, but he was church deacon and Sunday School Superintendent, and, more important than that, he had money enough to allow him to insult his customers, especially the colliers' wives. He was a 'success'.

Phoenix 2 592–3   My mother was, I suppose, superior. She came from town, and belonged to the lower bourgeoisie. She spoke King's English, without an accent, and never in her life could even imitate a sentence of the dialect which my father spoke, and which we children spoke out of doors. She wrote a fine Italian hand, and a clever and amusing letter when she felt like it. And as she grew older she read novels again,

8a Victoria Street, Eastwood, Lawrence's birthplace, as it was in 1930. It is now a museum.

and got terribly impatient with *Diana of the Crossways* and terribly thrilled by *East Lynne*.

But she was a working man's wife, and nothing else, in her shabby little black bonnet and her shrewd, clear, 'different' face.

She stored up resentment against her husband. He loved making and mending things about the house, cobbling, soldering, making fuses for the pit, and singing old ballads about tailors or gipsies. He had 'a certain warm, uncurbed vitality that made a glow in the house, when he was not in an evil temper'.

He would tell the children stories from the pit, about Taffy the horse stealing tobacco from his pocket or a mouse running up his sleeve, stories told with such colour and excitement that the children would remember them long after they had forgotten the Hans Andersen stories their mother told them. He was happiest frying a rasher of bacon or a herring for his breakfast in that hour before dawn when the others were still asleep. But his wife even resented his occasional happiness, and his love for his children, turning them against him. In Ada's words:

Ada 26–7   As we grew older we shut him more and more out of our lives, and instinctively turned more to mother, and he, realizing this, became more and more distasteful in his habits. He was never really intolerable, and if, instead of wanting the impossible from him, we had tried to interest ourselves in the things for which he really cared, we should have been spared many unhappy and sordid scenes.

Arthur John Lawrence. 'He was well set-up, erect, and very smart. He had wavy black hair that shone again, and a vigorous black beard that had never been shaved. His cheeks were ruddy, and his red, moist mouth was noticeable because he laughed so often and so heartily.' (Sons and Lovers)

For years Bert prayed that his father would either be converted to a chapel man or die. It was the best prayer he could think of for his mother. When he was fourteen, and his father, whose leg had been smashed in an accident at the mine, came home at last from the convalescent home, Bert saw for the first time that his mother loved her husband like any girl, and had constantly to fight against her own love for him, vindictively. She half despised her own children because they were also his, and therefore her inferiors. Bert was heard to praise his father for one thing only, his dancing; but whenever he found wild mushrooms he filled his pockets with them for his father's tea, knowing how much he liked them. Bert and his father were both very interested in wild life, and knowledgeable about it, but it was an interest they seldom shared. Sometimes Arthur brought little wild animals home, which usually sulked and pined and refused to live, causing storms of tears. Adolf, a wild rabbit which did thrive, caused even more trouble. There was trouble over the white rats Arthur built a hutch for; and more trouble over Rex, an uncle's puppy which the children kept for a while. Where animals were concerned Mrs Lawrence thought they were all lunatics.

'Getting On'   Bert was delicate, 'a pale-faced, dirty-nosed frail boy'. At Beauvale School he was a good scholar, but was too sensitive to mix well. He was small and sickly and shy and proud. He did not join in the rough and tumble of the play-ground, preferring the company of girls. The Breach boys called him 'mardarse' and chanted after him, 'Dicky Dicky Denches plays with the wenches.'

Bert was six when the Lawrences moved up the hill (and up the social scale) to a new house at 3 (now 8) Walker Street. It commanded a panorama Lawrence never forgot. In 1926 he wrote to Rolf Gardiner:

Lydia Lawrence.

Lawrence's class at Beauvale Boys' School, 1894. Lawrence is on the third row from the back, second from left. Immediately in front of Lawrence is his friend George Henry Neville.

Moore 952   Go to Walker St – and stand in front of the third house – and look across at Crich on the left, Underwood in front – High Park woods and Annesley on the right: I lived in that house from the age of 6 to 18, and I know that view better than any in the world.

Just opposite the house stood an ancient ash tree which became the focus for the children's play, though its moaning scared them on winter nights, and Lawrence was later to use it as an image of the discord within the house. Usually the father's physical blustering was no match for the mother's tongue. 'I'll make you tremble at the sound of my footstep,' he would shout. 'Which boots will you wear?' she replied. 'Never mind which boots I shall wear.' But she had made him ridiculous and taken the wind out of his sails. Young Bert soon learned to use his tongue to defend himself against physically superior boys at school.

Life was by no means gloomy or boring for the Lawrence children. There was always a houseful of youngsters. Though Bert disliked sports, he loved indoor games, was very good at them, invented a great many himself, played wholeheartedly, and cared a great deal that he or his side should win. His favourite game, even as an adult, was charades. Then there were sing-songs. Mother, or Ada in later years, would play the piano, and they would sing all the songs from the *Oxford Song Book*. When mother was out Emily would read to the younger children from *Coral Island* or *Swiss Family Robinson* or *The Gorilla Hunters*.

Bert and his sisters made frequent excursions into the surrounding fields and woods, picking blackberries, collecting coltsfoot for mother's herb beer, searching for holly at Christmas. Bert always seemed to notice things before anyone else, and pointed them out so enthusiastically and knowledgeably that he enhanced everything for others.

Friday and Sunday were days to be feared. On Friday Bert had to collect his father's wages. He suffered the tortures of the damned having to submit himself to the jibes of the cashier, Alfred Brentnall: 'Ho, lad, wheer's your Pa – too drunk to come and collect the pay hissen?' But there was consolation in the evening when mother went out to do the week's shopping, leaving the children with the house to themselves. In her absence they would dress up in her clothes, or try experiments in cookery. Most of all they hated 'the stiff null propriety which used to overcome us, like a sort of deliberate, self-inflicted cramp, on Sundays'; but there were stirring hymns to sing, and Bert's imagination was fired by the Bible, with its golden and glamorous words like 'Galilee' and 'Canaan'.

Christmas was, of course, the climax of the year, when they decorated the house with holly, mistletoe, angels, glass balls and anything that shone, and waited for Christmas morning when each stocking would be filled with toys and books, with a sugar pig and a mince pie on top.

Eastwood was not entirely off the cultural map. Teddy Rayner's travelling theatre company (known as 'The Blood Tub'), which performed in a tent, was very popular there, with its repertory of classic Victorian melodramas or even Shakespeare:

The Breach, with Brinsley colliery beyond, from the junction of Walker Street and Lynn Croft. The Lawrence house was at the lefthand end of the righthand block.

When I was a child I went to the twopenny travelling theatre to see *Hamlet*. The
Ghost had on a helmet and a breastplate. I sat in pale transport.
  ''Amblet, 'Amblet, I *am* thy father's ghost.'
Then came a voice from the dark, silent audience, like a cynical knife to my fond
soul:
  'Why tha arena, I can tell thy voice.'

Eastwood had its fair share of local 'characters' to gossip about. The Barber family,
of Barber, Walker and Co., the local coal-owners, experienced two tragedies in
Lawrence's childhood. Thomas Barber's wife had died when she was twenty-five. In
1890 his eldest son, Thomas Philip, accidentally shot and killed his younger brother.
Two years later, during the water party at Moorgreen Reservoir (held on Whit
Monday and August Bank Holiday Monday every year) his daughter Cecilia fell from
a steam launch and was drowned. She was seven. The reservoir was drained all night.
Next morning her body was found, with her arms locked round the neck of young Dr
Bingham who had gone in after her. Six-year-old Bert may well have been there. Over
twenty years later he was to describe it all vividly in *Women in Love*. Within a year of
that accident Thomas Barber himself had died, at the age of fifty. His son Thomas
Philip took over, mechanized the pits, and instituted a more efficient and less humane
regime.

Major Thomas Philip Barber, the original model for Gerald in Women in Love.

Lamb Close House, home of the Barber family; Highclose in The White Peacock; *Shortlands in* Women in Love.

Another local character was George Henry Cullen, a man with a talent for grandiose doomed enterprises – such as London House (Manchester House in *The Lost Girl*) where he tried to sell high fashions indeed more suitable for a London clientèle, Throttle Ha'penny pit with its coal not fit to burn, a cinema at Langley Mill, and many other such speculations.

Lawrence's first childhood sweetheart was probably Mabel Thurlby, though he unchivalrously hid when she was bullied by other boys, and warned her early that she could entertain no hopes:

Nehls 1, 29   When I grow up, I will write poetry like Miss Matthews reads to us. I will marry a pretty lady, not like you. She will have blue ribbon in her hair, not wool. I will earn a lot of money and buy my mother a pretty bonnet, and she will have a garden full of flowers. 'What will you buy your father?' Mabel asked. Bert replied, 'I only love my mother.'

Nehls 1, 31   Mabel has recorded other stories about the young Lawrence:
On Boxing Day every year, the miners' children from many miles around were invited to Lamb Close House, the home of the colliery owner, Mr Barber, and were given one new penny and one large orange each. On one occasion Bertie dared not to go forward, so I took my presents, gave them to him, and then went back for his. As we walked home and crossed the brook by the alder trees, we polished our new coins on our sleeves, and changed our minds so often as to how we would spend them. Bertie decided he would give his to his mother, and with mine we would buy sweets and divide them.

Mabel's father had lost an arm in a pit accident, and become keeper of the Moorgreen crossing, near Lamb Close House. One day Mabel and Bert were waiting for a train to pass when Thomas Philip Barber rode up on horseback and demanded to be let through. 'Are you going to make that horse's mouth bleed?' said Mr Thurlby, and refused to open the gates. Lawrence used this incident in *Women in Love*.

In the summer of 1897 the Lawrences and the Thurlbys were packed into a carrier's cart in their Sunday best to be taken to Nottingham to have their photographs taken. The fathers went ahead on foot so that they could call for drinks. Bert was eleven. That same summer he wrote a little poem for Mabel:

We sit in a lovely meadow
My sweetheart and me
And we are oh so happy
Mid the flowers, birds, and the bees.

Nehls 2, 32

Perhaps that was not too unlike what Miss Matthews read to them.

When he was twelve Bert Lawrence became the first boy from his school to win one of the recently instituted County Council Scholarships, worth £12 a year and a place at Nottingham High School. The money hardly covered the expenses, and Lawrence's health suffered from the daily travelling – two hours each way. But for the next three years he received an excellent education there. Most of the boys were middle-class, sons of lace manufacturers and shop-keepers. They were respectful, even kindly, to the few 'common' scholarship boys, but the two groups never truly mixed. In his first term Lawrence came second in his form, top in French, German and Arithmetic, second in English, third in Algebra, fourth in Writing, eleventh in Scripture, twelfth in Drawing, and fifty-fourth (out of seventy-eight) in Science. His diligence and conduct were 'very good'. At Easter 1900 he was top of his form, and later that year won a Mathematics prize. His performance fell away in his last year, partly through ill-health, partly through his inability to compete, in that form, with boys most of whom were older than himself. He left school in July 1901.

Left to right, front row: Lettice Ada (1887–1948), Lydia (1851–1910), David Herbert (1885–1930), Arthur John (1846–1924); back row: Emily Una 'Pamela' (1882–1962), George Arthur (1876–1967), William Ernest (1878–1901).

William Ernest Lawrence. 'He was so fiery that only his good-nature and his size protected him. All the things that men do – the decent things – William did. He could run like the wind. . . . Also he danced – this in spite of his mother. All the life that Bestwood offered he enjoyed, from the sixpenny hops down Church Street, to sports and billiards.' (Sons and Lovers)

2 His Mother's Darling

Bert had a most friendly relationship with his older brother Ernest, from whom, at the age of twelve, he received a letter beginning:

My Dear William Whytteun,
    You whitenobbed rascal. Has thy most noble brother lived all these weary years, only at the end to be called 'Red Nob'. For this my punishment for thee shall be swift and sure, therefore know that when I land home I shall carry in a hand bag a beautiful mahogany coffin, and our people will all indulge in a free ride to the cemetery. But I have a better revenge. Know that when I come to visit my distant home though thou mayest question and cross-question me all the time I am there, yet will I not tell thee of one animal at the Zoo. No! I have not been and if I went a million times, my visits should be as a sealed book.

Ernest was his mother's pride and joy, popular, intelligent, humorous, handsome, athletic; he would never climb a fence or open a gate if he could jump it. His promising career in a London shipping office was ended when, at twenty-three, he made a flying visit home for Goose Fair while ill with erysipelas, contracted pneumonia on his return to London, and died a few hours after his mother reached his bedside. He had been weakened by overwork, but perhaps a factor was also the split in him caused by his mother's disapproval of his fiancée, whom she rightly saw to be a frivolous good-time girl. His mother had urged him on with that typical non-conformist confusion of worldly success with righteousness which expresses itself in such phrases as 'making the most of yourself' and 'leaving your mark in the world'. He over-extended himself. He was his mother's unwitting sacrifice to (in Ruskin's words) 'the great Goddess of "Getting-on" '.

Lawrence had just left school. On his last visit home Ernest had written for him an application for a job as junior clerk at Haywood's surgical goods manufacturers in Nottingham. Lawrence got the job at 13s. a week. He quickly settled down and enjoyed the comradeship of the work. But Haywood's had no proper ventilation. The job was twelve hours most days, six days a week, with all that travelling. After three months, Lawrence also became desperately ill with pneumonia. Having nursed him through the crisis, his mother transferred to him all the intense love and all the ambitions she had had for Ernest. Thus, at sixteen, at that very moment in his life when he left school, started work, met his first serious girlfriend, and should have

Goose Fair, Nottingham, October 1900.

been given his first push towards independence by his mother, she tightened her emotional grip on him almost to strangulation. On him alone rested the responsibility for making up to her for the failure of her marriage and for all her suffering.

Young Bert was not only tied to his mother's apron strings, he would frequently wear the apron, making bread or potato cakes. He would help his mother with such jobs as blackleading or scrubbing the floor, establishing early an aptitude for and enjoyment of traditionally feminine tasks which was to last a lifetime. He was loath to begin shaving, because that would be to admit that his boyhood was over, and he did not feel ready to assume the independence of a young man.

The Lawrence children went to the 'Congo' (the Congregational Chapel) three times every Sunday, to morning and evening services and to Sunday School. One Sunday evening in 1898 Mrs Lawrence struck up a friendship with Mrs Chambers, whose husband had recently acquired Haggs Farm, a couple of miles north of Eastwood. She invited Mrs Lawrence to visit her there, but apparently two or three years elapsed before the visit was actually made. Lawrence, then fifteen and dressed in the Eton coat and collar of Nottingham High School boys, accompanied his mother and met the

J. H. Haywood's factory. 'The girls were ordinary working girls. Yet not one of them ever flicked the least spot of dirt on the boy. Paul liked them all very much, they were all fond of him. It came to be that, when he took down the orders in the morning, he sat on one of the high stools and gossiped for a quarter of an hour.' (Paul Morel)

Haggs Farm. 'In front, along the edge of the wood, was a cluster of low red farm buildings. Some cows stood in the shade. The farm and buildings, three sides of a quadrangle, embraced the sunshine towards the wood. It was very still.' (Sons and Lovers)

Chambers children. Alan was then eighteen, May, seventeen, Jessie, fourteen, Hubert, thirteen, Bernard, eleven, Mollie, six, and David, three.

For years Lawrence visited the Haggs at least once a week. The whole family looked forward to these visits with eager anticipation; they knew there would be never a dull moment. When he recovered his health, Lawrence would work all day in the hayfields. 'Work goes like fun when Bert's there,' said Mr Chambers. Jessie added:

Jessie 31   It was true; in those early days Lawrence seemed so happy that merely to be alive and walking about was an adventure, and his gift for creating an atmosphere of good fellowship made work a joy. One could not help being affected by his vitality and charm.

He would teach them part songs from tonic sol fa while they were milking. In the evening, round the parlour fire, he would organize readings (sometimes of whole plays) and discussions of Maupassant, Ibsen, Tolstoy (he suffered deeply with Anna Karenina), Darwin and Schopenhauer. The questioning of all existing moral and religious values sometimes went too far for Mrs Chambers, who would retire early rather than be exposed to it. Nevertheless she said, 'I should like to be next to Bert in heaven.'

What drew Lawrence to be such a frequent visitor to the Haggs was, first, the place, which was so different from the squalor of Eastwood, with an abundance of wildlife, and many jobs to help with, which for him were like play; and second, the family which accepted him so cheerfully and made no demands on him, his beloved 'Haggites'.

If he went to see any one person, it was certainly not Jessie, whose painful shyness kept her in the background, but her elder sister May, who had got to know Bert years earlier, when she delivered milk at the Lawrences' every day. Lawrence insisted on helping her with her homework so that he could then drag her off to look for rare flowers or birds' nests. Lawrence was certainly attracted by May, who was just the opposite of Jessie, 'fearless, gay and tempestuous', as her brother David called her. Lawrence was later jealous of her fiancé Will Holbrook, and once smashed two effigies that Will, a stone mason, had made for May. The family had to avoid having Lawrence and Will Holbrook at the house together. But May was two years older than Lawrence, and never succumbed to his spell as Jessie did. There was some rivalry between the sisters for Lawrence's attention before Will came along. As for the rest of the family, it was the eldest son Alan with whom Lawrence became particularly friendly and spent most of his time. Jessie could not understand what her brother had to offer Lawrence, but with Alan he could work or talk or sing without the emotional pressure continually exerted by Jessie.

Jessie's own account in *A Personal Record*, is not wholly reliable because of its excessively 'personal' slant. She cannot help seeing herself, from the beginning, at the centre, the betrayed heroine of a great romantic melodrama. They undoubtedly had a close and rewarding relationship for a while, though there were aspects of Jessie which grated on Lawrence from the start – her over-intensity and

The Chambers family in 1906. Left to right: May, Mollie, Alan, Edmund, Jessie, David, Hubert, Sarah Ann, and Bernard. In The White Peacock, *Alan is the model for George, and Jessie for Emily. In* Sons and Lovers, *Jessie is Miriam, May Agatha, Alan Edgar and Hubert Maurice.*

humourlessness, her inability to relax and be ordinary. They shared many discoveries, in nature and in literature, but Jessie was too much the submissive, adoring acolyte for that to form the basis for a mature and lasting partnership. *A Personal Record* is of great value for its account of the voracious reading of the pair in their most formative years, and the eagerness with which they approached learning and shared their doubts and enthusiasms, though in reality the sharing was less exclusive than Jessie suggests, taking in the whole family and many of Lawrence's other friends.

From 1902 to 1906 Lawrence taught as a pupil-teacher at the British School next to the Congregational Chapel in Albert Street, Eastwood, at half-a-crown a week for the first year. It was an exhausting daily battle to impose some sort of discipline on the unruly colliers' lads. In 1903 a new system of teacher-training came into operation whereby Lawrence spent half his time at a pupil-teacher centre at Ilkeston. Apparently conditions there were little better than at Eastwood, but at least Lawrence had the pleasure of travelling to and from Ilkeston with a lively group of Eastwood pupil-teachers who formed the nucleus of the 'Pagans'. The Pagans included, apart from Lawrence and his sisters, three other teachers from Albert Street school; Richard Pogmore, Kitty Holderness (whose father was headmaster of that school) and Alice Hall (whose husband later threatened a lawsuit over her portrayal as Alice Gall in *The White Peacock*; she is also Beatrice Wyld in both *A Collier's Friday Night* and *Sons and Lovers*); other Pagans were Jessie and Alan Chambers, George Henry 'Diddler' Neville (Lawrence's particular friend), several of the Lawrences' neighbours after their move to 97 Lynn Croft in late 1904 or early 1905 (the five Cooper girls from next door, especially Gertrude 'Grit' and Frances 'Franky', four of whom died in their twenties of consumption, and whose father was the original of Aaron Sisson in *Aaron's Rod*), Polly Goddard, Agatha Kirk (who taught with Ada),

Left: On 25 March 1905 Lawrence's photograph appeared in The Teacher *together with his answers to a questionnaire – his first appearance in print.*

Right: Lawrence was in great demand for illustrations in albums. This one is dated 1 July 1905.

her future husband Steve Bircumshaw and his sister Blanche (Agatha and Steve appear as Agatha Sharp and her 'best boy' Freddy in *Mr Noon*), Emmie and Mabel Limb, Leonard Watts, Fred Stevenson, and Louie and Ethel Burrows. There was always some rivalry between Louie and Jessie over Lawrence, but it was not until the end of 1910 that Louie displaced Jessie as his fiancée.

97 Lynn Croft, just round the corner and up the hill from Walker Street, was the best of the Lawrence family homes, with bay windows at the front and a large garden at the back overlooking fields. There was an attic where Bert and his friends could have parties, dances, charades and little plays. But the principal activity of the Pagans seems to have been walking – to Annesley, to Watnall Woods, or more ambitious walks to Matlock or to Wingfield and Crich, returning by train. The girls all felt safe with Bert, since he invariably behaved like a brother towards them all. His was a ready shoulder to cry on, for he was very compassionate, and not only towards people – he was sickened by having to dissect a frog at school.

Life must have been very full for Lawrence at this time. Before he went to college in 1906 he had read several Shakespeare and Ibsen plays, and several of the novels of Fielding, Dickens, George Eliot, Fenimore Cooper, Flaubert, Stevenson, Rider Haggard and J. M. Barrie; he had also read other fiction by Reade, Blackmore, Anthony Hope, Hugo, Maupassant, Tolstoy, Borrow, Emily Brontë, Carroll, Daudet, Mrs Gaskell, Gissing, Pierre Loti, Mark Rutherford, Wilde and many others; poems by Longfellow, Blake, Fitzgerald, Tennyson, Petrarch, Shelley and, of course, everything in Palgrave's *Golden Treasury*; essays by Bacon, Emerson, Lamb, Schopenhauer and Carlyle; and Thoreau's *Walden* and Darwin's *Voyage of the Beagle*.

He was fond of painting floral designs on plaques and fire-screens and copying reproductions from magazines: for several years these served as birthday and wedding presents. His attempt to learn the piano lasted only half an hour – the 'beastly scales' exasperated him. But he sang duets with Ada, and bought her songbooks and music by Chopin, Tchaikovsky and Brahms.

In December 1904 Lawrence sat for the King's Scholarship and was placed in the First Division of the First Class with thirty-six other men and nineteen women. In June 1905 he matriculated, and so qualified himself to study at Nottingham University College either for a London external degree or for a teacher's certificate. But the Lawrences could not raise the £20 needed for advance fees (the scholarship paid the rest) and Bert had to continue for another year at Albert Street School to save it. He entered college in September 1906 to read for an Arts degree.

It was about this time that Lawrence began to write. The earliest surviving poems are 'Campions' and 'Guelder Roses'. Both express metaphorically what 'Virgin Youth' expresses quite overtly – the torment of baffled desire. The guelder rose is clearly Jessie,

> . . . too chaste and pure
> Ever to suffer love's wild attack.

Lawrence on his twenty-first birthday, 11 September 1906. ' "Ah, the pity! I shall never be as nice as I was at twenty-one, shall I ?" He glanced at his photo on the mantlepiece . . . which had been called the portrait of an intellectual prig, but which was really that of a sensitive, alert, exquisite boy.' ('A Modern Lover')

*Jessie Chambers in 1906. 'The girl was romantic in her soul. She herself was something of a princess turned into a swine-girl in her own imagination. She could not be a princess by wealth or standing. So she was mad to have learning whereon to pride herself. Her beauty – that of a shy, wild, quiveringly sensitive thing – seemed nothing to her.' (*Sons and Lovers)*

(During a reading of *Hedda Gabler* at the Haggs, Jessie could not bring herself to utter the words 'keep mistresses'.)

In 1928 Lawrence wrote of these poems:

Poems 27   The first poems I ever wrote, if poems they were, was when I was nineteen: now twenty-three years ago. I remember perfectly the Sunday afternoon when I perpetrated those first two pieces: 'To Guelder-Roses' and 'To Campions'; in spring-time, of course, and, as I say, in my twentieth year. Any young lady might have written them and been pleased with them; as I was pleased with them. But it was after that, when I was twenty, that my real demon would now and then get hold of me and shake more real poems out of me, making me uneasy.

However the dead hand of Georgian convention was stifling the voice of the demon, as his mother stifled it, and college stifled it.

The poems and the first scraps of Lawrence's first novel *Laetitia* (later to become *The White Peacock*) had to be written furtively, when he was at home, into college exercise books so that he would seem to be working. His father hated books and study. His mother thoroughly approved of study, which was part of the process of 'getting on', but would have thought imaginative writing a waste of valuable time. Great sacrifices had been made to send Lawrence to college in order to pass examinations. The work was shown only to Jessie, who thought everything wonderful. At first Lawrence was wholly dependent on her encouragement, but he soon came to find it too uncritical to be of real value.

Eventually Mrs Lawrence discovered what was in the exercise books. She read the passage in the novel where the bride runs up the church path, and said, in a mocking tone, 'But my boy, how do you *know* it was like that?' It was presumptuous of him to claim to know things he had not learned at school. Later she said, with disgust, 'To think a son of mine should have written such a story.'

The conflict that developed between Lawrence and Jessie was superficially sexual. Both were 'fiercely virgin'. Lawrence strove to break down this resistance to life and the body in both of them, but Jessie unwittingly conspired with the whole ethos of that place and time to make him feel ashamed of desire. It was partly the influence of

Nehls 3, 533   her mother, who, in the words of David Chambers, 'had absorbed with passionate intensity the puritan message of nineteenth-century nonconformity' and 'used to shudder when the subject of sex was mentioned'.

Yet we cannot attribute the problems of Bert Lawrence and Jessie Chambers solely to a puritanical culture and ultra-puritanical mothers. Jessie was considered odd even within her own family. And the same culture and mothers did not stop their brothers and sisters participating in the usual adolescent experiments, such as 'spooning' in shop doorways after chapel – Lawrence's brother Ernest had been famous for it. Nor did it always stop at spooning. Lawrence's early works are full of illegitimate babies, and this was sociologically accurate. His best friend George Neville was to father two of them.

Bert and Jessie were more sensitive and fastidious than most, so the split went deeper. But Bert's backwardness suggests something more than this:

Letters 1, 99   I have kissed dozens of girls – on the cheek – never on the mouth – I could not.

Perhaps Lawrence was less sure than other young men of his age just what he wanted from girls, and what he wanted from other young men. In *The White Peacock* Cyril, the Lawrence figure, says that his friendship with George Saxton (Alan Chambers) was 'more perfect than any love I have known since, either for man or woman'. In the rejected opening chapter to *Women in Love*, the Lawrence figure, Rupert Birkin, is more explicit:

Phoenix 2 103–4   All the time, he recognized that, although he was always drawn to women, feeling more at home with a woman than with a man, yet it was for men that he felt the hot, flushing, roused attraction which a man is supposed to feel for the other sex. Although nearly all his living interchange went on with one woman or another, although he was always terribly intimate with at least one woman, and practically never intimate with a man, yet the male physique had a fascination for him, and for the female physique he felt only a fondness, a sort of sacred love, as for a sister.

Lawrence felt that it was Jessie, not his mother, who was making him abnormal. In January 1908 he wrote to her:

Letters I, 43   Look, you are a nun, I give you what I would give a holy nun. So you must let me marry a woman I can kiss and embrace and make the mother of my children.

It was difficult to admit defeat, partly because they had shared so much of real value, but a marriage would have been disastrous. Years later Lawrence said:

Nehls 1, 71   It would have been a fatal step. I should have had too easy a life, nearly everything my own way, and my genius would have been destroyed.

Jessie 186   Though Lawrence came to blame his mother – 'They tore me from you. It was the slaughter of the foetus in the womb' – and she was certainly motivated by extreme possessiveness, she may also have sensed the wrongness of Jessie and Lawrence for each other. He needed a woman not only free from that puritanical inheritance, but strong enough to shake him out of his own narcissistic puritanism and priggishness.

It is easy to condemn the chapel for the predicament of many young people of whom Lawrence and Jessie were representative. But the chapel influence was by no means wholly negative. Lawrence's formal education had behind it that strong tradition of self-education, open serious discussion, wide reading (thanks to the Mechanics' Institute library) and free-thinking that is associated – in a strange, uneasy alliance – both with Congregational/Unitarian nonconformity and with a largely atheistic socialism of which Willie Hopkin was the shining local example – councillor and magistrate, host to many of the great left-wing figures of the day and to weekly meetings of Eastwood 'progressives', shaper of local opinion for many years in his weekly column in the *Eastwood and Kimberley Advertiser*, and vocal participant in the meetings of the Literary Society. Lawrence later gave us two friendly portraits of him, as Willie Houghton in *Touch and Go* and as Lewis Goddard in *Mr Noon*.

The Congregational Chapel provided not only stimulating sermons but also a social meeting place and an active Literary Society, founded by the minister, Robert Reid, in 1899, which provided visiting lecturers (about half of them nonconformist minsters) on a wide range of literary, philosophical and scientific topics, but very rarely on theological topics, papers read by members, debates and socials. At some of the early meetings there were audiences of over two hundred for lectures or papers on such subjects as Burns, Thomas Hood, Browning, Early English Drama, Tennyson and Longfellow. Relative to the paucity of the rest of Eastwood's cultural life, the chapel was an oasis, as Lawrence was to testify in *The Lost Girl*:

> The Congregational Chapel provided Alvina with a whole outer life, lacking which she would have been poor indeed.

The Congregational background helped to foster in Lawrence some of his most 'Lawrentian' qualities – independence ('Dare to be a Daniel. Dare to stand alone'), earnestness, whole-heartedness, enthusiasm, a sense of deep responsibility both for oneself and for others, and that prophetic, crusading, evangelical, hortatory, not to say self-righteous spirit which sallies out and seeks its adversary, though in later life adversary number one was to be the puritan to whom all things are impure (a relatively uncommon type at the Congregational/Unitarian end of the nonconformist spectrum). As an adolescent Lawrence had alread heard the jibe 'Here comes Jehovah Junior!' Though he thought at one stage that he might enter the ministry, Lawrence soon came to reject the negative morality his mother had mediated to him:

Lawrence's year at Nottingham University College, probably 1907. Lawrence is at the righthand end of the next-to-back row. Three rows in front of him, arms folded, is Ernest Weekley. Bottom righthand corner is Louie Burrows.

Jessie 856   The chapel system of morality is all based upon 'Thou shalt not'. We want one based upon 'Thou shalt'.

In 1907 Lawrence experienced a crisis of faith and confided in Robert Reid that his reading of Darwin, Herbert Spencer, Renan, J. M. Robertson, Blatchford, and Vivian in his *Churches and Modern Thought*, had 'seriously modified' his religious beliefs. He asked Reid to tell him the 'precise position of the Church of today' on such matters as evolution, the origin of sin, heaven and hell. He was worried also by the problem of suffering, and could no longer believe in 'a personal, human God'. He revealed to Reid his belief that men are born twice, the second time on entering manhood:

Letters I, 40   Then they are born to humanity, to a consciousness of all the laughing, and the never-ceasing murmur of pain and sorrow that comes from the terrible multitudes of brothers. Then, it appears to me, a man gradually formulates his religion, be it what it may. A man has no religion who has not slowly and painfully gathered one together, adding to it, shaping it; and one's religion is never complete and final, it seems, but must always be undergoing modification. So I contend that true Socialism is religion; that honest, fervent politics are religion; that whatever a man will labour for earnestly and in some measure unselfishly is religion.

Lawrence was soon disillusioned by college, with its atmosphere of repression. His English mistress made him write his first essay again:

Jessie 79   I know it isn't an ordinary essay; it wasn't meant to be; and I thought she'd have the wit to perceive it. But I'll give her the kid's stuff she evidently wants.

Jessie 76   The only member of staff he admired ('he really *is* a gentleman') was Ernest Weekley, head of the Department of Modern Languages.
    By the end of his first year, Lawrence had completed the first draft of *Laetitia*. At that point, to his mother's chagrin, he transferred to the 'normal' (that is non-degree) course, which would be less demanding, so that he could read novels during lectures and work on *Laetitia* in his own time. He rewrote it many times, hewing it out, he claimed, with infinitely more labour than his father hewed out coal.
    In the Autumn of 1907 the *Nottinghamshire Guardian* announced a Christmas literary competition, with three prizes of £3 for the best stories on three themes: 'An enjoyable Christmas', 'An amusing Christmas', or 'Some historic building'. Lawrence was so determined to win that he decided to cheat by persuading Jessie and Louie Burrows (who was now at college with him) to submit stories for him so that he could enter all three categories. The stories were 'A Prelude' (Jessie), 'The White Stocking' (Louie) and 'Legend' (Lawrence). 'The White Stocking' is an excellent story, and 'Legend' (collected in *The Prussian Officer* as 'A Fragment of Stained Glass') is interesting. 'Prelude' is a sentimental confection probably written for the occasion; it won its class and was published in the *Guardian* on 7 December over Jessie's name.
    Lawrence was awarded his teacher's certificate in June 1908, with distinctions in Maths, History and Geography, French, and Botany, and began looking for a job. He refused to consider anything under £90 a year. In desperation he even wrote after a

N.U.C. 1908.

'College gave me nothing, even nothing to do – I had a damnable time there, bitten so deep with disappointment that I have lost forever any sincere boyish reverence for men in position.'

job in Egypt. In October he was offered a post at Davidson Road School, Croydon, at £95 a year.

That summer was a long farewell to the country of his heart for a young man who felt himself condemned to exile. He spent much of it at the Haggs, or harvesting with the Chamber boys in the fields below Greasley Church. Lawrence knew it was a critical time for him:

I had a devil of a time, getting a bit weaned from my mother, at the age of 22.

Belatedly, he strove to enter his manhood. He became very self-conscious about his body, no longer admiring its slimness. In an attempt to become more manly, he worked hard at his dumb-bells when he was not exhausted with harvesting, and cultivated an image of himself as sweating in an open-neck shirt, gruff-voiced and horny-handed.

Still virgin, his emotions at this time were like dry tinder. On 15 June he saw Sarah Bernhardt (then aged sixty-four) play *La Dame aux Camélias* in Nottingham. The performance disturbed him so much that he battered at the doors to be let out. He warned Blanche Jennings not to go to see Bernhardt 'unless you are very sound':

Letters I, 59 She represents the primeval passions of woman, and she is fascinating to an extraordinary degree. I could love such a woman myself, love her to madness; all for the pure, wild passion of it. . . . When I think of her now I can still feel the weight hanging in my chest as it hung there for days after I saw her. Her winsome, sweet, playful ways; her sad, plaintive little murmurs; her terrible panther cries; and then the awful, inarticulate sounds, the little sobs that fairly sear one, and the despair and death; it is too much in one evening.

Lawrence knew that after his departure to London, nothing would ever be the same again. After saying goodbye to the Chambers family, he stopped at the gate and looked back.

Jessie 150 'La dernière fois,' he said. Jessie burst into tears. 'I'm so sorry,' he said, 'but it can't be helped, it can't be helped.'

3 Stranger in a Strange Land

Lawrence's first letter to Jessie from Croydon was 'like a howl of terror'. To Blanche Jennings he wrote:

Letters I, 85   Think of a quivering greyhound set to mind a herd of pigs and you see me teaching.

After a month, the struggle was obviously taking its toll – he wrote to Louie:

Letters I, 93   It is the cruellest and most humiliating sport, this of teaching and trying to tame some fifty or sixty malicious young human animals. I have some days of despair myself – this has been one. We are not allowed to punish, you know, unless we send to the boss' desk for the regulation cane, and enter up full particulars of the punishment in the cane-book. The boss is nice, but very flabby; the kids are rough and insolent as the devil. I had rather endure anything than this continual, petty, debasing struggle. Shortly I shall be good for very little myself.

A week later he affirmed his faith in 'a good stinging cane':

Letters I, 94   I am making things hum this week: you can guess what things.

By February he had settled as much as he was ever to settle at Croydon:

Letters I, 117   School is really very pleasant here. I have tamed my wild beasts – I have conquered
my turbulent subjects, and can teach in ease and comfort. But still I long for the
country and for my own folks.

His headmaster, P. F. T. Smith, has testified to the quality of his school work, and the
quantity:

Nehls 1, 86   He shirked none of the drudgery of the details which hamper the routine of a
teacher's life. He was interested in Art, English and Biology. I kept for some years
his note book recording a year's work in biology. The water colour drawings and
details of experimental exercises were models of correctness and clarity. . . .
    Lawrence hated the slightest interference with his class work. On one occasion I
followed a Ministerial Inspector into his room. The intrusion was unexpected and
resented. A curious wailing of distressed voices issued from a far corner. The
sounds were muffled by a large covering blackboard. The words of a familiar song
arose from the depths:

> Full fathom five thy father lies;
> Of his bones are coral made.

The class was reading *The Tempest*. The presentation expressed the usual
thoroughness of Lawrence's attitude to the exercise in progress. It must not be
spoiled by even official comment. Lawrence rushed with outstretched hands to the
astounded visitor: 'Hush! Hush! Don't you hear? The sea chorus from *The
Tempest*.'

In those days of desk-bound chalk and talk, such methods were revolutionary. The
experts at the Art Department at Kensington highly approved the work of his boys.
Enthusiasm for the weekly composition soared when, with Lawrence's help, several
boys had articles published in small magazines and were actually paid for them. He
Nehls 1, 87   put in extra work on school plays and in the school library – 'Let them read any
rubbish they like as long as they read at all. They will very soon discard the bad'.
    Throughout his time at Croydon Lawrence lodged with John Jones, the school
attendance officer, and his wife. 12 Colworth Road was a substantial semi-detached
house in an aspiring middle-class part of Croydon, a house which would have been
the answer to Mrs Lawrence's dreams. There Lawrence began to cultivate a new,
genteel, image of himself. He found the streets he walked through every day 'sordid'
and 'mean'. He was very conscious of the class differences in his boys, most of whom
Phoenix 2 24–5   were 'coarsely dressed'. He preferred the boys 'from a fairly well-to-do Home for the
children of actors'; they were 'a pleasure even to look at', 'polite and obedient', 'all of
them more or less gentlemanly'.
Letters I, 94   Lawrence amused himself painting, playing chess with Mr Jones, and 'larking

with Hilda Mary, our eight month, jolly baby'. He was reading as keenly as ever – Thackeray, Meredith, Hardy, George Moore, Wells, Bennett, Galsworthy, Conrad and Forster, Stendhal, Balzac, Zola, Verlaine, Baudelaire, Tolstoy, Dostoevsky, Turgenev, Gorky, Chekhov, Ibsen, Nietzsche . . . He was also, of course, writing – poems about London, school, Hilda Mary . . . and 'that old work of mine', *Laetitia*. On 20 January 1909 he wrote to Blanche Jennings:

Letters I, 106   Since coming back I have set down to write in earnest – now verses – now *Laetitia*: I am astonished to find how maudlin is the latter. I needed to come out here to toughen me off a bit; I am a fearful, sickly sentimentalist.

Blanche Jennings was four years older than Lawrence. She lived in Liverpool, but Lawrence had met her at the home of Alice Dax, with whom she shared an interest in socialism and women's rights, in Eastwood. He adopted her as an emancipated elder sister, to whom, through 1908 and 1909, he poured out his thoughts and feelings in many long letters, embarrassingly callow and self-conscious effusions, flaunting his flirtations, and simultaneously defending and castigating the sloppiness of *Laetitia* in pirouetting prose.

During the summer of 1909 Lawrence and Louie Burrows were working together on short stories, one of which, 'Goose Fair', they had sent to an agency, with no success. The previous year *The English Review* had had 'a glorious rebirth under Ford Madox Hueffer,' encouraging what Lawrence called 'the new young school of realism'. Jessie suggested that Lawrence should submit some of his own work; he finally agreed to let her send some poems. In June 1909 she sent 'Discipline', 'Dreams Old and Nascent', 'Baby Movements' and 'A Still Afternoon'. The reply came from Hueffer in August:

Jessie 158   If you would get him to come and see me some time when he is in London perhaps something might be done.

Lawrence took the letter to show his mother, and Jessie never saw it again. When he returned to Croydon, Lawrence went to see Hueffer, and wrote to Jessie:

Letters I, 138   He is fairish, fat, about forty, and the kindest man on earth.

Hueffer was indeed kind to Lawrence. He launched him in *The English Review*, found him a publisher for *The White Peacock*, and introduced him to the London literary scene. Very soon Lawrence had met Ernest Rhys, editor of the Everyman's Library,

Letters I, 144   H. G. Wells ('He is a funny little chap: his conversation is a continual squirting of thin little jets of weak acid: amusing, but not expansive. There is no glow about

Letters I, 145   him'), Ezra Pound ('He is 24, like me, – but his god is beauty, mine, life. He is jolly nice – a good bit of a genius, and with not the least self consciousness') and W. B. Yeats.

The Rhymers' Club, which had in its heyday met at the Cheshire Cheese, still met, informally, at Ernest Rhys's home. Hueffer took Lawrence to a meeting where he read (interminably) from his love poems and dialect poems. Other readers included Yeats and Pound, who was so impressed by Lawrence's dialect poems that he proposed him for the Polingnac Prize on the strength of them. It was here that Lawrence heard

*Ford Madox Hueffer in 1909. 'He is a really fine man, in that he is generous, so understanding,
and in that he keeps the doors of his soul open.'*

Florence Farr intoning Yeats to the psaltery. His imitation of her 'ping-wanging'
became his favourite party-piece for the rest of his life.

Lawrence's poems took up the first six pages of the handsome blue volume of *The
English Review* for November 1909. That same month Jessie spent a weekend in
London with Lawrence and met Hueffer, Violet Hunt and Pound. Lawrence also
introduced her to his new girlfriend, Agnes Holt, whom he had almost made up his
mind to marry (though he wrote of her to his confidante, Blanche Jennings, 'I can't

Letters I, 141 help it: the game begins, and I play it, and the girl plays it'). His account of their
failure could equally well be about either of his next two girlfriends, Helen Corke and
Louie Burrows:

Letters I, 153 She's so utterly ignorant and old fashioned, really, though she has been to college
and has taught in London some years. A man is – or was – a more or less interesting
creature, with whom one could play about with smart and silly speech – no more –
not an animal – mon dieu, no! – I have enlightened her, and now she has no
courage. She still judges by mid-Victorian standards, and covers herself with a
woolly fluff of romance that the years will wear sickly. She refuses to see that a
man is a male, that kisses are the merest preludes and anticipations, that love is
largely a physical sympathy that is soon satisfied and satiated. She believes men
worship their mistresses; she is all sham and superficial in her outlook, and I can't
change her. She's frightened. Now I'm sick of her. She pretends to be very fond of
me; she isn't really; even if she were, what do I care! – but if she were, she

wouldn't be the timid duffer she is, declaring things dreadful, painful, hateful; life not worth living, life a degradation etc etc.; she would be interested in life; she lapses into sickly sentimentality when it is a question of naked life.

Much of this had also applied, until very recently, to Jessie. But the letter goes on:

At Christmas an old fire burned up afresh . . . She is coming to me for a week-end soon; we shall not stay here in Croydon, but in London. The world is for us, and we are for each other – even if only for one spring.

At last he had declared his love to Jessie and persuaded her to give herself to him. In his extremity he no doubt believed what he said. She was the only woman he knew who might accept him, with whom he could hope for the great healing and religious experience he expected sex to be. Their coming together, with a complete lack of spontaneity, in conditions Jessie described as 'both difficult and irksome', was surely doomed to failure. Afterwards he wrote to her:

Letters I, 157 You have done me a great good, my dear. Only I want you here with me. It is as if I cannot rest without you near me, you goodly thing, good to be near, to touch and to hold.

He was fooling himself; just as he was fooling himself when he wrote:

Delavenay 1, 702 If only we could have a little house . . . it would be the most wonderful castle in Spain come true.

It was probably shortly after this that Lawrence began his affair with Alice Dax, the wife of an Eastwood chemist. They had known each other for several years, having probably met at the home of Willie Hopkin. His daughter Enid later recalled:

Nehls 1, 135–6 Alice Dax and my mother were *years* ahead of their time. . . . Alice was almost completely uninhibited in an age when you just weren't. . . . Together she and my mother worked for the women's cause. . . . Alice Dax carried her ideas almost to extremes. Gradually she became a NAME in the district, a person to whom people turned in trouble, and who initiated all the good community enterprises, such as nursing associations, local forms of health insurance and so forth. She successfully tackled the school system too, and new modern schools arose. Alice Dax was one of the kindest persons I have ever met, but most of the men of her generation feared her.

Alice, who, because of the behaviour of her father, had grown up hating men, and had married out of hate, fell in love for the first time with Lawrence and offered herself to him. In the spring of 1910 they had spent a weekend in London together, but Lawrence remained faithful to Jessie. It was probably during the summer holidays that the incident occurred which Alice later described to Sallie Hopkin:

Priest 112 Sallie, I gave Bert sex. I had to. He was over at our house, struggling with a poem he couldn't finish, so I took him upstairs and gave him sex. He came downstairs and finished the poem.

Alice Dax and her daughter.

It was not as coldly done as these words suggest. In 1935 she wrote to Frieda Lawrence: 'It was from that one hour that I began to see the light of life.' She did not try to hold Lawrence, knowing she was not 'meet' for him, but suffered deeply after giving him up.

Tedlock 245

It is more difficult to know what Lawrence's feelings were towards her. He wrote affectionately of her (though somewhat in awe of her) to their mutual friend Blanche Jennings. But in December 1910 he wrote to his then fiancée, of the women he had known:

Letters I, 208   One is a little bitch, and I hate her: and she plucked me, like Potiphar's wife.

Yet the affair with Alice must have continued at least until March 1912. She hoped that the child she conceived in January might be Lawrence's, though in the event she was sure that it was not. And insofar as Alice was a model for Clara in *Sons and Lovers*, we must deduce that he got some satisfaction from their relationship.

⌒

Lawrence was very lonely in Croydon. Agnes Mason, an older woman on the staff at Davidson Road, befriended him and, in the spring of 1909, introduced him to her younger friend Helen Corke. Helen had little interest in Lawrence, for she was preoccupied with her affair with a married man fifteen years older than herself. That summer, after five days in the Isle of Wight with Helen, he returned home and hanged himself. The shock of this experience left Helen like a sleepwalker. Gradually Lawrence coaxed her back to life. He read *The Trojan Women* with her, so that her

Agnes Mason and Helen Corke in 1909.

own grief might be subsumed in the larger rhythms of Hecuba's. He sought her help with the final revision of *Nethermere* (his new title for his novel).

Helen had kept a record of her experience, her Freshwater Diary. Lawrence asked to see it, and suggested, with great enthusiasm, that she should help him to make it into a novel. She agreed. In three months the first draft of *The Saga of Siegmund* was finished. Helen was amazed that Lawrence, never having met Siegmund, and with so little help from her, could recreate that relationship so fully. In fact it was all too easy for Lawrence to identify himself with Siegmund, not only because he had fallen in love with Helen, but also because the pressures which had driven Siegmund to his death were the very pressures under which Lawrence also writhed, and which drove him to write to Helen (who, still living in the past, had returned to Freshwater):

Letters I, 173   [Jessie] came to see me yesterday. She kisses me. It makes my heart feel like ashes. But then she kisses me more and moves my sex fire. Mein Gott, it is hideous. . . . I must tell her that we ought finally and definitely to part: if I have the heart to tell her . . . I am a rather despicable object. But can I hurt her so much. I wish I had not come home. I wish fate wouldn't torture one with these conjunctions – and you in Freshwater.

Helen was a much more extreme example than Jessie of 'the dreaming woman':

Corke 162–3   My early religious training had divided soul and body, and presented the body as the inferior, rightly subordinate to the soul. The literary patterns of the period mostly enhanced this teaching. They tended to exhibit physical passion as a gross manifestation, linking man with the animal, but, in the case of man, properly controlled by reason and the will. Love was either divine or human. Religion imposed no prohibition against *spiritual* intimacy, for which it claimed complete essential detachment from bodily functions.

Judged by the standards of *my* ethical code, it had been found guilty and condemned.

Therefore she had tried to impose on her lover a purely spiritual relationship, forcing him always to struggle against the demands of a passionate nature. She had made him hate his own ungovernable body to the point where, 'in an extremity of mental torture', he had destroyed it.

Lawrence was putting himself into Siegmund not only on paper. In real life he knew that he was merely 'filling the place of a ghost with warmth', and that if he could eventually make Helen aware of him as a living man, history could only repeat itself. As for Helen, she knew that he would ultimately make an impossible demand upon her; but she had become dependent on him:

Corke 191   Since the early summer of this year I have been increasingly aware of the demand that he, instinctive man, makes upon me as a woman. I cannot definitely ignore it, but there is no physical response from my own body. My desire is not towards him. I do not want either to marry him and bear him children, or to be his mistress.

In August 1910 Mrs Lawrence became ill, and it soon became obvious that she was dying of cancer. Lawrence was under a terrible strain. It was a time when all his relationships seemed particularly tangled and hopeless. And now his mother, the stable centre of his life, was being taken from him. And he must watch her dying by degrees. On 3 December he went by train to Leicester and met Louie Burrows. On the return journey he proposed to her. Three days later he wrote to her:

Letters I, 195   It is morning again, and she is still here. She has had the 'thrush' rather badly: they say one must have it, either on coming or going. Many have it when they are little babies: and others when they're dying. Mother's is nearly better. But she looks so grievous, pitiful this morning, still and grey and deathly, like a hieroglyph of woe. One mustn't be bathetic: but there, one is vitiated by sitting up: Ada and I share the night.

I look at my mother and think 'Oh Heaven – is this what life brings us to?' You see mother has had a devilish married life, for nearly forty years – and this is the conclusion – no relief. What ever I wrote, it could not be so awful as to write a biography of my mother. But after this – which is enough – I am going to write romance – when I have finished Paul Morel, which belongs to this.

This anxiety divides me from you. My heart winces to the echo of my mother's pulse. There is only one drop of life to be squeezed from her, and that hangs trembling, so you'd think it must fall and be gone, but it never will – it will evaporate away, slowly. And while she dies, we seem not to be able to live.

So if I do not seem happy with the thought of you – you will understand. I must feel my mother's hand slip out of mine before I can really take yours. She is my first, great love. She was a wonderful, rare woman – you do not know; as strong, and steadfast, and generous as the sun. She could be as swift as a white whip-lash, and as kind and gentle as warm rain, and as steadfast as the irreducible earth beneath us.

But I think of you a great deal – of how happy we shall be. This surcharge of grief makes me determine to be happy. The more I think of you, the more I am glad that I have discovered the right thing to do. I have been very blind, and a fool. But sorrow

Mrs Lawrence in the garden at Lynn Croft at the beginning of her last illness.

Louie Burrows. 'She is a glorious girl: about as tall as I, straight and strong as a caryatid (if that's how you spell them) – and swarthy and ruddy as a pomegranate, and bright and vital as a pitcher of wine. . . . The rest can go to the devil, so I have Louie.'

opens the eyes. When I think of you, it is like thinking of life. You will be the first woman to make the earth glad for me: mother, J – all the rest, have been gates to a very sad world. But you are strong & rosy as the gates of Eden. We do not all of us, not many, perhaps, set out from a sunny paradise of childhood. We are born with our parents in the desert, and yearn for a Canaan. You are like Canaan – you are rich & fruitful & glad, and I love you.

Lawrence and his sister could not bear to watch the pointless suffering of their mother. They put morphine in her milk. Three days later she died.

An advance copy of *The White Peacock* had been rushed through to Lawrence. He had put it into his mother's hands, but she had been beyond reading it. After the funeral, his father 'struggled through half a page, and it might as well have been Hottentot':

Phoenix 232

'And what dun they gi'e thee for that, lad?'
'Fifty pounds, father.'
'Fifty pounds!' He was dumbfounded, and looked at me with shrewd eyes, as if I were a swindler. 'Fifty pounds! An' tha's niver done a day's hard work in thy life.'

Letters I, 220

The death of his mother did not soften Lawrence's detestation of his father. The following month he wrote of him to the minister Robert Reid as 'disgusting, irritating, and selfish as a maggot. Yet I am sorry for him: he's old, and stupid, and very helpless and futile'.

4 Death in Life

Lawrence now turned to Louie for his life. What he thought she could offer was 'a fine, warm, healthy natural love'. But he had known for years how ingenuous and conventional and well-brought-up Louie was, both arch and frivolous. 'You would make a good Bacchante,' he had told her, 'but for your training.' She was yet another worshipper of the beautiful rather than the true. In March 1909 he had written to her:

Letters I, 124   Louisa, my dear, thou art a century or so behind – and I am at the tip of the years. So thou art very comfortable and charming, and I am uncomfortable and a nuisance.

Once again he had underestimated the strength of 'time-long prudery'. He was soon to find that Louie could only be to him the

Poems 129   Betrothed young lady who loves me, and takes good care
                            Of her womanly virtue and of my good name.

So the old struggle began again, but it seems, despite the engagement, with less passion, less real hope. Now a sister's jealousy and possessiveness replaced a mother's. As early as February 1911 Lawrence was writing to Ada:

Letters I, 231   There is more *real* strength in my regard for you than there is for Louie.

It is clear that Lawrence soon realized that he had made a mistake, but, not knowing how to extricate himself without hurting Louie, he let things drift.

He turned to Helen Corke again and proposed marriage to her, but she was wiser than Louie. The situation was now complicated by her growing intimacy with Jessie. She has recorded that she was more in love with Jessie than with Lawrence; and that throughout her life sex had no interest for her. At times Lawrence wanted to strangle her. On 12 July 1911 he wrote to Helen:

Letters I, 286   On Sunday night, after I left you, I threw away, over St James' railway bridge, the two little articles Jones gave me months back, and which were my articles of temptation. . . . Another little death I died.

At the end of *The Saga of Siegmund* Lawrence brings together the heroine Helena and the Lawrence figure Cecil Byrne. But the short story 'Witch à la Mode', probably written in the summer of 1911, is virtually a sequel to the novel, and ends with an image of raw agony:

> His whole body ached like a swollen vein, with heavy intensity, while his heart grew dead with misery and despair. This woman gave him anguish and a cutting-short like death; to the other woman he was false.

In a flash of rage he kicks over a lamp which sets fire to her dress. He extinguishes the blaze with his arms.

> In another instant he was gone, running with burning-red hands held out blindly, down the street.

In September 1911 Lawrence sent this and another story to Edward Garnett, editor of the *Century*. Garnett, destined to take over from Hueffer as Lawrence's mentor, was enthusiastic and invited Lawrence to let him see more of his work and to visit him at his house, the Cearne, in Kent. There Lawrence heard conversation so free and frank on such taboo subjects as sex that in later life he claimed that the seed of *Lady Chatterley's Lover* had been sown there.

Edward Garnett.

Lawrence's health and spirits were very low. After one visit to the Cearne in late October, he had a long wait at the station in the rain and contracted pneumonia. He was severely ill for several weeks. The doctor warned him that if he went back to school he would be consumptive. Convalescing in Bournemouth in January, he began to rewrite *The Saga*, now called *The Trespasser*, and to make plans to visit his Aunt Hannah Krenkow at Waldbröl in Germany in the spring. On 4 February he wrote to Louie that the doctors had told him he ought not to marry:

Letters I, 361   Then, seeing I mustn't teach, I shall have a struggle to keep myself. I will not drag on an engagement – so I ask you to dismiss me. I am afraid we are not well suited.

Louie remained devoted to Lawrence, though she never saw him again.

That same month Lawrence resigned his post at Croydon. He could not settle down to any work, but mooned about 'like a moulting bird'. He invited Helen Corke to spend a night with him at the Cearne, assuring her that Garnett was 'beautifully free
Letters I, 362   of the world's conventions'. Miss Corke was not. He turned again to Alice Dax. But he felt he was going round in a squirrel cage; that his life had lost all direction and purpose. Later he looked back on that last year as one of the worst of his life. He was derelict, his mother dead and the family home broken up; his relationships with Jessie, Helen, Louie, were all turned to ashes; his health was in ruins, his early career prematurely ended, and he was unable to see any way forward:

Phoenix 253   Then, in that year, for me everything collapsed, save the mystery of death, and the haunting of death in life. I was twenty-five, and from the death of my mother, the world began to dissolve around me, beautiful, iridescent, but passing away substanceless. Till I almost dissolved away myself, and was very ill: when I was twenty-six. Then slowly the world came back or I myself returned but to another world.

✍

At least Lawrence was now launched as a writer. *The White Peacock* had appeared in January and had been, on the whole, favourably received. *The Trespasser* was finished and both Heinemann and Duckworth had offered to publish it; the first version of *Paul Morel* was finished; and poems were appearing regularly in the *English Review*; Secker had asked for a volume of short stories; Garnett was active about the publication of the poems and plays. But little money had yet come in, and Lawrence had no reason to think that he could support himself by writing. Nor could he yet have a justified conviction that he had it in him to be a major writer. Everything he had so far written was immature. He had indeed already written two of his finest stories, 'Odour of Chrysanthemums' and 'Daughters of the Vicar', but in versions which fall far short of the versions later prepared for inclusion in *The Prussian Officer*. His fine play, *The Widowing of Mrs Holroyd*, based like 'Odour of Chrysanthemums' on the true story of his aunt Polly and uncle James Lawrence, was also to be much altered in 1913. Hueffer said that *The White Peacock* had every fault the English novel could have – 'but you've got GENIUS', and accurately described
Letters I, 178   *The Trespasser* as 'a rotten work of genius'. The genius was not at that stage self-evident, and Hueffer and Garnett deserve much credit for recognizing it.

The White Peacock is a clumsy story told by an insufferably priggish narrator about tiresome people in a socially artificial environment, accurately described by Lawrence as:

Letters I, 44

> All about love – and rhapsodies on spring scattered here and there – heroines galore – no plot – nine-tenths adjectives – every colour in the spectrum descanted upon – a poem or two – scraps of Latin and French – altogether a sloppy, spicy mess.

For the reviewers the 'rhapsodies' redeemed it, though one found the style cloying and 'intolerably eloquent'. Violet Hunt seemed to think it was a realistic picture of the lives of the 'lower orders'. One reviewer amused Lawrence by wondering if he were a woman. In fact, if the novel is redeemed at all, it is by the gamekeeper Annable, added at a late stage, irrelevant to the plot, but looming out of the novel 'like some malicious Pan' with a solidity which makes all the other characters seem like flitting shadows; and by two consecutive excellent chapters towards the end of the novel, 'A Poem of Friendship' and 'Pastorals and Peonies'. Here the essential theme of the novel, that woman, like the white peacock, is 'all vanity and screech and defilement', degrading both man and nature by her insistence on rejecting everything which cannot be reduced to the aesthetic/spiritual, is given the kind of concrete realization and embodiment we take for granted in the mature Lawrence.

The Trespasser returns obsessively to the theme of the destructive woman:

> These deep, interesting women don't want *us*; they want the flowers of the spirit they can gather of us. We, as natural men, are more or less degrading to them and to their love of us; therefore they destroy the natural man in us – that is, us altogether.

Lawrence began *Paul Morel* as a tribute to his mother. Paul is clearly Lawrence, so the title invites us to expect the novel to be highly autobiographical. In fact it is highly fictionalized. Jessie (Miriam) is there, but transposed to another family, the Cullens. There is a great deal of material about the Cullen family (here called Staynes of Belfast House). Miss Wright, the Cullen family governess whom Lawrence much admired, is a major character, Miss May, who later marries Mr Revell, the incompetent Congregational minister of whom Mrs Morel has tired. They go to live at the Haggs, taking Miriam with them. When her father dies she inherits some money. She proposes (like Flossie Cullen) to become a nurse, but becomes a peripatetic music teacher instead. It is Paul's younger brother Arthur who goes to Nottingham High School and to University. He quarrels with his father who throws a steel at him, killing him (this actually happened to an uncle of Lawrence's). The father is imprisoned, and dies of grief.

All this Cullen material disappeared later from this novel, but reappeared in 1912 in *The Insurrection of Miss Houghton*.

Lawrence showed what he had written to Jessie:

Delaveney I, 670   Then in October (or it might have been November) 1911 Lawrence suddenly sent the entire M.S. to me, and asked me to tell him what I thought of it. He had written about two thirds of the novel and appeared to have come to a standstill. In reading the M.S. I felt oppressed by a sense of strain, as though he had had to force himself to write it. There was no spontaneity, no sparkle. It was his mother's story, told rather sentimentally; a young non-conformist minister whose sermons she composed was there as a set-off to the brutal husband. Our household of Willey Farm (I think he calls it that; I am writing absolutely from memory) was not there at all, and the character he calls Miriam was placed in a suburban atmosphere in Eastwood. In my reply to Lawrence I suggested that he should relate the story of his mother's married life as it had actually happened, and include his brother Ernest, whose story was omitted in the first draft. It seemed to me that the reality was so much more poignant and interesting than his semi-fictitious account. Not only that, I felt that if he could work out artistically and *within himself* all the issues of his mother's life and their implications, not only would he write a magnificent novel, but he would rid himself of his obsession with regard to his mother, and be a free and a whole man. My advice arose purely from intuition. I knew Lawrence and his situation so well, and I felt that this was his way out of his dilemma. He took me at my word, and entirely recast his novel. He included also the story of our household, which I had *not* suggested.

Lawrence even incorporated several passages written by Jessie. But the new version, which Lawrence passed to Jessie a dozen pages at a time through February and March 1912, hurt her deeply. It seemed to her a betrayal of her, and of the truth, to justify the mother. Jessie wanted him to write autobiography as autotherapy:

Jessie 204   I could hear in advance Lawrence's protesting voice: 'Of course it isn't the truth. It's an adaptation from life, as all art must be. It *isn't* what I think of you; you know it isn't'.

Lawrence was caught between two imperatives, the need to avoid hurting Jessie yet again, and the need to produce art rather than reproduce life, to go for the deeper, not exclusively personal, significance. Miriam was to be not a picture of Jessie Chambers but yet another embodiment of the destructive woman, taking her place in the sequence – Lettie, Helena, Miriam, Hermione, and many more. Jessie thought that the Jessie 202 character of Clara was 'a clever adaptation of elements from three people, Miss Burrows, Miss Corke, and Mrs Dax'. In fact there is little of Louie in Clara and less of Helen. What Jessie could not see (and could hardly have been expected to see, given the outward closeness of Miriam to herself, which she had herself insisted on) was that Miriam is also a composite character with elements of several real women including Helen, Louie and Agnes Holt. Lawrence's scheme for the novel at that stage was that Paul, drawing on standards embodied by his mother, should discover the deadliness of wholly 'spiritual' love, and the inadequacy of wholly carnal love, so that on the death of the mother he will be left, as Lawrence was at the time of writing, with nothing to hold on to but a determination that his mother should not have suffered in vain.

Lawrence always wrote about what most deeply concerned him at the time of writing. At the beginning of 1912 Jessie was already part of his past. Much more fresh were the scars of his relationship with Helen Corke. All the bitterness against her which we glimpse in the 1911 poems and stories had to be carried in the novel by Miriam. Perhaps this was why his first instinct had been to give Miriam an outer life utterly different from Jessie's. Jessie was right that Lawrence at that stage had not realized that his mother had been the most destructive woman of them all (perhaps he had unconsciously sought girlfriends who were images of her). That realization, when it came, involved a reassessment of the father, but not of Miriam, who reappears, much more cruelly exposed, as Hermione in *Women in Love*.

Early in March 1912 Lawrence went to lunch with Ernest Weekley, his former teacher, to discuss the possibility of getting some teaching post in Germany. Weekley had many German connections. Indeed he had a German wife, Frieda, the daughter of Baron Friedrich von Richthofen. She was fifteen years younger than her husband and six years older than Lawrence. She had been a handsome and high-spirited girl of seventeen when she had met Ernest, then a Lektor at Freiburg University. Three years later she had married him and come to England to become a Nottingham

The Weekley family on the occasion of Ernest's parents' Golden Wedding, 23 September 1911. At the front are Frieda's three children, Monty, Barby and Elsa.

Lawrence and Meg Brinton at Kew Gardens. Photograph by Irene Brinton. The Brinton sisters were fellow guests (possibly the 'very proper and proprietous maidens' referred to in Lawrence's letter of 7 January) at the Bournemouth boarding house where Lawrence convalesced in January 1912.

housewife. Her marriage was a bitter disappointment to her from the first night. Ernest was good and honourable and adored her, but he was interested only in books. She bore him three children, Monty in 1900, Elsa in 1902 and Barbara in 1904. She went through the motions of respectability in England, and had lovers in Germany, including Otto Gross, a disciple of Freud and free love, who helped her to the

Lucas 39 realization that she was 'living like a somnambulist in a conventional set life' and made her determined to discover and assert her 'own proper self'.

We have seen how desperately at this time Lawrence needed a woman who could release his manhood and his demon. Frieda had also reached the end of her tether. Both later felt that 'fate' had set up their meeting at that moment:

Frieda 22　I see him before me as he entered the house. A long thin figure, quick straight legs, light, sure movements. He seemed so obviously simple. Yet he arrested my attention. There was something more than met the eye. What kind of bird was this?

Letters I, 376　Soon afterwards he wrote to her: 'You are the most wonderful woman in all England', and to Garnett:

Letters I, 384　She is ripping – she's the finest woman I've ever met – she's splendid, she is really. . . . Oh but she is the woman of a lifetime.

At first Frieda would probably have settled for an affair, but for Lawrence it was all or nothing. He insisted that she tell her husband and go away with him. On an excursion into the Derbyshire countryside she watched Lawrence playing with her children, crouching by a stream to sail the paper boats he had made, and suddenly she knew she loved him. The last weekend in April Lawrence and Frieda spent at the Cearne. The following day she took the girls to their grandparents in London and left

Frieda 24　them, feeling 'blind and blank with pain'. On 3 May she met Lawrence at Charing Cross Station. He had eleven pounds in his pocket. They crossed the grey Channel sitting on some ropes, watching England slowly submerging like a long, ash-grey coffin. The past, the old life, sank into the sea.

Frieda 25　There was nothing but the grey sea, and the dark sky, and the throbbing of the ship, and ourselves.

5 The Best I Have Known

The Von Richthofens were all gathered in Metz for the fiftieth anniversary of the Baron's entry into the army. Lawrence, a forlorn figure in his raincoat and cloth cap, stayed at a small hotel, while Frieda had to spend most of her time with her family. She quickly introduced him to her sisters:

Letters I, 395   You should see the Richthofens at home – three sisters – one, the eldest, a professor of psychology and economics – left her husband, gone with two other men (in succession) – yet *really* good – good, the sort of woman one reverences. Then there's Frieda. Then the youngest sister, very beautiful, married to a brute of a swanky officer in Berlin – and, in a large, splendid way – cocotte. Lord, what a family. I've never seen anything like it.

On the fourth day Lawrence and Frieda were lying on the obsolete fortifications talking in English, when they were overheard by a policeman, who arrested Lawrence as a spy – an English officer in disguise. Frieda could secure his release only through the influence of her father, so the cat was out of the bag. Lawrence was obliged to flee eighty miles to Trier, and then to Waldbröl, to stay with his relatives the Krenkows. From Waldbröl Lawrence wrote Frieda several wonderful love-letters, though she was so bewildered that the depth of their feeling did not touch her. She went to one of her lovers, and even told Lawrence about it to try to make him jealous, but he refused to be shaken from his conviction:

Letters I, 403   Can't you feel how certainly I love you and how certainly we shall be married. Only let us wait just a short time, to get strong again. Two shaken, rather sick people together would be a bad start. A little waiting, let us have, because I love you. Or does the waiting make you worse? – no, not when it is only a time of preparation. Do you know, like the old knights, I seem to want a certain time to prepare myself – a sort of vigil with myself. Because it is a great thing for me to marry you, not a quick, passionate coming together. I know in my heart 'here's my marriage'. It feels rather terrible – because it is a great thing in my life – it is *my life* – I am a bit awe-inspired – I want to get used to it. If you think it is fear and indecision, you wrong me. It is *you* who would hurry, who are undecided. It's the very strength and inevitability of the oncoming thing that makes me wait, to get in harmony with it. Dear God, I am marrying you, now, don't you see. It's a far

The von Richthofen matriarchy; Else, the Baroness, and Frieda.

greater thing than ever I knew. . . . It's a funny thing, to feel one's passion – sex desire – no longer a sort of wandering thing, but steady, and calm. I think, when one loves, one's very sex passion becomes calm, a steady sort of force, instead of a storm. Passion, that nearly drives one mad, is far away from real love. I am realising things that I never thought to realise. – Look at that poem I sent you – I would never write that to you. I shall love you all my life. That also is a new idea to me. But I believe it.

At last, on 25 May, Lawrence and Frieda began a week of real honeymoon at Beuerberg in the valley of the Isar in the Bavarian Tyrol. The first night was a failure:

Poems 204

> I could not be free,
> not free myself from the past, those others.

But that could not spoil their happiness. The week was idyllic:

Frieda 52–3

> The Alps floated above us in palest blue in the early morning. The Isar rushed its glacier waters and hurried the rafts along in the valley below. The great beechwoods stretched for hours behind us, to the Tegernsee.
>
> Here we began our life together. And what a life! We lived on black bread that Lawrence loved, fresh eggs, and 'ripple'; later we found strawberries, raspberries and 'heidelbeeran'.
>
> We had lost all ordinary sense of time and place. Those flowers that came new to Lawrence, the fireflies at night and the glow-worms, the first beech leaves spreading on the trees like a delicate veil overhead, and our feet buried in last year's brown beech leaves, these were our time and our events.
>
> When Lawrence first found a gentian, a big single blue one, I remember feeling as if he had a strange communion with it, as if the gentian yielded up its blueness, its very essence, to him. Everything he met had the newness of a creation just that moment come into being.

Thus the gentian stands at Lawrence's entry into life, as at his exit from it, as an image of wholeness and selfhood. In terms of it he was to ask of himself and others, in his life and works:

Poems 684

> Oh what in you can answer to this blueness?

From Icking in June Lawrence wrote to Sallie Hopkin:

Letters I, 414

> The world is wonderful and beautiful and good beyond one's wildest imagination. Never, never, never could one conceive what love is, beforehand, never. Life *can* be great – quite god-like. It *can* be so. God be thanked I have proved it.

Yet all was not well. The past pulled at Frieda also. When Frieda was consumed with wild longing for her children, Lawrence hardened himself against her by fusing her with the image of his own now repudiated mother, and cursing

Poems 208

> All mothers who fortify themselves in motherhood, devastating the vision.

The thought of losing her was an agony to him, as of cutting his very connection with the universe. His first mention of the dark Gods is to invoke them to help him to hold on to her:

Poems 213   And if I never see her again?

I think, if they told me so
I could convulse the heavens with my horror.
I think I could alter the frame of things in my agony.
I think I could break the System with my heart.
I think, in my convulsion, the skies would break.

She too suffers
But who could compel her, if she chose me against them all?
She has not chosen me finally, she suspends her choice.
Night folk, Tuatha De Danaan, dark Gods, govern her sleep,
Magnificent ghosts of the darkness, carry off her decision in sleep,
Leave her no choice, make her lapse me-ward, make her,
Oh Gods of the living Darkness, powers of Night.

There was the constant worry about money. And of course the inevitable difficulties of reconciling two such strong and different beings. Frieda amoral, disorderly, wasteful, utterly helpless in the house, lying in bed late, lounging about all day with a cigarette dangling from her mouth, expecting service and deference from everyone as her birthright. Lawrence fiercely puritanical even in his sensuality, tidy, frugal, omnicompetent at household tasks, energetic and industrious, at ease with common people. If he was jealous of her children and her lovers, she was jealous of his work, not only the time and energy he put into it, excluding her, but the way he seemed to draw life out of her to turn it into stories and plays and poems.

Frieda was an extraordinary mixture of openness and prejudice, naïvety and low cunning, intelligence and stupidity (she convinced Aldous Huxley that Buddha was right to make stupidity one of the deadly sins). She was utterly amoral, sexually. In the midst of their happiness in Gargnano, she kept Harold Hobson at home, while Lawrence and David Garnett went botanizing in the mountains. Her relationship with Angelo Ravagli in Lawrence's last years was more or less open. Immediately after Lawrence's death Murry accepted the relationship she had offered him several years earlier. She loved Lawrence and depended on him totally, as did he on her; affairs did not seem to her to affect that relationship. Lawrence from the first tried to bully her. She took her revenge in several ways. If Lawrence was an irresistible force, Frieda was an immovable object. The reverberations of their conflict still echo down the years.

Look! We Have Come Through! is a poetic record of the first stages of that conflict, with its joys and miseries. Gradually Frieda came to realize the greatness of the man she had chosen, and that for him there was no distinction between the creativeness *Poems* 191 which brought him and Frieda through to 'some condition of blessedness' and the creativeness which issued in art. Neither is an achievement of the deliberate self; both are products of the wind that blows through him to which he must open and attune himself:

Poems 250   Oh, for the wonder that bubbles into my soul
                       I would be a good fountain, a good well-head
                       Would blur no whisper, spoil no expression.

It was true instinct that led Frieda, twenty years later, to choose as the title of her book about this marriage *'Not I, But the Wind'*. The huge strides Lawrence began to
Poems 184 take in his art were a matter of breaking down all the 'artificial conduits and canals through which we do so love to force our utterance', to allow the spontaneous, uniquely appropriate form to emerge. The success of his marriage was equally a matter of breaking through old dead ideas and life-modes:

Letters I, 424–5   F. wants to clear out of Europe, and get to somewhere uncivilised. It is astonishing how barbaric one gets with love : one finds oneself in the Hinterland der Seele, and – it's a rum place. I never knew I was like this. What Blasted Fools the English are, fencing off the big wild scope of their natures.

It was ten years before F. got her wish. But they had their freedom, and they asserted it by setting off in August, with rucksacks on their backs, to walk from the Isartal over the Alps to Mayrhofen. There they stayed for a fortnight, then on to Riva on Lake Garda, accompanied by David Garnett and his friend Harold Hobson as far as Sterzing. The first leg took them a week, the second ten days. Frieda always remembered this as one of the highlights of her life with Lawrence. They never knew

'Gargnano is a tumbledown Italian place straggling along the lake. It is only accessible by steamer, because of the rocky mountains at the back.'

what shelter they would find for the next night, and usually slept in hayhuts. They bought food in the villages they passed and cooked over a spirit stove by the mountain streams. They had learned to live in the present, letting their love carry them forward into the adventure of each new day. They felt like Adam and Eve setting out to regain Paradise.

Letters I, 440–1   For ourselves, Frieda and I have struggled through some bad times into a wonderful naked intimacy, all kindled with warmth, that I know at last is love. I think I ought not to blame women, as I have done, but myself, for taking my love to the wrong women, before now. Let every man find, keep on trying till he finds, the woman who can take him and whose love he can take, then who will grumble about men or about women. But the thing must be two-sided. At any rate, and whatever happens, I do love, and I am loved – I have given and I have taken – and that is eternal. Oh, if only people could marry properly, I believe in marriage.

At Gargnano Lawrence plunged into the rewriting of *Paul Morel*. Of course Frieda had read it, and they had fought 'like blazes' over it. She told Lawrence that he had *Letters* I, 449 'quite missed the point'; the point being that Paul was a classic case of the Oedipus complex. She wrote a skit called *Paul Morel, or His Mother's Darling*, which left Lawrence unamused. But he did come round to a new, radically altered, assessment of his mother and, consequently, of his father. We do not know exactly what changes Lawrence made in this final version. His new title, *Sons and Lovers*, first suggested in October 1912, is significant. But it was impossible at this late stage to alter a novel which had begun its life as a tribute to a wonderful woman to accommodate a totally opposite evaluation of her. Years later he said:

Frieda 74   I would write a different *Sons and Lovers* now; my mother was wrong, and I thought she was absolutely right.

And again:

Brewster 255   All self-righteous women ought to be martyred.

In fact, of course, his mother had been neither right nor wrong, or both right and wrong, and the novel as we have it, making no such judgements, is the better for its ambiguity.

There was no place in *Sons and Lovers* for his new insights. It was a document from his past. Sending it off to the publishers on 18 November was like writing 'Finis' to that phase of his life. It came as a severe blow to Lawrence when he received a 'wigging' from Garnett, who saw that it still carried too much slack. Lawrence asked Garnett to make the necessary cuts himself, and Garnett much improved the novel by removing about a tenth. When Lawrence saw the proofs he wrote to Garnett:

Letters I, 517   You did the pruning jolly well, and I am grateful. I hope you'll live a long long time, to barber up my novels for me before they're published.

Lawrence himself hated such 'pidgilling' work. Besides, he had conceived a new novel, 'purely of the common people', which was clamouring for his attention:

Letters I, 487 It is to be a life of Robert Burns – but I shall make him live near home, a Derbyshire man – and shall fictionalise the circumstances. . . . I think I can do him almost like an autobiography.

Only a couple of fragments survive, but they are enough to suggest that this hero, Jack Haseldine, was a first sketch for Tom Brangwen in *The Rainbow*, the first of a long list of Lawrence heroes whose essential qualities were qualities he now belatedly recognized his father to have had – instinctive, non-intellectual and non-moral warmth, spontaneity and passion: qualities of the blood rather than of the mind. Italian men were the same:

Letters I, 460 I think they haven't many ideas, but they look well, and they have strong blood.

Lawrence's elopement had been his declaration of war against society, and much of his subsequent work was a rationalization of or generalization from his personal revolt against his own past and whatever survived from it, against his mother and Eastwood and England and, ultimately, the basic values of Western civilization. His works are all metaphors for this revolt. New ideas came flooding in with the new experiences. Lawrence tried to jettison all the old beliefs and morality, but, unlike Frieda, it was not in his nature to live without a metaphysic, so he tried to forge a new one partly out of the raw material of his own personal experiences, partly by a simple reversal of the old metaphysic.

His first attempts to state his new credo are coherent but extreme. On 17 January 1913, the day after he had watched the passionate actor Enrico Persevalli 'put himself through the creepings and twistings' of *Hamlet*, Lawrence wrote to Ernest Collings:

Letters I, 503–4 My great religion is a belief in the blood, the flesh, as being wiser than the intellect. We can go wrong in our minds. But what our blood feels and believes and says, is always true. The intellect is only a bit and a bridle. What do I care about knowledge. All I want is to answer to my blood, direct, without fribbling intervention of mind, or moral, or what not. I conceive a man's body as a kind of flame, like a candle flame forever upright and yet flowing: and the intellect is just the light that is shed onto the things around. . . . That is why I like to live in Italy. The people are so unconscious. They only feel and want: they don't know. We know too much. No, we only *think* we know such a lot. A flame isn't a flame because it lights up two, or twenty objects on a table. It's a flame because it is itself. And we have forgotten ourselves. We are Hamlet without the Prince of Denmark. We cannot *be*. 'To be or not to be'— it is the question with us now, by Jove. And nearly every Englishman says 'Not to be'. So he goes in for Humanitarianism and suchlike forms of not-being. The real way of living is to answer to one's wants. Not 'I want to light up with my intelligence as many things as possible'—but 'For the living of my full flame—I want that liberty, I want that woman, I want that pound of peaches, I want to go to sleep, I want to go the pub, and have a good time, I want to look beastly swell today, I want to kiss that girl, I want to insult that man.'

The ideas Lawrence expressed to Collings seem commonplace enough to us now, and their dangers, with our historical hindsight, clear. But they seemed very new to

Lawrence, whose only precedent was Nietzsche. His early formulations are a mixture of Nietzschean tendentiousness and inverted Protestant theology. Three days later Lawrence developed these ideas further in his Foreword to *Sons and Lovers*, where he becomes incoherent and even more extreme:

Huxley 98   But if in my passion I slay my neighbour, it is no sin of mine, but it is his sin, for he should not have permitted me.

The incoherence, which persisted through the *Study of Thomas Hardy* and was not resolved until 'The Crown' in 1915, is the result of Lawrence, in his anxiety to reverse traditional values, accepting the dualism responsible for the antinomies; and his absurd thesis, following the sudden apotheosis of his father, was that the Father is the Flesh, but Woman, as mother, is also the Flesh, and therefore the Father is Woman. No wonder Lawrence told Garnett:

Letters I, 510   I would die of shame if that Foreword were printed.

6 Terra Incognita

With *Sons and Lovers* out of the way, Lawrence embarked on a period of incredible creativity, with more poems for *Look!*, two plays, (*The Fight for Barbara* and *The Daughter-in-Law*), *Twilight in Italy*, and the abortive Burns novel which he abandoned in January 1913 in favour of *The Insurrection of Miss Houghton*. In mid-February he wrote to Garnett:

Letters I, 517
> This new novel is going quite fast . . . exciting, thrilling, to my mind – a bit outspoken, perhaps.

Letters I, 526
By mid-March he had written 200 pages, but though he still loved it, he decided that it was *'too improper'*, and set it aside to write an 'absolutely impeccable' pot-boiler. On 4 October Lawrence had read *Anna of the Five Towns*:

Letters I, 459
> I hate England and its hopelessness. I hate Bennett's resignation. Tragedy ought really to be a great kick at misery. But *Anna of the Five Towns* seems like an acceptance – so does all the modern stuff since Flaubert. I hate it. I want to wash again quick, wash off England, the oldness and grubbiness and despair.

He had resolved his own tragedy with a great kick at misery, and come through; he had washed off England in the Mediterranean sun; he had found new hope and energy in the creative conflict of marriage. He wanted to write an answer to Anna, embodying what he felt he had 'proved'. The idea lay dormant for three months. Then he remembered Flossie Cullen, the Eastwood girl who had nursed his mother in her last illness, and played the piano in her father's cinema, and whose family he had begun to describe in that earliest version of *Paul Morel* and again as the Culverwells in *My mother made a failure of her life*. . . . She became Alvina Houghton and her insurrection is against the living death of Woodhouse (Eastwood) and England. Alvina runs away with an Italian circus performer Ciccio. Their lovemaking is important; but Lawrence's answer to 'the real deep want of the English people' is not
Letters I, 544 simply 'a making free and healthy of the sex' – it is a religious conviction that the potentiality for rebirth is there at the heart of every living man and woman. He felt
Letters I, 526 that he had gone 'really a stratum deeper' in this novel because he created Woodhouse in all its Bennett-like 'reality' of character and society and money and clothes and furniture and grubbiness and 'local colour', only for an absurd troupe of phony Indians to make it disappear at the toss of a feathered head.

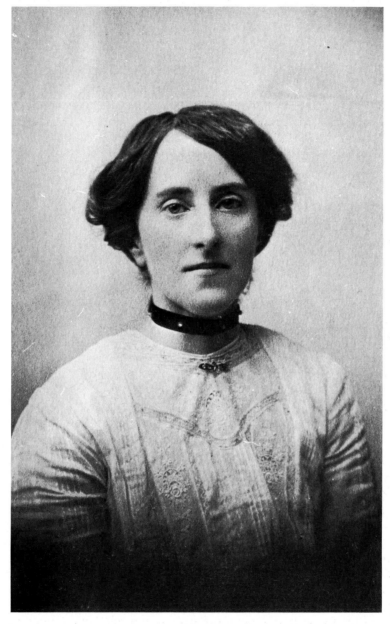

*Flossie Cullen (1879–1924). 'She grew up a slim girl, rather distinguished in appearance, with a slender face, a fine slightly arched nose, and beautiful grey-blue eyes over which the lids tilted with a very odd, sardonic tilt.' (*The Lost Girl*)*

Alvina's throwing overboard of everything which had bound her to a false reality is for Lawrence a paradigm of the function of any truly creative imagination:

Moore 189   Isn't it hard, hard work to come to real grips with one's imagination, – throw everything overboard. I always feel as if I stood naked for the fire of Almighty God to go through me – and it's rather an awful feeling. One has to be so terribly religious, to be an artist.

One of the things which had to be thrown overboard was the idea of novelistic form held by Bennett, Galsworthy, Garnett and almost everyone else at that time. Only Frieda knew what Lawrence was after and encouraged him. She wrote to Edward Garnett:

Tedlock 185–6   I have heard so much about 'form' with Ernest; why are you English so keen on it? Their own form wants smashing in almost any direction, but they can't come out of their snail house. I know it is so much safer. That's what I love Lawrence for, that he is so plucky and honest in his work, he dares to come out in the open and plants his stuff down bald and naked; really he is the only revolutionary worthy of the name, that I know; any new thing must find a new shape, then afterwards one can call it 'art'. . . . I am sure he is a real artist; the way things pour out of him, *he* seems only the pen, and isn't that how it ought to be?

But what hope was there of a readership for an art so challengingly new that the author himself could not understand it?

Letters I, 544   I am doing a novel which I have never grasped. Damn its eyes, there I am at page 145, and I've no notion what it's about. I hate it. F. says it is good. But it's like a novel in a foreign language I don't know very well – I can only just make out what it is about.

Letters I, 536   This new novel was *The Sisters*, the pot-boiler, now 'developed into an earnest and painful work', which was to develop further over the next four years into two of the greatest English novels, *The Rainbow* and *Women in Love*.
It is clear from the letter that *The Sisters* is to be about marriage:

Letters I, 546   I can only write what I feel pretty strongly about: and that, at present, is the relations between men and women. After all, it is *the* problem of today, the establishment of a new relation, or the re-adjustment of the old one, between men and women.

It was now just a year since Lawrence and Frieda had made their break. They were living (since the middle of April) in Irschenhausen, in 'a jolly little wooden house standing in a corner of a fir-wood, in a hilly meadow all primulas and gentians and looking away at the snowy Alps':

Letters I, 543   F. and I are quite alone. The place is a little summerhouse belonging to her brother in law, which he has lent us for a month or two. It is lonely. The deer feed sometimes in the corner among the flowers. But they fly with great bounds when I

'I have been married for this past year. . . . And this is the best I have known, or ever shall know.'

go out. And when I whistle to a hare among the grass, he dances round in wild bewilderment.

Already Lawrence was benefiting from his knack of finding beautiful places to live; but he and Frieda carried their happiness with them.

In June 1913, at Irschenhausen, Lawrence wrote two of his best stories, 'The Prussian Officer' and 'A Thorn in the Flesh'. But there was still a thorn in his own flesh. Frieda could wait no longer to see her children. They quarrelled. She broke a plate over his head (the first of many), and ran away for two days. Then they agreed to return to England together. If *Sons and Lovers* did not bring in enough money, Lawrence would have to teach again. They arrived at the Cearne on 19 June. Two days later came a cheque for £50 from Duckworth.

Katherine Mansfield was born Katherine Beauchamp in New Zealand in 1888. Her father was chairman of the Bank of New Zealand. She had gone to England at fifteen to complete her education, and quickly showed her propensity for exploiting anyone willing to be exploited by turning her college friend Ida Baker into her lifelong slave. Later she was quite prepared to use her sexual attractiveness for the same purpose, as she did with both S. S. Koteliansky and Mark Gertler. She unscrupulously accelerated her acceptance as a short story writer by lifting stories from Chekhov. She

John Middleton Murry and Katherine Mansfield in London, 1913.

struck most people as simultaneously pushing and furtive, yet she could also be clever and charming.

John Middleton Murry, a lower-middle-class scholarship boy from Camberwell, was a year younger than Katherine. After Oxford, he had gone to Paris to shed some of his inhibitions, and had returned to Oxford to found *Rhythm*, which was to bring a splash of Paris to England. He met Katherine in 1911, by which time she had already had a husband, several lovers, and two abortions. At her invitation, he moved in with her. Murry was both arrogant and wheedling. In any situation he was likely to do the wrong thing, half on purpose, in order to give himself plenty of opportunities for exercising his talent for self-laceration.

In January 1913 Katherine had written to Lawrence inviting him to contribute to *Rhythm*. Lawrence contributed a review of *Georgian Poetry: 1911–1912*, an anthology in which he was himself represented (by 'Snapdragon'). The review appeared in the March number, which was the last. But Murry and Mansfield immediately bobbed up again with *The Blue Review*. Again Lawrence made one contribution, an essay on Thomas Mann, in what again turned out to be the last number (July 1913). In the essay Lawrence takes the opportunity to define his own artistic credo by attacking that of such writers as Flaubert and Mann:

Phoenix 312   Physical life is a disordered corruption, against which he can fight with only one weapon, his fine aesthetic sense, his feeling for beauty, for perfection, for a certain

Lawrence photographed by W. G. Parker, 26 June 1913. 'With his broad, jutting brow, and clear, sensitive, extremely blue eyes – very wide apart – he looked half fawn, half prophet, and very young. He had not yet grown the tawny beard with which most people remember him. He wasted no time – he never did – on small talk, but dived with a clean plunge into some subject that interested him, and he could not fail to make it interest everyone else. Words welled out of him. He spoke in flashing phrases; at times colloquially, almost challengingly so, but often with a startling beauty of utterance. His voice was now harsh, now soft. One moment he was lyrically, contagiously joyous; the next sardonic, gibing.' (Lady Cynthia Asquith)

fitness which soothes him, and gives him an inner pleasure, however corrupt the stuff of life may be. . . . And even while he has a rhythm in style, yet his work has none of the rhythm of a living thing.

Frieda 85   Lawrence called on the Murrys (as I shall call them, though they were unable to marry until 1918), and the two couples soon became friends. Frieda recalled that 'theirs was the only spontaneous and jolly friendship that we had'. She fell for them at once when she caught them making faces at one another on a bus. The Lawrences invited them down to Broadstairs, where they lived for most of July, and they all bathed naked.

Another guest at Broadstairs was Edward Marsh, editor of the Georgian anthologies:

Moore 215   We are quite swells. Edward Marsh came on Sunday (he is the Georgian Poetry man and Secretary in the Admiralty to Winston Churchill) and he took us in to tea with the Herbert Asquiths – jolly nice folk – son of the Prime Minister. Today I am to meet there Sir Walter Raleigh. But alas it is not he of the cloak.

Marsh wrote to Rupert Brooke, whom he was later to introduce to Lawrence, that the Lawrences had been a tremendous success:

Nehls 1, 199   He looks terribly ill, which I am afraid he is – his wife is a very jolly buxom healthy-looking German, they seem very happy together.

Lawrence later apologized to Marsh for introducing Frieda as his wife. When he returned to Eastwood at the beginning of August, he had to go without Frieda, because, though Ada herself knew about her, neither Emily nor George did.

Frieda had been unable, after all, to see her children, and when Katherine went to St Paul's school as go-between, Monty sent word by another boy 'that he was not to talk to people who came to the school to see him'. Frieda returned to Irschenhausen alone and Lawrence joined her there on 8 August.

In England Lawrence had worked mainly on short stories and poems; now he returned to *The Sisters*. The first version had been narrated in the first person by the heroine Ella Templeman, modelled on both Louie and Frieda. Lawrence knew, before Garnett told him, that this would not do:

Moore 208   But it did me good to theorize myself out, and to depict Frieda's God Almightiness in all its glory. That was the first crude fermenting of the book. I'll make it into art now.

There were two false starts, but by the time they left Germany for Switzerland and his 'beloved' Italy in mid-September, he had written a hundred pages. At Lerici, Moore 223   where they were to live for eight months, the novel came very quickly: 'my autumn burst of work'.

Lawrence had walked, alone, through Switzerland into Italy. The last chapter of *Twilight in Italy* records his emerging sense of the Alps as an image of death:

The very pure source of breaking-down, decomposition, the very quick of cold death, is the snowy mountainpeak above. There, eternally, goes on the white foregathering of the crystals, out of the deathly cold of the heavens; this is the static nucleus where death meets life in its elementality. And thence, from their white, radiant nucleus of death in life, flows the great flux downwards, towards life and warmth.

He goes on to associate this 'death of life' with 'the perfect mechanizing of human life' in modern industry, thus prefiguring the ending of *Women in Love*, where Gerald Crich, a captain of industry, meets a death by perfect cold in these very mountains. This is not so surprising when we realize that the *Sisters* material Lawrence had been working on up to this time was the story of two 'remarkable females', Ella (later Ursula) and her sister Gudrun (based on Nusch) and their respective lovers, Birkin (closely modelled on Lawrence himself) and Gerald Crich (whose family history is that of the Barbers, the Eastwood coal-owners), in other words material exclusively from *Women in Love*, which was not finished until late in 1916, rather than from *The Rainbow* which was finished early in 1915. In December Lawrence decided on a new title, *The Wedding Ring*. The wedding in question is clearly that of Birkin and Ursula:

Moore 207 (margin)

Moore 263 (margin)

> I *must* have Ella get some experience before she meets her Mr Birkin. I also felt that the character was inclined to fall into two halves – and gradations between them. It came of trying to graft on to the character of Louie, the character, more or less of Frieda.

Garnett had objected to 'the Templeman episode' – presumably an affair between Ella and her cousin out of which grew the Skrebensky episode in *The Rainbow*. When Lawrence begins again at the beginning of February, he describes the new version almost as though it were a new novel with a new theme:

Moore 273 (margin)

> In the *Sisters* was the germ of this novel: woman becoming individual, self-responsible, taking her own initiative.

All this has to happen before Ursula will be ready to meet Birkin. So it seems that *The Rainbow* grew from its germ in *The Sisters* backwards; from the need to give his heroine 'some experience of love and of men'; which called for an account of her adolescence; which could not be handled adequately without her childhood and relationship with her parents, her region, class and culture. Lawrence realized that by beginning with Ursula's grandparents, yeoman farmers whose way of life had not changed for generations, he could condense into the three generations of Brangwens a social history of English life from before the industrial revolution to the present day. The second draft was finished in May 1914 and the title changed to *The Rainbow* – 'a better title than *The Wedding Ring* for the book as it is'. The new title spans the generations as the old did not, for though the rainbow is also a symbol of marriage, of any harmonious creative relationship, it has many other complex symbolic potentialities, from the geometrical to the metaphysical, which Lawrence could exploit slightly differently for each generation.

Moore 276 (margin)

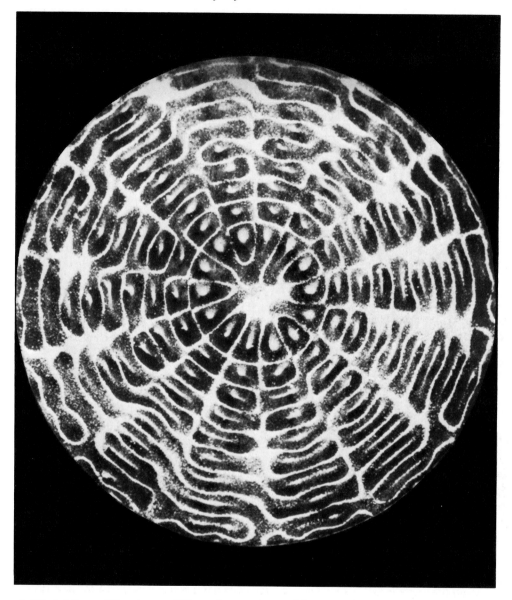

A Chladni figure. Vibrations at different frequencies would arrange the sand in different patterns, all intricate, balanced, beautiful, and strongly resembling the structure of living organisms.

The new emphasis on Ursula's early development meant that Lawrence needed to draw a great deal on Frieda's recollection of her own and Else's adolescent experiences. In February she wrote to Garnett:

Tedlock 202   I am going to throw myself into the novel now and you will see what a gioia it will be.

Two months later Lawrence wrote to Murry:

Moore 269–70   I have written quite a thousand pages that I shall burn. But now, thank God, Frieda and I are together, and the work is of me and her, and it is beautiful.

Lawrence had to rely more and more on Frieda also for constructive criticism, for he was now pushing into new ground where Garnett was unable or unwilling to follow:

Moore 273   You know how willing I am to hear what you have to say, and to take your advice and to act on it when I have taken it. But it is no good unless you will have patience and understand what I *want* to do. I am not after all a child working erratically. All the time, underneath, there is something deep evolving itself out in me. And it is *hard* to express a new thing, in sincerity. And you should understand, and help me to the new thing.

Lawrence felt that his second year with Frieda had been a lazy year, but in addition to those thousand pages he had written several fine stories, added several poems to *Look!*, and finished *Twilight in Italy*. Certainly they had taken full advantage of the pleasures of Lerici, bathing, picnicking, collecting shell-fish, exchanging visits with other English families, being honoured guests at peasant weddings and entertainments:

Huxley 181   Oh, it is so beautiful here, I feel as if my heart would jump out of my chest like a hare at night – it is such lovely spring. The sea is blue all day, and primrose dusking to apricot at evening. There are flowers, and peach trees in bloom, and pink almond trees among the vapour grey of the olives.

Lawrence had no wish to leave Lerici. But Frieda's divorce was declared absolute in May. She received 'a saner letter' from Ernest, and began to hanker again for her children. They decided to go to England and marry there, intending to return to Italy in August.

Lawrence's last letter from Lerici was a final desperate attempt to explain to Garnett what he was trying to do in *The Rainbow*. Garnett had not liked it, thinking the psychology wrong. But there was no common language available to Lawrence in which to describe his new psychology; he had to resort to obscure metaphors, most of them drawn from the jargon of futurism, or from Chladni's experiments.

Moore 282   Again I say, Don't look for the development of the novel to follow the lines of certain characters: the characters fall into the form of some other rhythmic form, as when one draws a fiddle-bow across a fine tray delicately sanded, the sand takes lines unknown.

7 Rananim

While Frieda visited her family, Lawrence walked with a friend, Lewis, an engineer from Spezia, across Switzerland, and joined her at Heidelberg where they stayed with Else's lover Max Weber, from whom Lawrence heard 'the latest things in German philosophy and political economy':

Unpub.   I am like a little half fledged bird opening my beak *very* wide to gulp down the fat phrases.

By 24 June Lawrence was back in London, where one of his first priorities was to get an advance on *The Rainbow*. Negotiations so far had been with Duckworth (who had published *The Trespasser*, *Love Poems* and *Sons and Lovers*) through Edward Garnett.

The Lawrences and the Murrys at 9 Selwood Terrace on Lawrence's wedding day. 'Lawrence was slim and even boyish; he wore a large straw hat that suited him well. Mrs Lawrence a big Panama over her flaxen hair. Straw hats, and sunshine, and gaiety. . . . Heavens, how happy we all were! The time of being jolly together had really begun. Frieda had a brand-new wedding-ring, and gave her old one to Katherine.' (J. M. Murry)

But Duckworth had lost money (a mere £15 or so) on *Sons and Lovers* and neither he nor Garnett was showing much enthusiasm for the new novel. The agent J. B. Pinker had offered Lawrence an advance of £300 from Methuen. Lawrence went to see Duckworth, who refused to make any offer, so Lawrence appointed Pinker as his agent, signed the agreement with Methuen, and opened a bank account with the cheque. He needed the money for his impending marriage. As a sop to Garnett, Lawrence offered Duckworth a volume of short stories, which he wanted to call *The Thorn in the Flesh*. Much to his disgust, it was published as *The Prussian Officer*.

The Lawrences stayed at Gordon Campbell's house in South Kensington. There Lawrence rewrote many of the early stories, much improving them. He was also busy reading everything of Hardy's he could lay his hands on in preparation for a little book on Hardy he had been invited to write for Nisbet.

Moore 287   At 10.30 on Monday 13 July 1914 at Kensington Registrar's Office, Lawrence and Frieda were married – 'a very decent and dignified performance'. The Murrys and Gordon Campbell were the witnesses. Frieda didn't care about being married; it was Lawrence who wanted to be 'respectable'. Eddie Marsh, generous as ever, sent Lawrence as a wedding present a set of the complete works of Thomas Hardy:

Moore 287   I rushed round the room almost cracked, between shame of having made it possible, and horror at your spending so much money on me, and joy of having the books.

Frieda has still not managed to contact her children. On 17 July Lawrence wrote to Edward Garnett:

Unpub.   She has seen them – the little girls being escorted to school by a fattish white unwholesome maiden aunt who, when she saw their mother, shrieked to the children – 'Run, children, run' – and the poor little things were terrified and ran. Frieda has written to her mother to come. I *do* hope that old Baroness will turn up in a state of indignation. Then we shall see sparks fly round the maggoty Weekley household – curse the etiolated lot of them, maggots.

Eventually Frieda went to the house and crept in by the back way. Many years later her daughter Barbara recalled:

She entered the nursery and found us at supper with Granny and Aunt Maude. She put her foot in it that evening; the law was invoked to restrain her. And while she stood at bay before our relations, we children gazed in horror at the strange woman she had then become. The stuffy old show: yes, indeed.

In 1925, by which time the girls were frequent visitors of the Lawrences, Lawrence, working largely from information supplied by Barbara, made that 'stuffy old show' the subject of his novel *The Virgin and The Gipsy*.

The Lawrences' circle of friends was rapidly expanding. In the summer of 1914 they met for the first time Catherine Carswell, Amy Lowell (who gave Lawrence his first typewriter and published him in the Imagist anthologies), Richard Aldington and his wife Hilda Doolittle, Ivy and Barbara Low, David Eder and Viola Meynell. Several of these new friends recorded the immediate and powerful effect Lawrence had on them. Catherine Carswell reported:

Nehls 1, 227   I was sensible of a fine, rare beauty in Lawrence, with his deep-set jewel-like eyes, thick dust-coloured hair, pointed underlip of notable sweetness, fine hands, and rapid but never restless movements. . . . It seemed a waste of time to talk about anything with him except one's real concerns.

It was the eyes they all remembered. Richard Aldington recalled this first sight of Lawrence:

Nehls 1, 236   A tall slim young man, with bright red hair and the most brilliant blue eyes, came in with a lithe, springing step. As a rule I don't remember people's eyes, but I shall not forget Lawrence's – they showed such a vivid flame-like spirit.

Another of Lawrence's new friends was Samuel Solomonovich Koteliansky. Kot (as he was known to all his friends) had come to England from Russia in 1911, and was working at the Russian Law Bureau, or at least spending his time there. He was never observed actually working. Katherine used to tell how Kot organized a revolution in Kiev against the Tsarist régime, but on the day appointed no one else turned up, so he started walking and did not stop till he got to Tottenham Court Road. Kot had no creative gifts, but he was an expert on Russian literature, and was absolutely dependable.

Katherine Mansfield and S. S. Koteliansky (Kot).

At Lerici Lawrence had met an engineer from Spezia called Lewis, who had accompanied him in his walk across Switzerland in June. They had arranged a walking tour in the Lake District: the tour began on 31 July. They were accompanied by a lawyer called Horne who brought his colleague from the Law Bureau, Kot. On 5 August they came down to Barrow-in-Furness, where Lewis lived, to find that war had been declared. In January 1915 Lawrence wrote:

Moore 309

The War finished me: it was the spear through the side of all sorrows and hopes. I had been walking in Westmorland, rather happy, with water-lilies twisted round my hat – big, heavy, white and gold water-lilies that we found in a pool high up – and girls who had come out on a spree and who were having tea in the upper room of an inn, shrieked with laughter. And I remember also we crouched under the loose wall on the moors and the rain flew by in streams, and the wind came rushing through the chinks in the wall behind one's head, and we shouted songs, and I imitated music-hall turns, whilst the other men crouched under the wall and pranked in the rain on the turf in the gorse, and Koteliansky groaned Hebrew music – Ranani Sadekim Badanoi.

It seems like another life – we *were* happy – four men. . . . And since then, since I came back, things have not existed for me. I have spoken to no one, I have touched no one, I have seen no one. All the while, I swear, my soul lay in the tomb – not dead, but with a flat stone over it, a corpse, become corpse-cold.

Kot became Lawrence's staunchest friend. And the song Lawrence had first heard Kot sing on that fatal day provided him, when he rose from the tomb six months later, with the name of the little colony on which he pinned all his fragile hopes – Rananim. 'Ranani Sadekim Badanoi' means 'Rejoice, O ye righteous in the Lord'. 'Ra'annanim' means green, fresh or flourishing. Rananim was to be a monastic community secluded from the sick world, of some twenty righteous or at least like-minded people dedicated to fostering 'new shoots of life' within themselves, and subsequently to seeding the sterile ruins of Western civilization.

Back in London there was a shock waiting for Lawrence. Methuen had returned *The Rainbow* saying that it was unpublishable as it stood, presumably because of 'flagrant love passages', though the passages which were subsequently to offend the reviewers were not in this version. Lawrence was so discouraged that he did not feel able to tackle the novel again for several months. There was also an invitation waiting for the Lawrences and the Murrys to a party at the home of H. G. Wells. Murry wanted to go in

Nehls 1, 239

flannels, but Lawrence insisted on wearing his new dress-suit. In Murry's words 'this initiation into the dress-suit world was for him a serious and ritual affair'. Lawrence was stiff, the party dismal. Afterwards he denounced Wells, who had been very pleasant with him. Wells had been an early enthusiasm of Lawrence's, especially *Tono-Bungay*, 'a great book'. In January 1910 he had read *Ann Veronica* and thought it 'not very good', but he took (and of course transformed) a good deal from it for the story of Ursula Brangwen. Though Lawrence came to find Wells stale, 'suburbanian', he never lost his enthusiasm for *Tono-Bungay* and 'The Country of the Blind'.

Moore 289   We can't go back to Italy as things stand, and I must look for somewhere to live. I think I shall try to get a tiny cottage somewhere, put a little bit of furniture in it, and live as cheaply as possible.

By 22 August, twelve days later, the Lawrences were settled at The Triangle, Bellingdon Lane, Chesham, Bucks.

Moore 289   This is a delightful cottage, really buried in the country.

But one of their first visitors, Compton Mackenzie, thought it was the ugliest cottage he Huxley 208 had ever seen, and buried in nettles, and Lawrence was soon calling it 'this God-forsaken little hole'. Certainly the cold and damp that winter were bad for Lawrence's health.

Nehls 1, 242   Mackenzie ('very flourishing and breezy: a nice fellow, I think, – for somebody other than me') had been brought by the Cannans, who lived near by and were friends of the Murrys. The Murrys themselves soon came to live only three miles away. Gilbert Cannan was a prolific but conventional novelist who had run away with J. M. Barrie's wife Mary and was now married to her. What a way Lawrence had come since, only five years before, he had gasped to the Chambers girls:

Nehls 3, 582   Barrie's wife's left him for a writer he had helped ever so much. Don't let's ever read any of his books. VOW never to read any of his books. Let's make a pact!

He did not, in fact, read many of Cannan's books, but only because he found them journalistic, vulgarizing and boring. That pact had been made in another life.
At Chesham Lawrence began his Hardy book:

Moore 290   What a miserable world. What colossal idiocy, this war. Out of sheer rage I've begun my book about Thomas Hardy.

It turned out to be 'about anything but Thomas Hardy' – a first working out of his Lowell 279 philosophy of life and art, his 'metaphysic' ('a sort of Confessions of my Heart'). The rage showed clearly in the wild gestures of the prose, the strident tone and uncontrolled form, the vast generalizations and assumption of omniscience. Much of it is tedious, turgid, or incomprehensible. Yet there is also much that is fine. What Lawrence most admired in Hardy was his perspective, setting his individuals not just Phoenix 419 against 'society' but against 'the terrific action of unfathomed nature'; not just against a system of human morality, but against 'the vast, uncomprehended and incomprehensible morality of nature or of life itself, surpassing human consciousness'. *The Study of Thomas Hardy* was part of Lawrence's search for a vision of reality Moore 291 to replace the madness of the war and the war-fever – a vision 'that contains awe and dread and submission, not pride or sensuous egotism and assertion'. He felt he had seen such a vision at work in Egyptian and Assyrian sculpture on a recent visit to the British Museum:

We want to realize the tremendous *non-human* quality of life – it is wonderful. It is not the emotions, nor the personal feelings and attachments, that matter. These are all only expressive, and expression has become mechanical. Behind it all are the tremendous unknown forces of life, coming unseen and unperceived as out of the desert to the Egyptians, and driving us, forcing us, destroying us if we do not submit to be swept away.

The £300 did not last long. Frieda could no longer get money from Germany. Lawrence could not afford to pay for the typing of the *Study*, but Kot volunteered to do it for love. Lawrence had to swallow his pride and accept loans from such friends as Eddie Marsh, and £50 from the Royal Literary Fund:

Priest 208   There is no joy in their tame thin-gutted charity. I would fillip it back at their cold noses, the stodgy, stomachy authors, if I could afford it. But I can't.

There was real joy, however, in Amy Lowell's gift of a typewriter:

Lowell 277   It goes like a bubbling pot, frightfully jolly.

In November Lawrence resumed work on *The Rainbow*, 'working *frightfully* hard'. In December they spent a few days in the Midlands. Frieda paid a surprise visit to Ernest Weekley, announcing herself to the landlady as Mrs Lawson. Lawrence told the whole story to Amy Lowell:

Moore 298   'You –' said the quondam husband, backing away – 'I hoped never to see you again.'
Frieda: Yes – I know.
Quondam Husband: And what are you doing in *this* town?
Frieda: I came to see you about the children.
Quondam Husband: Aren't you ashamed to show your face where you are known! Isn't the commonest prostitute better than you?
Frieda: Oh no.
Quon. Husb.: Do you want to drive me off the face of the earth, Woman? Is there no place where I can have peace?
Frieda: You see I must speak to you about the children.
Quon. Husb.: You shall *not* have them – they don't want to see you.
   Then the conversation developed into a deeper tinge of slanging – part of which was:
Q.H.: If you had to go away, why didn't you go away with a *gentleman*?
Frieda: He is a *great* man.
   Further slanging.
Q.H.: Don't you know you are the vilest creature on earth?
Frieda: Oh no.
   A little more of such, and a departure of Frieda. She is no further to seeing her children.
Q.Husb.: Don't you know, my solicitors have instructions to arrest you, if you attempt to interfere with the children?
Frieda: I don't care.
   If this weren't too painful, dragging out for three years, as it does, it would be very funny, I think. The Quondam Husband is a Professor of French Literature,

great admirer of Maupassant, has lived in Germany and Paris, and thinks he is the tip of cosmopolitan culture. But poor Frieda can't see her children. – I really give you the conversation verbatim.

A year or two later Weekley was at last persuaded to allow the children half an hour with their mother in a solicitor's office. At parting she gave them ten shillings each. Ernest formally returned the money.

◢◢

In December Gilbert Cannan introduced Lawrence to Lady Ottoline Morrell. Lady Ottoline, thirteen years older than Lawrence, was the daughter of Arthur Cavendish Bentinck and Lady Bolsover. Her half-brother was the Duke of Portland. She had been brought up at Welbeck Abbey in Nottinghamshire, so they were able to share childhood memories at their first meeting. Lady Ottoline was larger than life, unconventional in both appearance and behaviour. Her hair was red. Her face seemed to some witchlike. Augustus John, who had painted her, and whom she had *Album 32* loved, was horrified by her 'prognathous jaw and bold baronial nose'; but she could make even these features majestic by her bearing. She reminded Lawrence of Queen Elizabeth. She accentuated her tallness with huge hats and vivid sweeping gowns. Sometimes she would dress as a shepherdess, complete with crook. She moved in a magic circle of beauty and lofty ideas, and gathered around her many of the leading thinkers, artists and writers of her time, especially the Bloomsbury group – Lytton Strachey, Dora Carrington, Mark Gertler, Virginia and Leonard Woolf, Vanessa and Clive Bell, Duncan Grant, Morgan Forster, Aldous Huxley, Dorothy Brett . . . At Oxford she had met and married Philip Morrell, now a Liberal M.P. and a pacifist. At the time she met Lawrence she was involved in a tempestuous affair with Bertrand Russell.

Lady Ottoline Morrell at Garsington. 'If you know her, be patient and go to the real things, not to the unreal things in her: for they are legion. But she is a big woman – something like Queen Elizabeth at the end.'

Dikran Kouyoumdjian (Michael Arlen), Philip Heseltine (Peter Warlock) and Lawrence at Garsington. 'Heseltine is a bit backboneless and needs stiffening up. But I like him very much; Kouyoumdjian seems a bit blatant and pushing.'

Garsington Manor, the Breadalby of Women in Love. *'So much beauty and pathos of old things passing away and no new things coming: this house of the Ottoline's – it is England – my God, it breaks my soul – their England, these shafted windows, the elm trees, the blue distance – the past, the great past, crumbling down, breaking down, not under the weight of many exhausted coming birds, but under the weight of many exhausted lovely yellow leaves, that drift over the lawn, and over the pond, like the soldiers, passing away, into winter and the darkness of winter – no, I can't bear it.'*

Aldous Huxley, Dorothy Brett and Mark Gertler at Garsington.

Lady Ottoline and Bertrand Russell.

Garsington

Lawrence became a frequent guest throughout 1915, first at Ottoline's London house in Bedford Square, then at Garsington Manor in Oxfordshire. Through her he met many important new friends (and potential recruits for Rananim). At Garsington Lawrence planted hedges and flowers and built a wooden rose-arbour. He visited the 'dead and useless' Oxford colleges with Ottoline, but enjoyed copying illuminated missals in the Bodleian.

As Christmas approached, with *The Rainbow* going well, Lawrence's spirits rose. Frieda recalled:

Frieda 99   Christmas came. We made the cottage splendid with holly and mistletoe, we cooked and boiled, roasted and baked. Campbell and Koteliansky and the Murrys came, and Gertler and the Cannans. We had a gay feast.

Lawrence's letters began to speak of resurrection rather than crucifixion, and of Rananim. The fullest account of Lawrence's 'pet scheme' is in a letter to Willie Hopkin of 18 January 1915:

Moore 307   I want to gather together about twenty souls and sail away from this world of war and squalor and find a little colony where there shall be no money but a sort of communism as far as necessaries of life go, and some real decency.

But already the 'assumption of goodness in the members' on which it was to be established had been thrown into doubt, at a less successful Christmas party, the Cannans', which had ended on a sour note when the Murrys and Gertler, having had too much to drink, acted out as a charade before the rest the real-life problems of their relationship. Lawrence was later to base the Gerald-Gudrun-Loerke triangle in *Women in Love* upon this. Gertler, in reality, was in love with Dora Carrington, who was in love with Lytton Strachey, who was a homosexual . . . It is no wonder that Lawrence later insisted that only married couples should be allowed aboard his Ark.

On 23 January 1915 the Lawrences drove 'in the Motor Car' through deep snow to the cottage Viola Meynell had lent them at Greatham, near Pulborough in Sussex:

The cottage is rather splendid – something monastic about it – severe white walls & oaken furniture – beautiful. And there is bathroom and all. And the country is very fine.

Lawrence felt the move had given him 'a new birth of life'. But still there was the problem of finding someone worthy to fight alongside him. On 28 January he confessed to Forster:

Delany 51   I can't find anybody. Each man is so bent on his own private fulfilment . . . And they make me tired, these friends of mine. They seem so childish and greedy, always the immediate desire, always the particular outlook, no conception of the whole horizon wheeling round.

Moore 323 Forster did not pass the test either; he seemed to Lawrence to be 'dying of inanition':

'I've been seedy, and I've grown a red beard, behind which I shall take as much cover henceforth as I can, like a creature under a bush.' Photo Bassano and Vandyke.

E. M. Forster.

Moore 315   We have talked so hard – about a revolution – at least I have talked – it is my fate,
God help me – and now I wonder, are my words gone like seed spilt on a hard floor,
only reckoned an untidiness there.

Lawrence scolded Forster so much on his visits to Greatham that at last the worm
turned:

Dear Lawrences

Delany 54   Until you think it worthwhile to function separately, I'd better address you as one
. . . As for coming again to Greatham, I like Mrs Lawrence, and I like the Lawrence
who talks to Hilda, and sees birds and is physically restful and wrote *The White
Peacock*, he doesn't know why; but I do not like the deaf impercipient fanatic who
has nosed over his own little sexual round until he believes that there is no other
path for others to take: he sometimes interests and sometimes frightens and angers
me, but in the end he will bore me merely, I know. So I can't yet tell about coming
down.

Forster's path was, of course, homosexual. He did not go to Greatham again, finding
Lawrence more admirable at a distance. 'I don't know where you've got to after
Howards End,' Lawrence had written. Forster cannot have told Lawrence of his
recently completed, unpublishable, homosexual novel *Maurice*.

Delany 52

When Lawrence had first read *Howards End*, in 1911, it must have made a deep
impression, for Forster's rainbow image clearly contributed to Lawrence's in *The
Rainbow*:

Howards End

... the rainbow bridge that should connect the prose in us with the passion.
Without it we are meaningless fragments, half monks, half beasts, unconnected
arches that have never joined into a man. . . . The bridge would be built and span
their lives with beauty.

The next candidate was Bertrand Russell:

Moore 314

Tomorrow Lady Ottoline is coming again & bringing Bertrand Russell – the
Philosophic-Mathematics man – a Fellow of Cambridge University – F.R.S. – Earl
Russell's brother. We are going to struggle with my island idea – *Rananim*. But
they say, the island shall be England, that we shall start our new community in the
midst of the old one, as a seed falls mong the roots of the parent. Only wait, and we
will remove mountains & set them in the midst of the sea.

Russell found Lawrence irresistible:

He is amazing; he sees through and through one. He is infallible. He is like Ezekiel
or some other Old Testament prophet, prophesying. Of course, the blood of his
nonconformist preaching ancestors is strong in him, but he sees everything and is
always right.

On 12 February Lawrence wrote to Russell:

Moore 317

There must be a revolution in the state. It shall begin by the nationalizing of all
industries and means of communication, and of the land – in one fell blow. Then a
man shall have his wages whether he is sick or well or old – if anything prevents
his working, he shall have his wages just the same. So we shall not live in fear of the
wolf – no man amongst us, and no woman, shall have any fear of the wolf at the
door, for all wolves are dead.
Which practically solves the whole economic question for the present.

And in his innocence Lawrence hoped to recruit the greatest living economist, John
Maynard Keynes, to his cause!

Lawrence invited Murry to Greatham. Murry was desolate, having been abandoned
by both Katherine, who had gone off to her lover Francis Carco in France, and Gilbert
Cannan, who had simply had enough of him. He walked four miles through floods to
Lawrence's cottage, caught influenza, and had to be nursed back to health by
Lawrence, on whom he became totally dependent. Lawrence wanted to give Murry too
a new birth of life, so that they could become partners in 'some great and all-inclusive
religious purpose', which meant that first the old Murry had to be broken down,

crucified. But Katherine returned after a week, and Murry fled back to her.

Lawrence had come to feel that the situation was so critical that art was a luxury. An artist is an explorer – 'one sent out from a great body of people to open out new lands for their occupation' – but what is the good of that if the people are chained and cannot follow. And the chains can be broken only by direct revolutionary action. Lawrence's own contribution would be to give joint lectures with Russell, to pull all Russell's Cambridge contacts into the cause ('I feel frightfully important coming to Cambridge – quite momentous the occasion is to me'), and to publish a new book about Life in weekly pamphlets – 'my initiation of the great and happy revolution'. It was in this mood of buoyant optimism that Lawrence finished *The Rainbow*.

Moore 319
Moore 327–8
Moore 328

Lawrence sent this drawing to Viola Meynell on 2 March 1915. 'I have finished my Rainbow, *bended it and set it firm. Now off and away to fine the pots of gold at its feet.'*

8 England, Their England

There was to be no 'great and happy revolution', no pots of gold at the feet of *The Rainbow*. Five days after finishing it, Lawrence went to Cambridge, and the bubble burst:

Nehls 1, 302
> When I saw Keynes that morning in Cambridge it was one of the crises of my life. It sent me mad with misery and hostility and rage.

What most upset Lawrence was the charming, sophisticated, witty, brittle, but Moore 332 essentially shallow and irresponsible talk ('never a good or real thing said') which passed for intelligence and civilization in the senior common rooms of Cambridge and Nehls 1, 302 on the lawns at Garsington. Lawrence knew that these people were 'done for forever'. Keynes later conceded that this judgement was not baseless, and even Russell thought for a time that Lawrence might be right. Lawrence was particularly sickened by the prevalent homosexuality of the Bloomsbury–Cambridge crowd:

Moore 333
> These horrible little frowsty people, men lovers of men, they give me such a sense of corruption, almost putrescence, that I dream of beetles.

Lawrence had a lifelong horror of homosexuality, in reaction against a strong tendency towards it in himself. But he did believe in the closest bonds of friendship and brotherhood between men, cemented not by sexual love (though he believed that the avoidance of physical contact between men in our society was a crippling inhibition), but by an impersonal commitment to a common cause, a sense of working shoulder to shoulder towards a large creative goal. Murry and Russell were to stand on either side of him. Murry had been at home with the Rananim idea, without really believing in it:

Nehls 1, 277
> I crystallized my daydreams about it as freely as he did his own.

But when Lawrence sought to enrol him under the banner of Revolution he was out of his depth. Murry, without in the least understanding what was being asked of him, set out to be what Lawrence desired. He was flattered that Lawrence should lean on him, but at the same time knew himself to be in a false position, and that he must sooner or later let Lawrence down.

Even after the Cambridge fiasco Lawrence tried to hold on to Russell:

Moore 330   But I wanted to write this to ask you please to be with me – in the underworld – or at any rate to wait for me. Don't let me go, that is all. . . . I wish you would swear a sort of allegiance with me.

Lawrence was certainly, at that moment in early April, on the brink of madness:

Huxley 237   I have a great struggle with the Powers of Darkness lately. I think I have just got the better of them again. Don't tell me there is no Devil; there is a Prince of Darkness. Sometimes I wish I could let go and be really wicked – kill and murder – but kill chiefly. I do want to kill. But I want to select whom I shall kill. Then I shall enjoy it.

Lawrence had come to feel that England was sick, in need of drastic surgery:

Huxley 234   I thought the war would surgeon us. Still it may.

Moore 336   For I am hostile, hostile, hostile to all that is, in our public and national life. I want to destroy it.

In April Lawrence turned once more to Rananim. Philip Morrell had offered to adapt an old 'monastic building' for the purpose at Garsington. Once more Lawrence's hopes were raised only to be dashed: the estimate from the contractors Schorer 51 was 'impossible beyond all consideration', and the idea had to be abandoned.

On 30 April 1915 Lawrence wrote one of his finest letters, to Lady Ottoline:

Moore 337–8   I wish I were going to Thibet – or Kamschatka – or Tahiti – to the ultima, ultima, ultima Thule. I feel sometimes I shall go mad, because there is nowhere to go, no 'new world'. One of these days, unless I watch myself, I shall be departing in some rash fashion to some foolish place . . .

I almost wish I could go to the war – not to shoot: I have vowed an eternal oath that I won't shoot in this war, not even if I am shot. I should like to be a bus conductor at the front – anything to escape this, that is.

The death of Rupert Brooke fills me more and more with the sense of the fatuity of it all. He was slain by bright Phoebus' shaft – it was in keeping with his general sunniness – it was the real climax of his pose. I first heard of him as a Greek god under a Japanese sunshade, reading poetry in his pyjamas, at Grantchester, – at Grantchester upon the lawns where the river goes. Bright Phoebus smote him down. It is all in the saga.

O God, O God, it is all too much of a piece: it is like madness.

Yesterday, at Worthing, there were many soldiers. Can I ever tell you how ugly they were. 'To insects – sensual lust'. I like sensual lust – but insectwise, no – it is obscene. I like men to be beasts – but insects – one insect mounted on another – oh God! The soldiers at Worthing are like that – they remind me of lice or bugs: 'to insects – sensual lust'. They will murder their officers one day. They are teeming insects. What massive creeping hell is let loose nowadays.

It isn't my disordered imagination. There is a wagtail sitting on the gate-post. I see how sweet and swift heaven is. But hell is slow and creeping and viscous and insect-teeming: as is this Europe now, this England.

That it is not indeed his disordered imagination is guaranteed not only by the wagtail but by the perfect living expressiveness of his prose. Writing many such letters was one way of asserting the possibility of sanity in a mad world.

Lawrence's attitude to the war was at this stage highly ambivalent. If 'the world of men' was so far gone that only the end of that world could create the conditions for a fresh start, then apocalypse was to be welcomed, and perhaps the war was apocalypse. But for a fresh start there had to be some survivors:

Moore 347   Death, and ever more death, till the fire burns itself out. Let it be so – I am willing. But I won't die. Let us remain and get a new start made, when we can get a look in.

But Lawrence did not always insist on being Noah when the flood came. There are moments when his acquiescence seems to include the possibility of his own annihilation. At Brighton he was strongly tempted to walk off the cliffs. His desperation was no doubt increased by incessant rows with Frieda. It seemed for a while that they must live apart. On 2 June Lawrence told Forster that Frieda was flathunting in London, 'unless a bomb has dropped on her – killed by her own countrymen – it is the kind of fate she is cut out for'.

Lawrence's first work of fiction after *The Rainbow*, and the first in which he wrote of the war, was 'England, My England', written at the beginning of June 1915. It is a bloodless, disembodied tale, but not inappropriately so, since it depicts a sort of Heartbreak House where the protagonist, Edgar, lives 'as a sort of epicurean hermit', tampering with the arts, committed to nothing. Lawrence had seen and lived among many such families these last months. They seemed to him essentially English in their niceness and ineffectuality. The tone of the story is, at the outset, clearly ironic, but in the last few pages, after the outbreak of war, the irony disappears, as Lawrence associates himself more and more closely with Egbert. Egbert's last thoughts, as he lies dying in No Man's Land, echo several of Lawrence's 1915 letters:

Better the terrible work should go forward, the dissolving into the black sea of death, in the extremity of dissolution, than that there should be any reaching back towards life.

In July Russell sent Lawrence his lecture notes, under the title 'Philosophy of Social Reconstruction'. Lawrence returned them much defaced with NO!s:

Moore 354   You *must* work out the idea of a new state, not go on criticizing this old one.

The word 'must' he underlined fifteen times. Lawrence gave Russell *his* idea of a new state. The great enemy was democracy: 'Liberty, Equality & Fraternity is the three-fanged serpent.' Lawrence proposed a three-tier structure: the workers to elect only management and local government; then 'a body of chosen patricians'; finally 'an absolute *Dictator*, & an equivalent *Dictatrix*' (for women were to govern equally with men at every stage, being responsible for 'the things relating to private life'). Russell accused Lawrence of wanting tyrants. He denied the charge, claiming that what he
Moore 355   wanted was 'an elected King, something like Julius Caesar'. What ailed Russell,

Lawrence told Lady Ottoline, was 'the inexperience of youth'. Russell was forty-three, Lawrence twenty-nine.

Russell, like so many others, had been swept away by Lawrence's visionary enthusiasm. At first, in Russell's phrase, 'all went merry as a marriage bell':

Nehls 1, 282   For a time I thought he might be right. I liked Lawrence's fire, I liked the energy and passion of his feelings, I liked his belief that something very fundamental was needed to put the world right. I agreed with him in thinking that politics could not be divorced from individual psychology. I felt him to be a man of certain imaginative genius and, at first, when I felt inclined to disagree with him, I thought that perhaps his insight into human nature was better than mine. It was only gradually that I came to feel him a positive force for evil and that he came to have the same feeling about me.

Russell's letters to Lady Ottoline Morrell in the early months of 1915 reveal the fluctuations of his feelings:

Ottoline 56–9   His intuitive perceptiveness is *wonderful* – it leaves me gasping in admiration. . . .
        I love him more and more. I couldn't dream of discouraging his socialist revolution. He has real faith in it, and it absorbs his vital force – he must go through with it. He talks so well about it that he almost makes me believe in it. . . .
        His attitude is a little mad and not quite honest, or at least very muddled. He has not learnt the lesson of individual impotence. And he regards all my attempts to make him acknowledge facts as mere timidity, lack of courage to think boldly, self-indulgence in pessimism. When one gets a glimmer of the facts into his head, as I did at last, he gets discouraged, and says he will go to the South Sea Islands, and bask in the sun with six native wives. He is tough work. The trouble with him is a tendency to mad exaggeration. . . .
        I don't know whether I shall be able to feel any faith in my own ideas after arguing with him, although my reason is all against him. I am depressed, partly by Lawrence's criticism. I feel a worm, a useless creature, sometimes I enumerate my capacities, and wonder why I am not more use in the world.

Lawrence's letter of 14 September had a devastating effect:

Nehls 1, 284–5   For twenty four hours I thought that I was not fit to live and contemplated committing suicide. But at the end of that time, a healthier reaction set in, and I decided to have done with such morbidness. When he said that I must preach his doctrines and not mine I rebelled and told him to remember that he was no longer a schoolmaster and I was not his pupil. He had written:

        The enemy of all mankind you are, full of the lust of enmity. It is not a hatred of falsehood which inspires you, it is the hatred of people of flesh and blood, it is a perverted mental blood-lust. Why don't you own it? Let us become strangers again. I think it is better.

I thought so too. But he found a pleasure in denouncing me, and continued for some months to write letters containing sufficient friendliness to keep the correspondence alive. In the end it faded away without any dramatic termination.

The joint lectures were abandoned. Abandoned too, for the time being, was Rananim:

Moore 363   I had hoped and tried to get a little nucleus of living people together. But I think it is no good. One must start direct with the open public, without associates. But how to begin, and when, I don't know yet.

At the beginning of August the Lawrences had moved to the Vale of Health, Hampstead, and so now saw more of the Murrys. In September they decided to launch a periodical called *The Signature*. Lawrence's contribution, his 'first try at a direct approach to the public', was to be his brilliant but obscure metaphysical
Moore 368   fantasia 'The Crown'. Subscriptions to *The Signature* were for six issues; there were only about fifty. After three issues 'the helpless little brown magazine' died. Ten years later Lawrence blamed Murry for the fiasco:

Phoenix 2, 364   John Middleton Murry said to me: 'Let us do something'. The doing consisted in starting a tiny monthly paper, which Murry called *The Signature*, and in having weekly meetings somewhere in London – I have now no idea where it was – up a narrow stair-case over a green-grocer's shop: or a cobbler's shop. The only thing that made any impression on me was the room over the shop, in some old Dickensey part of London, and the old man downstairs. We scrubbed the room and colour-washed the walls and got a long table and some windsor chairs from the Caledonian market. And we used to make a good warm fire: it was dark autumn, in the unknown bit of London. Then on Thursday nights we had meetings of about a dozen people. We talked, but there was absolutely nothing in it. And the meetings didn't last two months.

On 30 September *The Rainbow*, undoubtedly the finest novel of its time, was
Draper 91–7   published. Robert Lynd described it as 'a monotonous wilderness of phallicism' and advised his readers to leave it alone. On 22 October James Douglas's review appeared in *Star*. *The Rainbow*, he said, had 'no right to exist':

Why open all the doors that the wisdom of man has shut and bolted and double-locked?

A similar review appeared the following day, in *Sphere*, by Clement Shorter:

There is no form of viciousness, of suggestiveness, that is not reflected in these pages.

Proceedings were initiated against Methuen by Sir Charles Matthews, Director of Public Prosecutions, in the name of the Commissioner of Police. The solicitor acting for the prosecution was Herbert Muskett. The magistrate, Sir John Dickinson, was clearly influenced by Douglas and Shorter, who were much quoted in court. He described the novel as 'utter filth'. Douglas's review had concluded:

The young men who are dying for liberty are moral beings. They are the living repudiation of such impious denials of life as *The Rainbow*. The life they lay down is a lofty thing. It is not the thing that creeps and crawls in this novel.

This must have hit Sir John Dickinson hard: his son had been killed at the front six weeks earlier. Lawrence was known to be against the war, and to have a German wife. The dedication of *The Rainbow* to Else cannot have helped him. On 15 November *The Times* reported:

> At Bow Street Police Court on Saturday, Messrs Methuen and Co. (Limited), publishers, Essex Street, Strand, were summoned before Sir John Dickinson to show cause why 1,011 copies of Mr D. H. Lawrence's novel *The Rainbow* should not be destroyed. The defendants expressed regret that the book should have been published, and the magistrate ordered that the copies should be destroyed and that the defendants should pay £10.10s. costs.

The legend is that the confiscated copies were burnt by the public hangman outside the Royal Exchange. The publishers had not even informed Lawrence of the proceedings. They had offered no defence, and had agreed with the prosecution's description of the novel. They claimed that they had refused to publish until certain alterations had been made; that Lawrence's agent had assured them that their wishes had been carried out; that they had not discovered until proof stage that the book was still objectionable; and that Lawrence had then made further alterations but refused to make others. All this was true enough. Only three days before publication Methuen's had written to Pinker:

> I am afraid we are likely to get into trouble over D. H. Lawrence's new novel and we hope he will try to moderate his broadmindedness in the next novel.

By playing along with the prosecution Methuen's managed to divert all the obloquy on to the absent author and avoided a fine. They actively discouraged Clive Bell and Pinker from trying to get the decision reversed. They even asked Lawrence for their £300 back.

Philip Morrell twice asked questions about the case in the House of Commons. The Home Secretary, Sir John Simon, replied that the law had taken its proper course, but Delavenay 241 the mysterious note in red ink on his briefing: 'As to a Mrs Weekley living at address of D. H. Lawrence, see 352857' indicates a political motivation and significant Home Office involvement in the case.

On the day before the Douglas review Lawrence had written to Lady Cynthia Asquith to express his horror at the death of her brother:

Moore 371
> In this war, in the whole spirit which we now maintain, I do not believe, I believe it is wrong, so awfully wrong, that it is like a great consuming fire that draws up all our souls in its draught. So if they will let me I shall go away soon, to America. Perhaps you will say it is cowardice: but how shall one submit to such ultimate wrong as this which we commit, now, England – and the other nations? If thine eye offend thee, pluck it out. And I am English, and my Englishness is my very

vision. But now I must go away, if my soul is sightless for ever. Let it then be blind, rather than commit the vast wickedness of acquiescence.

Lawrence was almost the only English writer of the time (Shaw being an Irishman) who was not compromised by the government-sponsored propaganda campaign in the popular press. He knew that the spirit in which the war was waged would determine the spirit in which the peace was made, and the quality of life in England for generations to come. He knew that the decencies for which Asquith stood were rooted in nothing more vital than class privilege, sentimentality and nostalgia, and the debilitating refinement of a classical education. He knew that the future was in the hands of the indecent Lloyd George and his press-baron cronies, who were manipulating and pandering to the lowest instincts of the masses:

Moore 369   Only I feel, that even if we are all going to be rushed down to extinction, one must hold up the other, living truth, of Right and pure reality, the reality of the clear, eternal spirit. One must speak for life and growth, amid all this mass of destruction and disintegration.

On 30 October, Lawrence sent Lady Cynthia his war story 'The Thimble', with an impassioned letter:

Moore 373   If the war could but end this winter, we might rise to life again, here in this our world. If it sets in for another year, all is lost. One should give anything now, give the Germans England and the whole empire, if they want it, so we may save the hope of a resurrection from the dead, we English, all Europe. What is the whole empire, and kingdom, save the thimble in my story? If we could bring our souls through, to life.

The following day Lady Cynthia recorded her response to the story in her diary:

Asquith 95   It is extremely well written, I think, though the symbolism of the thimble is somewhat obscure. I *was* amused to see the 'word-picture' of me. He has quite gratuitously put in the large feet. I think some of his character hints are damnably good. He has kept fairly close to the model in the circumstances.

Lawrence had not sent her the story for her amusement. All her references to 'poor Lawrence' in her diaries are shallow and patronizing. All she could see in his diatribes against the war was that he seemed to think she ought to be able to stop it single-handed.

Perhaps Lawrence was a bit in love with Lady Cynthia, and, not wishing to admit to himself that he could be impressed by mere beauty and aristocratic charm, tried to convince both himself and Lady Cynthia that she had deeper qualities. Unfortunately she had not. Lawrence felt strongly the need for an aristocracy, but only if the aristocrats justified themselves by standing above the merely local and temporal. He was later to write to Lady Cynthia:

Moore 510   I feel angry with you, the way you have betrayed everything that is real, by admitting the superiority of that which is merely temporal and foul and external

upon us. If all the aristocrats have sold the vital principle of life to the mere current of foul affairs, what good are the aristocrats?

Murry's resistance to Lawrence's political and utopian notions is understandable, but this response to *The Rainbow* was, for a man in the process of becoming a professional literary critic, unforgivable:

Murry 2, 351   I could not understand it at all. I disliked it on instinct. There was a warm, close, heavy promiscuity of flesh about it which repelled me, and I could not understand the compulsion which was upon Lawrence to write in that fashion and of those themes; neither could I understand his surprise and dismay that the critics were out for his blood. As far as mere feeling went, I felt with them. I happened to be friends with Lawrence, and Robert Lynd didn't: that was about the only difference.

Nevertheless, he was still going through the motions of being Lawrence's lieutenant; and of preparing to start a new life with him in the New World. At the end of October Lawrence and Murry sat for hours in a shed at the Foreign Office trying to get passports. They had the offer of a cottage at Fort Myers in Florida. At last, with some help from the Asquiths, Lawrence got his passport. He was also totally without money. Lady Ottoline sent him £10, Eddie Marsh £20 and Bernard Shaw £5 towards his ticket to sail to New York on 24 November. But Lawrence postponed his sailing in the vain hope of action by the Society of Authors, which he had joined after the *Rainbow* verdict. Also he wanted to sail direct to Florida, not via New York; and a new acquaintance, the composer Philip Heseltine ('Peter Warlock'), was negotiating with Frederick Delius about his 'forsaken estate' in Florida. Delius replied:

Nehls 1, 330   I should have loved to be of use to Lawrence whose work I admire, but to let him go to Florida would be sending him to disaster.

On 25 November Lawrence wrote to the Murrys:

Moore 389   If only it will all end up happily, like a song or a poem, and we live blithely by a big river, where there are fish, and in the forest behind wild turkeys and quails; there we make songs and poems and stories and dramas, in a Vale of Avalon, in the Hesperides, among the Loves.

Another potential recruit at this time was Aldous Huxley. At Lady Ottoline's suggestion, Lawrence invited him to tea:

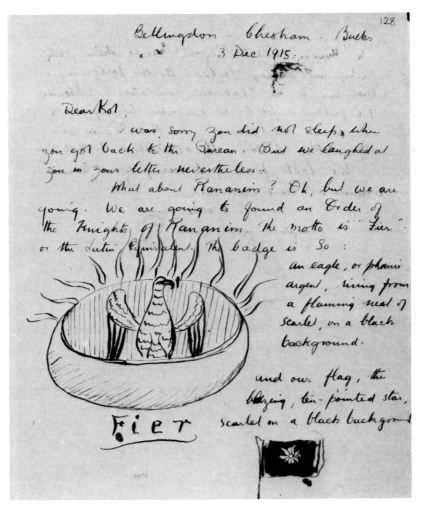

Lawrence copied his phoenix from Mrs Henry Jenner's Christian Symbolism.

Huxley xxix

Before tea was over he asked me if I would join the colony, and though I was an intellectually cautious young man, not at all inclined to enthusiasms, though Lawrence had startled and embarrassed me with sincerities of a kind to which my upbringing had not accustomed me, I answered yes.

But Huxley was relieved when the scheme fell through:

It was better that it should have remained, as it was always to remain, a project and a hope.

Huxley 284

Lawrence's next project was to sail by tramp steamer on 20 December, accompanied by Heseltine and Suhrawardy, 'a lineal descendant of the Prophet', whom Lawrence had met at Garsington. The lease of the Hampstead house was transferred from that date, the furniture sold. Then came the news that Lawrence would not be allowed to leave the country without exemption from military service. He went to a recruiting station at Battersea Town Hall, waited two hours, then came away. The repulsiveness of that degrading situation was stronger than the pull of America. He would go to Cornwall, to a house lent by J. D. Beresford at Porthcothan near Padstow:

Moore 403

Some members of our Florida expedition are coming down too – we begin the new life in Cornwall. It is real.

Russell 66

But only for a few weeks, or months. They would certainly be in Florida before the end of the summer. There were several young people 'anxious to come'. Russell was invited to 'come and be president of us'.

The Lawrences moved to Porthcothan on 30 December. Lawrence felt it was his

Huxley 301

'first move outwards, to a new life':

Eder 118

We arrived here to-night – a fine large house with clear, large rooms, and such lovely silence, with a little wind and a faint sound of the sea: such peace, I could cry. One only wants to be allowed to begin to love again – not all this friction and going apart. Only let us begin once more to love – I feel like imploring the winds and the waters. But one dare not address the people.

The people had chosen instead Horatio Bottomley as their spokesman, preaching jingoistic hatred and hypocritical puritanism in his weekly *John Bull*:

Kangaroo

It was in 1915 the old world ended. In the winter 1915–1916 the spirit of the old London collapsed; the city, in some way, perished, perished from being a heart of the world, and became a vortex of broken passions, lusts, hopes, fears, and horrors. The integrity of London collapsed, and the genuine debasement began, the unspeakable baseness of the press and the public voice, the reign of that bloated ignominy, *John Bull*.

As the year ended Lawrence nursed his fragile hopes:

Eder 118

There is a Florida to be – it must be so. We must all leave that complex, disintegrating life – London, England. Here one stands on tiptoe, ready to leap off.

9 The Nightmare

Lawrence did not go to Florida in 1916, or anywhere else. He never set foot outside Cornwall. Within a week he expressed himself willing to give up Florida, to give up people altogether, if only he could be left alone to get on with his 'intimate art'. He felt like a fox run to earth:

Delany 188   There is no Florida, there's only this, this England, which nauseates my soul, nauseates my spirit and my body – this England. One might as well be blown over the cliffs here in the strong wind, into the rough white sea, as sit at this banquet of vomit, this life, this England, this Europe.

Moore 411   He owned that he was beaten and would struggle and strive no more, just drift like thistledown, having no connection with the world, a world as unreal as 'the lights of last night's Café Royal'. 1916 he proclaimed 'Year 1 of the new world', a world with 'no people in it but new-born people: moi-même et Frieda'. Heseltine and Kouyoumdjian, the popular novelist, 'Michael Arlen', were staying with the Lawrences, but Lawrence now found them 'sick', 'disintegrated'. He still liked Heseltine, but Kouyoumdjian was too self-assertive and Lawrence sent him away.

Lawrence was in bed ill much of the time. Maitland Radford examined him and told him there was nothing organically wrong, that his nerves were the root of the trouble. At least he found Cornwall more congenial than anywhere else he had lived in England:

Moore 410   I like being here. I like the rough seas and this bare country, King Arthur's country, of the flicker of pre-Christian Celtic civilization. I like it very much.

Lawrence began his 'philosophy' again and was sure that this time he had 'got it':

Moore 414   It's come at last. I am satisfied, and as sure as a lark in the sky.

Moore 424   He had set himself the awesome task of defining the 'new world', for there was no hope left for the old one but to slide 'in horror down into the bottomless pit':

Huxley 319   We shall stay in Cornwall till our money is gone – which will take three or four months – then I think we may as well all go and drown ourselves. For I see no prospect of the war's ever ending, and not a ghost of a hope that people will ever want sincere work from any artist. It is a damned life.

Nevertheless, Lawrence felt that the only idea was to found a publishing company 'that publishes for the sake of the truth':

A book is a holy thing, and must be made so again.

Heseltine wrote and distributed the following prospectus:

THE RAINBOW BOOKS AND MUSIC

Nehls 1, 348–9 Either there exists a sufficient number of people to buy books because of their reverence for truth, or else books must die. In its books lie a nation's vision; and where there is no vision the people perish.

The present system of production depends entirely upon the popular esteem: and this means gradual degradation. Inevitably, more and more, the published books are dragged down to the level of the lowest reader.

It is monstrous that the herd should lord it over the uttered word. The swine have only to grunt disapprobation, and the very angels of heaven will be compelled to silence.

It is time that enough people of courage and passionate soul should rise up to form a nucleus of the living truth; since there must be those among us who care more for the truth than for any advantage.

For this purpose it is proposed to attempt to issue privately such books and musical works as are found living and clear in truth; such books as would either be rejected by the publisher, or else overlooked when flung into the trough before the public.

The method of private printing and circulation would also unseal those sources of truth and beauty which are now sterile in the heart, and real works would again be produced.

It is proposed to print first *The Rainbow*, the novel by Mr D. H. Lawrence, which has been so unjustly suppressed. If sufficient money is forthcoming, a second book will be announced: either Mr Lawrence's philosophical work, 'Goats and Compasses' or a new book by some other writer.

Heseltine wrote to Delius that it was a 'despairing project', and indeed there were only about thirty replies to the 600 circulars.

When Lawrence moved to Zennor in March, he hoped that Heseltine would join
Nehls 1, 351 him and the Murrys there. But in the meantime Heseltine had 'found him out' and decided to abandon any attempt at a personal relationship. He had probably discovered that Lawrence had been discussing his private life and his mistresses with Lady Ottoline Morrell. So Rainbow Books and Music collapsed. But Lawrence did finish 'Goats and Compasses'. Cecil Gray read a typescript in 1916 and described it as
Nehls 1, 582 'a bombastic, pseudomystical, psycho-philosophical treatise dealing largely with homosexuality'. Of the two copies which existed, Lawrence burnt one and Heseltine used the other for toilet paper. It is likely, however, that a good deal of 'Goats and Compasses' went into Lawrence's next attempt at his philosophy – 'The Reality of Peace'.

THE
RAINBOW

D. H.
LAWRENCE

This story, by one of the most remarkable of the younger school of novelists, contains a history of the Brangwen character through its developing crises of love, religion, and social passion. It ends with Ursula, the leading-shoot of the restless, fearless family, waiting at the advance-post of our time to blaze a path into the future.

METHUEN

THE RAINBOW
D.H. Lawrence

The dust-wrapper of the first edition of The Rainbow, Methuen 1915. *The synopsis is probably by Lawrence.*

I

'I think the greatest pleasure I ever got came from copying Fra Angelico's Flight into Egypt. . . . working from photographs and putting in my own colour. . . . Then I really learned what life, what powerful life has been put into every curve, every motion of a great picture.' (Making Pictures)

Portrait of Dorothy ('Arabella') Yorke by D. H. Lawrence.

Jan Juta's 1920 portrait of Lawrence 'looking with his penetrating eyes into the troubled future'.
Lawrence called it 'the Wild Man of Borneo'.

NUORO

One of Jan Juta's illustrations for Sea and Sardinia.

'*The lovely unapproachableness, indomitable. And the flash of the black and white, the slow stride of the full white drawers, the black gaiters and black cuirass with the bolero, then the great white sleeves and white breast again, and once more the black cap—what marvellous massing of the contrast, marvellous, and superb, as on a magpie.—How beautiful maleness is, if it finds its right expression.*'

'Gotzsche is doing a real forcible portrait of me in my leather shirt & blue overalls— if he doesn't spoil it.' 19 January 1923.

The Road to Mitla
by Brett and Lawrence.
'I hold up my painting proudly. "Oh, Brett", you say, testily, "Do look at the mountain. It has great bare toes, where it joins the desert. Here, let me have a try." Down you sit, and with delicate finger-touches, you proceed to give the mountain its toes. You roughen the fir-trees on the mountain and darken the blue of the sky. . . . "It needs some animals, but it is nice", you say; and you paint in the right hand corner some women, burros, goats and dogs. "I like my women better than yours," you remark.'

Brett: 'My big picture of the desert, with all our ranch life going on, is progressing. We are all working on it. You and I do most of it. . . . "Look at my Tepee and Indians. Aren't they much better than yours?" you ask. Then you say, "I'll put Timsy just there," and with careful fingers you paint Timsy arching her back. . . . You shove me aside. "If that is Susan, the Lord help her—she'll never stand on legs like that, let alone run". With careful fingers you make a wild, flying Susan.'

Lawrence and his Three Fates *by Brett. The women are Mabel, Frieda and Brett.*

The Finding of Moses

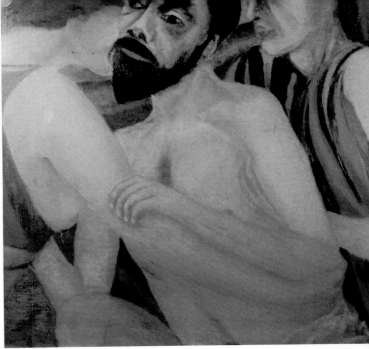

Resurrection

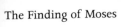
Boccaccio Story

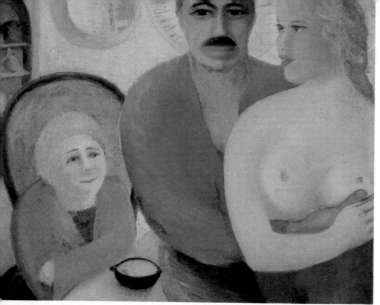

A Holy Family 'I call it the Unholy Family, because the bambino—with a nimbus—is just watching anxiously to see the young man give the semi-nude young woman un gros baiser. Molto moderno!'

Design by Lawrence from a Maya motif for the Black Sun Press edition of Sun.

Watercolour frontispiece by Lawrence for the Black Sun Press Escaped Cock.

Figure from the tomb of the Augurs at Tarquinia worked in wool by Lawrence and Frieda.

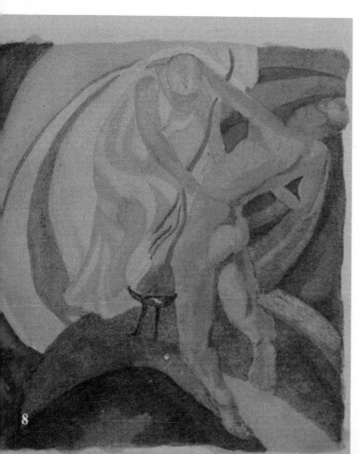

Higher Tregerthen, Zennor. 'I told you all about the house: the great grey granite boulders, you will love them, the rough primeval hill behind us, the sea beyond the few fields, that have great boulders half submerged in the grass, and stone grey walls. . . . And your tower-room is all wood and windows, panelled, with 3 big windows, and cosy as can be.'

Moore 440   At Zennor Lawrence felt he had found 'the best place to live in which we shall find in England'. He sent the Murrys drawings of the three cottages at Higher Tregerthen, 'like a little monastery . . . our Rananim':

Moore 441   Let it be agreed for ever. I am Blutbruder: a Blutbruderschaft between us all.

At the beginning of April the Murrys arrived, and they all worked furiously getting their cottage ready.

Lawrence's health improved with the coming of spring. In April he began *Women in Love*. As early as 1 May he had come to feel that the new novel was 'beyond all hope of ever being published' or even offered to 'a putrescent mankind like ours':

Moore 449

But a work of art is an act of faith, as Michael Angelo says, and one goes on writing, to the unseen witnesses.

Nevertheless the work went rapidly through May, and at the end of the month he wrote:

Moore 454   Two-thirds of the novel are written. It goes on pretty fast, and very easy. I have not travailed over it. It is the book of my free soul.

By the end of June the book was finished, except for the last chapter which he left for Moore 460 a time when his heart would be 'less contracted'.

Several things had happened to drain Lawrence of the faith he needed to finish the novel. There was the debilitating grind of poverty: at the end of April he had £15 between himself and complete starvation. There were the violent fights with Frieda, one of which was graphically described to Kot by Katherine:

Miscellany 132

Frieda said Shelley's 'Ode to a Skylark' was false. Lawrence said, 'You are showing off; you don't know anything about it.' Then she began. '*Now* I have had enough. Out of my house. You little God Almighty you. I've had enough of you. Are you going to keep your mouth shut or aren't you.' Said Lawrence: 'I'll give you a dab on the cheek to quiet you, you dirty hussy.' Etc. Etc. So I left the house. At dinner-time Frieda appeared. 'I have finally done with him. It is all over for ever.' She then went out of the kitchen and began to walk round and round the house in the dark. Suddenly Lawrence appeared and made a kind of horrible blind rush at her and they began to scream and scuffle. He beat her – he beat her to death – her heart and face and breast and pulled out her hair. All the while she screamed for Murry to help her. Finally they dashed into the kitchen and round and round the table. I shall never forget how L. looked. He was so white – almost green and he just hit, thumped the big soft woman. Then he fell into one chair and she into another. No one said a word. A silence fell except for Frieda's sobs and sniffs. I felt almost glad that the tension between them was over for ever, and that they had made an end of their 'intimacy'. L. sat staring at the floor, biting his nails. Frieda sobbed. . . . Suddenly, after a long time – about a quarter of an hour – L. looked up and asked Murry a question about French literature. Murry replied. Little by little, the three drew up to the table. . . . Then F. poured herself some coffee. Then she and L. glided into talk, began to discuss some 'very rich but very good macaroni cheese'. And next day, whipped himself, and far more thoroughly than he had ever beaten Frieda, he was running about taking her up her breakfast to her bed and trimming her a hat.

The Murrys left in mid-June for calmer waters:

Moore 452

They should have a soft valley, with leaves and the ring-dove cooing.

said Lawrence.
Katherine wrote:

Mansfield 68–9

He simply raves, roars, beats the table, abuses everybody. But that's not such great matter. What makes these attacks insupportable is the feeling one has at the back of one's mind that he is completely out of control. Swallowed up in acute insane irritation. After one of these attacks he's ill with fever, haggard and broken. . . . They are both too tough for me to enjoy playing with. I hate games where people lose their tempers in this way – it's so witless. In fact they are not my kind at all. I cannot discuss blood affinity to beasts for instance if I have to keep ducking to avoid the flat irons and the saucepans. And I shall *never* see sex in trees, sex in running brooks, sex in stones and sex in everything.

Moore 456

And Murry backed away from 'blutbruderschaft', which he envisaged as black magic on the moors. Then there was Lawrence's second medical examination, at Bodmin on 28 June, where he was 'marched like a criminal through the street to a barracks' and kept there all night. Next day they gave him a complete exemption:

Moore 457   If I had not escaped I should be dead.

Lawrence's sickness went into his novel. But the novel does not take the shape of that sickness. It objectifies the sickness in order to diagnose it. The world of the novel is larger than the 'real' world, because it contains those truths the real world has lost touch with in its living death:

Moore 477   I know it is true, the book. And it is another world, in which I can live apart from this foul world which I will not accept or acknowledge or even enter. The world of my novel is big and fearless – yes, I love it, and love it passionately.

Birkin, the hero, the Lawrence figure in *Women in Love*, re-enacts Lawrence's past by coming to the very brink of a series of almost deadly mistakes. He moves 'from death to death', from one hell to another, partaking of each, subscribing to and contributing to each for a while, because they seem to be all that life offers, and because he cannot yet bring into full consciousness, or articulate, his obscure sense of death or fatuity in each of them. There is the hell of Beldover where men are shoved underground to toil mechanically in darkness; the hell of Shortlands where the presiding devil Gerald lives, maintaining 'the plausible ethics of productivity'; the hell of Breadalby where the talk (much of it Birkin's) 'went on like a rattle of small artillery'; the hell of Soho Bohemia, a modern Sodom with its 'host of licentious souls'. Workers, bosses, aristocrats, intellectuals, artists . . . all living the life of the damned. So prevalent is the corruption that Birkin comes to feel that he must be living through the world's latter days, or at least humanity's, and that it would be more honourable to go through with the destructive process, to make way for a new phase of creation, than to struggle against it. He is saved, narrowly, from all these deaths, partly by Ursula and partly by his own unquenchable commitment to 'the old effort at serious living'.

In transforming the material left over from 1913, the 'original *Sisters*', into *Women in Love* in 1916, Lawrence set himself an almost impossible task. The novel he had set out to write in 1913 was to have been an epithalamium; the novel he felt the need to

Moore 519   write in 1916, expressing 'the results in one's soul of the war', was a jeremiad, an apocalypse. The overriding sense of the impending end of the world accounts for all the alternative titles Lawrence considered: *Noah's Ark, Dies Irae, Day of Wrath, The Latter Days*. The utterly different, almost opposite, metaphysic is not the only problem. The major characters already existed, based on models from Lawrence's pre-1913 experience; Gerald on Major Thomas Philip Barber, Gudrun on Ethelreda Burrows, Hermione on Jessie Chambers. In 1916 these characters had to incorporate also aspects of Murry and Katherine Mansfield and Lady Ottoline Morrell respectively. Murry can have had little in common with Major Thomas Philip Barber. It is remarkable that the seams show as little as they do.

Lawrence confronted his readers with so many difficulties and complexities in this novel that they were unable to read it (and critics today are deeply divided over it).

From Murry he might have expected more than that he should find the characters as 'indistinguishable as octopods in an aquarium tank':

Draper 168–72   Their creator believes that he can distinguish the writhing of one from the writhing of another; he spends pages and pages in describing the contortions of the first, the second, the third and the fourth. To him they are utterly and profoundly different; to us they are all the same.

Murry concluded his review by pronouncing the novel 'sub-human and bestial, a thing that our forefathers had rejected when they began to rise from the slime.'

When he was not making impossible demands, Lawrence had a wonderful gift for friendship. As Murry put it:

Nehls 1, 373

It wasn't what the man said, so much as the warm and irresistible intimacy with which he surrounded one, an atmosphere established as it were by a kindly gardener who had, very precisely, decided that you were to grow, and who, by that act, awakened in you the feeling that there was something in you which could grow.

Perhaps his friendships ripened too quickly. When his friends found themselves expected to become acolytes, they defected. Lawrence in 1916 felt himself a Jesus with twelve Judases for disciples. Catherine Carswell had warned him that the friends in whom he had invested his faith lacked the basic qualification for disciples: they did not ultimately believe in him. And this is not surprising, since, at this moment, he could not sustain his own belief in any kind of creative human future.

Lawrence demanded that his friends should all submerge their personalities in the common cause. But since he was to be the interpreter of that cause, and since this interpretation was liable to change from day to day, it seemed to them that they were being asked simply to submerge their personalities in his. They were all lesser men. They lacked his vision, his seriousness and his courage. Russell was insentient, Murry and Heseltine invertebrate. They were no doubt unworthy of him. He, on the other hand, made demands which would have been excessive upon the best of men.

In November Lawrence wrote to Forster:

Unpub.   I have not a friend in the world, nor an acquaintance, I have the honor to say. Neither have I any money at all, I have the dishonor to say. Neither have I much in the way of health: I seem to have spent a great deal of my time in bed, lately. Really, one looks through the window into the land of death, and it *does* seem a clean good unknown, all that is left to one.

The following day he wrote to Kot:

Moore 483   I tell you my Rananim, my Florida idea, was the true one. Only the *people* were wrong. But to go to Rananim *without* the people is right.

A colony without people. A sad conclusion.

On 20 November Lawrence finally sent off the manuscript of *Women in Love* to Pinker, in a spirit very different from that in which he had launched his *Rainbow* a mere eighteen months earlier:

Moore 485   Can I tell you how thankful I am to have the thing done, and out of the house!

He saw little hope that it would ever be published. He had neither the energy nor the faith to begin anything else:

Moore 486   Now I am not doing any work, we need books to read. . . . This is a kind of interval in my life, like a sleep. One only wanders through the dim short days, and reads, cooks, and looks across at the sea. I feel as if I also were hibernating, like the snakes and the dormice.

On 7 December 1916 Lawrence looked back over the year that was to have been Year 1 of the New World:

Irvine 8   I have been in Cornwall for twelve months now, never out of it, so I feel a stranger to the world. I find myself divested of all my friends, and much more confident and free, having no connections anywhere. Why should one seek intimacies – they are only a net about one. It is one's business to stand quite apart and single, in one's soul.

His hibernation was soon to be interrupted. Within three weeks another sort of net had entangled him.

In his first week at Zennor Lawrence had written:

Nehls 1, 361   We can be perfectly happy in Tregerthen Cottage, if only the world won't stare in at the windows with its evil face.

The words were more literally prophetic than he could have guessed. The first sign of trouble was on Christmas Eve 1916. An American journalist Robert Mountsier was visiting the Lawrences with his girlfriend Esther Andrews, when the police sergeant from St Ives called, wanting to know all about them. This inquiry had no immediate consequences, but the Lawrences were being watched.

There seemed no point in staying in England. His latest books could not be published, and there was no sale for those which were published:

Marsh 230   I know it is no good writing for England any more. England wants soothing pap, and nothing else, for its literature.

It seemed to him there was something in the very air he breathed, in England, which damaged his spirit. The only hope seemed to be America, a Rananim in the far west – perhaps as far west as the Marquesas Islands – with its back to mankind:

Huxley 393   The only way is the way of my far-off wilderness place which shall become a school and a monastry and an Eden and a Hesperides – a seed of a new heaven and a new earth.

Lawrence's sudden interest in the Pacific islands was inspired by his enthusiastic reading of Melville.

On 12 February Lawrence learned that they had refused to endorse his passport. He told Gertler that he would give up writing and become a farmer. And indeed he was to devote more and more of his time to his garden. He invested sixpence in *Culture of Profitable Vegetables in Small Gardens*, and this paid off with an excellent crop of carrots, parsnips, peas, broad beans, scarlet runners, marrows, beets, kohlrabi, lettuce, parsley, spinach and endives – more than the Lawrences themselves could eat:

Huxley 408   My gardens are so lovely, everything growing in rows, and so fast – such nice green rows of all kinds of young things. It looks like a triumph of life in itself.

Lawrence did not, of course, stop writing. After completing *Look! We Have Come* Moore 498 *Through!* ('a sort of final conclusion of the old life in me') he wrote a set of seven little essays called 'The Reality of Peace':

Moore 508   The pure abstract thought interests me now at this juncture more than art. I am tired of emotions and squirmings and sensations. Let us have a little pure thought, a little perfect and detached understanding.

Four of these essays appeared in the *English Review* that summer; a fifth, 'The Whistling of Birds' was published by Murry in *The Athenaeum* in 1919. The others are lost, as is the little book of about 140 pages, *At the Gates*, which Lawrence developed from these essays during the summer. He described it to Pinker as Huxley 414 'perfectly sound metaphysics, that will stand the attacks of technical philosophers', and to Kot as the final form, written four times since, of the material Kot had so Nehls 1, 452 laboriously typed for him in 1914. Heseltine read it, thought it 'the supreme utterance of all modern philosophy', and tried, without success, to get it published, by Maunsel of Dublin, to whom Lawrence himself offered, unsuccessfully, *Women in Love*.

Lawrence's next project was another set of essays, this time the long-planned critical work on 'The Transcendental Element in American (Classic) Literature':

Lowell 422   It sounds very fine and large, but in reality is rather a thrilling blood-and-thunder, your-money-or-your-life kind of thing: hands up America! – No, but they are very keen essays in criticism – cut your fingers if you don't handle them carefully. . . . Tis a chef-d'oeuvre of soul-searching criticism.

He began with Crèvecoeur. There followed essays on Franklin, Fenimore Cooper, Poe, Hawthorne, Dana and Melville. He completed the set in June 1918 with the final essay on Whitman. They were revised in 1919 and 1920 and rewritten in 1922 before publication as *Studies in Classic American Literature*. Lawrence, in this lively, witty, aggressive, buttonholing, and wholly original book, told the Americans that they had a classic native literature. The serious study of American literature derives entirely from this one book. His greatest affinity was with Whitman. His own poetry was to be transformed by this exposure to him.

The Lawrences were happier in the hot summer of 1917. Lawrence had become very friendly with the Hocking family, the neighbouring farmers, and would frequently help with the haymaking or harvesting. He spent many evenings at the Hockings' farm where he had his own seat by the range, chatting to everyone, especially William Henry, and teaching young Stanley French, chess and bridge, until his conscience would prick him for leaving Frieda alone. That short walk across the field must have been like walking into the past, reliving the best of his times at the Haggs, with William Henry almost another Alan Chambers. Sometimes he would walk the five miles to St Ives. On the hottest days he and Frieda would bathe at Wicca Pool.

But they were under suspicion. They could not hang out a towel without being watched. One day, coming home from shopping in Zennor, they were pounced on by coastguards who accused them of having a camera in their rucksack. Frieda opened it revealing nothing more incriminating than a loaf of bread. They knew there were men watching behind walls and boulders by day and listening outside the windows by night.

They were frequent visitors of Cecil Gray at Bosigran Castle near by. Gray was a musician, a friend of Heseltine, and a wealthy snob. He had come to Bosigran for romantic isolation. One night they were singing German folk-songs when half-a-dozen soldiers burst in and accused them of flashing lights towards the sea. A drawing pin holding a curtain had worked loose in the gale, allowing the curtain to flap. Gray was

Nehls 1, 425 fined heavily for violating the black-out regulations. He blamed the 'characteristically Cornish spirit of disinterested malevolence'. Lawrence was more vituperative. But it was hardly disinterested. There had been a submarine sighted off the coast that night. In fact there had been a dramatic increase in submarine activity since the arrival of the Lawrences, and ships were sunk within sight of Higher Tregerthen. Lawrence was known to the authorities as a subversive and anti-war writer. He entertained many strange foreign visitors. He was married to a German woman whose cousin was the famous Red Baron air ace, and who was in regular correspondence with her relatives via Switzerland. The authorities believed that some of the caves and coves once the haunt of smugglers were being used to smuggle provisions to the submarines, and that the submarines were receiving signals about the movements of British merchant shipping.

A few days later, on 11 October, the Lawrences returned home to find the cottage had been searched and papers taken. The following day a captain, two detectives and a constable came with a paper to the effect that the Lawrences must leave Cornwall within three days:

Moore 527 I cannot even conceive how I have incurred suspicion – have not the faintest notion. We are as innocent even of pacifist activities, let alone spying of any sort as the rabbits in the field outside. And we must report to the police. It is *very* vile. We have practically no money at all – I don't know what we shall do.

It was the beginning of a long period when the Lawrences were to be dependent on the kindness of friends for a roof over their heads.

10 Babes in the Wood

In desperation Lawrence turned yet again to the idea of Rananim. It was always his last resort. All his other ideas about human relationships were put to the test, if not in reality, then in his fiction. But he never dared follow through, imaginatively, the Rananim idea; it was too precious to put at risk. When he writes of it in his letters, his language lapses into Arcadian or Prelapsarian. On 27 October he wrote to a pregnant Catherine Carswell to invite her and her husband to 'sail away to our Island – at present in the Andes':

Moore 531

> We have got a much more definite plan of going away. There will be Frieda and I, Eder and Mrs Eder, and William Henry and Gray, and probably Hilda Aldington, and maybe Kot and Dorothy Yorke. We shall go to the east slope of the Andes, back of Paraguay or Colombia. Eder knows the country *well*. Gray can find £1000. The war will end this winter. In that case we set off in the spring.

David Eder was a leading Freudian psychoanalyst and Ivy Low's uncle. Lawrence had met him in 1914. Dorothy Yorke was a striking twenty-five-year-old American. She had rooms in the same house in Mecklenburgh Square as the Aldingtons, whose rooms the Lawrences were using in their absence. Mrs. Aldington was the poet Hilda Doolittle (H.D.). Wanting to avoid further sex with her husband after a miscarriage, she had encouraged him to take Dorothy Yorke as a mistress, and had expected their own relationship to become finer in its spirituality. But Aldington fell in love with Dorothy ('Arabella'), and subsequently lived with her. H.D. turned to Lawrence for her sublimated soul-marriage. He had given her some encouragement, partly for revenge on Frieda who having an affair with Cecil Grey, partly in the spirit of Orphic underworld 'marriage' he was to celebrate a few months later in one of the worst of his stories 'The Ladybird' (where it is clear that the acolyte he most desired was Lady Cynthia Asquith). Fortunately, Lawrence's saner instincts made him reject H.D.'s advances. Lawrence quarreled with Gray, and he and H.D. ran away together. The title of Gray's autobiography *Musical Chairs* seems particularly appropriate to the goings on at 44 Mecklenburgh Square at this time. Nor is it difficult to see why the prospect of joining Lawrence's colony in the Andes did not appeal to Gray:

Gray 133

> The idea of spending the rest of my life in the Andes in the company of Lawrence and Frieda, filled me with horror – the combination of the mountain heights and the psychological depths was more than I could sanely contemplate. Apart from

anything else, I was already weary and sceptical, sick and tired, of his dark gods, sensuous underworlds, and all the rest of his literary 'properties'. I accused him of allowing himself to become the object of a kind of esoteric female cult, an Adonis, Atthis, Dionysos religion of which he was the central figure, a Jesus Christ to a regiment of Mary Magdalenes.

By February Rananim had changed both its location and its personnel: it was now to be in the Abruzzi, with Kot, Gertler ('weaned from the paint brush'), Shearman, Campbell 'and anybody else that seemed particularly nice':

Kot 132   We'll cook for ourselves, and row in a boat, and make excursions, and talk, and be quite happy for a while.

In December 1917 the Lawrences moved to Chapel Farm Cottage, Hermitage, near Newbury, Berkshire. It was cold and comfortless. In February Dollie Radford needed
Moore 541 her cottage – 'so I suppose we are to camp out like babes in the wood, and ask the robins to cover us with warm leaves'. It never came to that; but Lawrence's financial situation was so bad that he had to sell his next collections of poems, *Bay*, for £10 outright. He wrote to Gertler:

Moore 541 I am at the dead end of my money, and can't raise the wind in any direction. Do you think you might know of somebody who would give us something to keep us going for a bit. It makes me swear – such a damned, mean, narrow-gutted, pitiful, crawling, mongrel world, that daren't have a man's work and won't even allow him to live.

He asked Pinker to approach Arnold Bennett on his behalf for support. Bennett had, at that time, a higher regard for Lawrence than had any other established writer (though George Moore, having read *Women in Love* in manuscript, said that it was a great book, and Lawrence was a better writer than himself).

Galsworthy called Lawrence a genius, but qualified it with the adjective 'provincial'. (People were always calling him a genius, Lawrence complained, as though to console him for lacking their own incomparable advantages.) Galsworthy had disliked *The Rainbow* intensely:

Art 69   I think it's aesthetically detestable. Its perfervid futuristic style revolts me. . . . I much prefer a frankly pornographic book to one like this. . . . A grievous pity – so much power, and vision (up to a point) run so young to seed.

When Lawrence had lunched with Galsworthy in November, he had found him a 'sawdust bore'. Bennett offered to give Lawrence £3 a week if Wells and Galsworthy would do the same. Lawrence rejected the offer as an insult, but Bennett secretly loaned him, through Pinker, £25. Shaw gave £40, but Lawrence was indignant that 'a
Kot 144   millionaire' should give so little. He applied for another grant from 'that dirty Royal Literary Fund', and, in July, got 'a miserable £50'. Lawrence's lack of grace or gratitude in receiving charity that he had himself asked for, is a measure of his humiliation.

Lawrence was working hard on his American essays, and at the end of February began serious work on 'another daft novel', *Aaron's Rod*:

Moore 543   It goes very slowly – very slowly and fitfully. But I don't care.

It continued to go slowly and fitfully – he did not finish it until May 1921 – partly because he needed to give his attention primarily to work which might bring him more immediate returns, but mainly because all Lawrence's fiction hitherto had been grounded in a deep belief in human relationships and potentialities which he could no longer sustain:

Moore 514   I find people ultimately boring: and you can't have fiction without people. So fiction does not, at the bottom, interest me any more.

Life at Chapel Farm Cottage improved with the spring. Frieda remembered it as a happy time:

Tedlock 142   Lawrence would write in the morning, while I fussed around the cottage. After lunch we would go for long walks over the fields and get mushrooms if there were any, and in the spring through the woods we found clearings where big primroses grew and pools of bluebells. In the spring we also got baskets full of dandelions and made dandelion wine. . . . After our afternoon exploring we came home with our loot, hungry, with muddy boots, changed into slippers and put the kettle on the fire and had tea.

Lawrence had kept up a close relationship with his sister Ada who was now married and living in Ripley. She was not badly off and offered to pay the rent if Lawrence would come and live near her. She found for him Mountain Cottage, Middleton-by-Wirksworth. And so, at the beginning of May 1918, Lawrence returned to live in the Midlands, some twenty miles from Eastwood, for the first time

Mountain Cottage. 'I think it will be nice. It is in the darkish Midlands, on the rim of a steep valley, looking over darkish, folded hills – exactly the navel of England, and feels exactly that.

since his elopement in 1912. At first, after the less dramatic landscape of Berkshire,
with its soothing 'tree-presences', he felt 'queer and lost and exiled . . . like Ovid in
Thrace', but there were frequent visitors to Mountain Cottage that summer to cheer
him up, especially his sisters and their children, his old Eastwood friend William
Hopkin with his wife Sallie and daughter Enid, and other friends from Eastwood and
London.

Moore 553

Lawrence's spiritual anchor at this time was Gibbon. He read the whole of *Decline
and Fall of the Roman Empire* between April and July 1918, and, as a result, was able
to impress Vere Collins so much with his knowledge of history, that Collins, who
worked for the Oxford University Press, got him a commission:

Nehls 1, 471

> I suggested to him that he might consider the idea of writing an elementary text-
> book for junior forms in grammar, or upper forms in primary schools, of European
> history. . . . I suggested that Lawrence should not attempt to write a formal,
> connected, text book, but a series of vivid sketches of movements and people. He
> suggested *Movements in European History* for the title.

Lawrence struggled for six months with the 'wretched piggling work', but the result
was approved by the eminent Oxford historian C. R. L. Fletcher, and duly published,
though not under the name of the author of *The Rainbow*. The innocents were to be
exposed only to the harmless Lawrence H. Davison. In fact it is difficult now, with
hindsight, to feel that the book was all that harmless. Lawrence told Cecil Gray at the
outset what was to be his controlling theme:

Moore 561

> I feel in a historical mood, being very near the end of Gibbon. The chief feeling is,
> that men were always alike, and always will be, and one must view the species
> with contempt . . . and find a few individuals . . . to rule the species.

He interprets history as the spirit of place and race surging into movement and
articulation through individual leaders, who are simultaneously heroes and puppets.
These surges are not predictable, not subject to laws of cause and effect; they have
their origins in the creative unknown. If one stands back far enough from history,
perhaps a certain pattern can be seen – the gradual decline of the military and
political power-struggle, and its replacement by an age of commerce. It is Lawrence's
faith (derived from Joachim of Flora) that this age will eventually be replaced by an
age of wisdom, when man has resolved the tugging dualities within him and learned
to live in intuitive atonement with the rest of creation. But this golden age would also
be dependent for its inauguration upon great men, the first to embody the new
wisdom.

The book is full of the worship of heroes, from Attila to Bismarck, and ends:

> The will of the people must concentrate in one figure, who is also supreme over the
> will of the people. He must be chosen, but at the same time responsible to God
> alone. Here is a problem of which a stormy future will have to evolve the solution.

Lawrence did not live to see how stormy.

On his thirty-third birthday, 11 September 1918, Lawrence was at a low ebb. He wrote to Amy Lowell:

Lowell 482

Frieda and I are here trying to be patient. I am slowly working at another novel: though I feel it's not much use. No publisher will risk my last, and none will risk this, I expect. I can't do anything in the world today – am just choked. – I don't know how on earth we shall get through another winter – how we shall ever find a future. Humanity as it stands, and myself as I stand, we just seem mutually impossible to one another. The ground dwindles under one's feet – what next, heaven knows.

What in fact came next, later the same day, was a summons to report to Derby for yet another medical examination. This time he was graded C3, which meant that he could be called up for light duties. Feeling that he would be more likely to avoid this if he had some regular employment, he got an introduction from Donald Carswell to G. S. Freeman, editor of the *Times Educational Supplement*, who encouraged Lawrence to submit some articles on education. In December Lawrence sent him four such essays, but they were rejected as more suitable for a book. In 1920 Lawrence extended them into a little book *Education of the People*, but it was not published in his lifetime.

The rejection of the essays is not surprising. *Education of the People* is one of Lawrence's worst productions, despite several splendid passages. His emphasis on education for life and individuality rather than jobs and social conformity is salutary, but undermined by his proposed caste system, based on the assumption that 'the uninstructible outnumber the instructible by a very large majority'. The challenge for Lawrence was to imagine new forms of 'instruction' suited to such potentialities as 'bottle-washing Jimmy Shepherd' had. Instead he gives us:

Phoenix 626–7

Abolish all the bunkum, go back to the three R's. Don't cultivate any more imagination at all in children: it only means pernicious self-consciousness. . . . The self-consciousness and all the damned high-flowness must be taken out of them, and their little personalities must be nipped in the bud.

We find the same sort of thing in other works of these misanthropic years.

Lawrence and Frieda with Willie and Sallie Hopkin (centre) and Kitty Allcock (right). The other couple is unidentified.

'We had such a good time at the week-end. Did your people enjoy it as much as we did? It was so jolly when we were all together. And it is the human contact which means so much to one, really. Do you know, I quite suffered when they had gone away on Monday – and usually I am so glad to be alone.'

Ada Clarke, Willie Hopkin, W. E. Clarke, Frieda, Sallie Hopkin, Gertie Cooper, Dr Feroze, and Lawrence.

Kitty Allcock, Dorothy (Arabella) Yorke, Lawrence and Willie Hopkin.

Lawrence with his nephew Jack Clarke, 'a very charming boy indeed'.

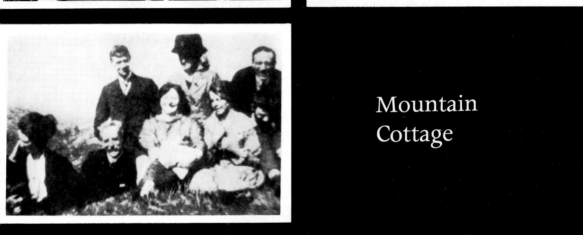

Mountain
Cottage

In October Lawrence blew on the embers of his hope in the world to produce his play *Touch and Go*, where several of the characters from *Women in Love* reappear in the context of an industrial dispute. The play works up to a confrontation between Gerald Barlow, the mine owner, and his striking men. Each side thinks that bullying, in one form or another, is the way to get what it wants. There is stalemate and the threat of serious violence. The point of the play seems to be to bring forward at the end Oliver Turton, the Lawrence/Birkin figure, to preach his simple solution:

> We're all human beings after all. And why can't we try to leave off struggling against one another, and set up a new state of things . . . It's life and living that matters, not simply having money . . . If you want what is natural and good, I'm sure the owners would soon agree with you.

But Oliver has already been shown to be ineffectual. The attack on Gerald is averted only by a desperate cry from the heroine Anabel – 'He's a man like you.' The play has neither the authenticity of a naturalistic play, nor the coherence and tight structure of a play of ideas.

Lawrence very much wanted it to be acted. In 1919 Douglas Goldring proposed that *Touch and Go* should be the first play to be performed by his People's Theatre Society, and the first to be published in his series *Plays for a People's Theatre*. On this understanding Lawrence let him have the play and its preface free. In the event Goldring was thwarted by a reactionary majority on the theatre committee. *Touch and Go* was not produced. The first play to be published in the series was Goldring's own *The Flight for Freedom*, which Lawrence despised. *Touch and Go* was published second, in 1920.

On 11 November came the armistice. The Lawrences were at Chapel Farm Cottage at the time. There was an impromptu party at Montague Shearman's flat in London. Most of Bloomsbury was there, including David Garnett, who had not seen Lawrence for three years, and approached him effusively. But Lawrence was the only man in the room who was not rejoicing. As Garnett remembered it, Lawrence said to him:

Nehls 1, 479
> I suppose you think the war is over and that we shall go back to the kind of world you lived in before it. But the war isn't over. The hate and evil is greater now than ever. Very soon war will break out again and overwhelm you. It makes me sick to see you rejoicing like a butterfly in the last rays of the sun before the winter. The crowd outside thinks that Germany is crushed forever. But the Germans will soon rise again. Europe is done for; England most of all the countries. This war isn't over. Even if the fighting should stop, the evil will be worse because the hate will be dammed up in men's hearts and will show itself in all sorts of ways which will be worse than war. Whatever happens there can be no Peace on Earth.

But Lawrence's mood could fluctuate wildly; it was by no means always dark. While in London Lawrence also visited Katherine Mansfield, who was ill:

Nehls 1, 477
> He was just his old, merry, rich self, laughing, describing things, giving you

pictures, full of enthusiasm and joy in a future where we become all 'vagabonds' – we simply did not talk about people. We kept to things like nuts and cowslips and fires in woods and his black self was not. Oh, there is something so loveable about him and his eagerness, his passionate eagerness for life – that is what one loves so.

During the following three months Lawrence wrote Katherine a series of delightful letters designed to bring some colour and gaiety into her life in her sickness. In one of them he confessed that all was not as it should be between himself and Frieda. It was no longer a matter of isolated rows:

Moore 565   In a way, Frieda is the devouring mother. It is awfully hard, once the sex relation has gone this way, to recover. If we don't recover, we die. But Frieda says I am antediluvian in my positive attitude. I do think a woman must yield some sort of precedence to a man, and he must take this precedence. I do think men must go ahead absolutely in front of their women, without turning round to ask for permission or approval from their women. Consequently the women must follow as it were unquestioningly. I can't help it, I believe this. Frieda doesn't. Hence our fight.

As Christmas approached Lawrence was low again:

Moore 569–70   We are going across to my sister's on Christmas Day, if ever I get so far – having got a bad cold, under which I crawl dismally for the time being. The weather is very dark and nasty, and Christmas is an institution that really should be abolished. I don't want to hear of it, it wearies me.

He made it to Ripley and thoroughly enjoyed himself:

Moore 571   My God, what masses of food here, turkey, large tongues, long wall of roast loin of pork, pork-pies, sausages, mince-pies, dark cakes covered with almonds, cheese-cakes, lemon-tarts, jellies, endless masses of food, with whisky, gin, port wine, burgundy, muscatel. It seems incredible. We played charades – the old people of 67 playing away harder than the young ones – and lit the Christmas tree, and drank healths, and sang, and roared – Lord above.

But the same letter ends:

Tonight we are going back to Middleton – and I feel infuriated to think of the months ahead, when one waits paralysed for some sort of release.

Lawrence still hankered for the Andes, but had now also conceived 'a hot little interest in Palestine', and begged David Eder to take him there. On 2 January 1919 he wrote to Eder:

Eder 121   Let me come and spy out the land with you – it would rejoice my heart into the heavens. And I will write you such a beautiful little book, 'The Entry of the Blessed into Palestine'.

Then suddenly, in the same letter, Lawrence launched into a constitution for Rananim sadly reminiscent of Gonzalo's commonwealth in *The Tempest*:

First Law: There shall be no laws: every man shall hold up his hand in token that he is self-responsible and answerable to his own soul. Second Law: Every man shall have food, shelter, knowledge and the right to mate freely – every man and woman shall have this, irrespective of any other claim than that of life-necessity: and every man who enters, and every woman, shall hold up a hand to signify that in these two principles we are at one. Then everything else can be done by arrangement, not by law. There are many deep and bitter and sweet things to know and learn, afterwards. But in accepting the first two principles, we put ourselves, like beginners, into the state of pure attention, like acolytes. And so our State begins.

It is hardly surprising that Eder went without him.

In November, probably as an excuse for not getting on with the history, Lawrence had turned to short stories: 'The Blind Man', 'The Fox' and, probably, 'Tickets Please'. That winter he also wrote 'Fannie and Annie' and 'Wintry Peacock'. At the beginning of February he finished *Movements*, but in the middle of the month became a victim of the influenza epidemic. He became so ill that he was taken to his sister's house at Ripley where there would be more warmth and comfort, and better nursing than he could expect from Frieda. For a few days Dr Feroze feared for his life. For a fortnight he was too ill to do anything:

Irvine 15   I am a wretched object like a drowned ghost creeping downstairs to tea.

It was a crisis in his relationship with Frieda. When he was fit enough to return to Middleton he took his sister with him:

Moore 581   I am not going to be left to Frieda's tender mercies until I am well again. She really is a devil – and I feel as if I would part from her for ever – let her go alone to Germany, while I take another road. For it is true, I have been bullied by her long enough. I really could leave her now, without a pang.

Kot 164   During his convalescence Lawrence received an invitation to contribute to the revived *Athenaeum* of which Murry had been appointed editor. Lawrence was pleased, but 'fearfully mistrustful of him – feel sure we shall be let down', and trod very carefully:

Moore 579   But you must tell me exactly what you would like me to do, and I will try to be pleasant and a bit old-fashioned. I don't mind if I am anonymous – or a *nom de plume*.

Murry 149 He submitted several pieces, only two of which can be identified. There was 'Whistling of Birds', a beautiful piece full of frail hope, and 'Adolf'. Murry published 'Whistling of Birds' (under the pseudonym Grantorto) in his second issue, but declined the rest:

He was not capable of writing *regular* articles for any journal with a public to consider. He wanted, no doubt, to do his best, and tried to do his best; but the 'contained murder' would out. He was festering with hatred of England. . . . And I certainly had not intention of risking offence to the readers and proprietors of *The Athenaeum* by publishing Lawrence's statements of a faith which would be offensive, and to which I personally was then bitterly opposed.

This seems plausible until one looks at the innocent 'Adolf', a charming piece about a pet rabbit Lawrence had kept as a child, as pleasant and old-fashioned and inoffensive as anything he ever wrote.

In spite of this rebuff, Lawrence was to send Murry some more articles a few months later. Murry returned them with a note to the effect that he didn't like them. Lawrence, in reply, called Murry a dirty little worm, to which Murry responded by promising to hit Lawrence in the face when they next met. That, for the time being, was the end of their alliance.

In the spring and summer of 1919 Lawrence wrote very little:

Lowell 493
> I feel I don't want to write – still less do I want to publish anything. It is like throwing one's treasures into a bog.

⁓

In May the Lawrences returned to Chapel Farm Cottage:

Moore 587
> Now the weather is warm I am quite happy – *dolce far niente*.

Occasionally he would walk five miles to visit the Farjeons. He wrote 'Fannie and Annie', 'Monkey Nuts' and 'You Touched Me', and perhaps tinkered with *Aaron's Rod*; but his mind was on Palestine, New York, or anywhere in the wide world outside England. In August he stirred himself to help Kot with his translation of Shestov's *All Things Are Possible*, then to find a publisher for it, only to find Kot and himself, after much labour, offered £20 between them for their pains. In September he did some more work on the American essays, and wrote to an interested American publisher, Huebsch, that they contained 'a new science of psychology' which the professional psychologists (he names Ernest Jones and the Eders) were trying to steal from him:

A Berkshire picnic with Herbert and Eleanor Farjeon and Rosalind Popham in the summer of 1919.

Lawrence and Frieda at Grimsbury Farm, near Newbury, September 1919. 'He informed me that these were now his only trousers – and that he had to wash them himself of a night-time after undressing so that they might be ready for wear again by the morning.' (Catherine Carswell)

Moore 596   I only know the psychoanalysts here – one of them – has gone to Vienna, partly to graft some of the ideas on to Freud and the Freudian theory of the unconscious – is at this moment busy doing it. I *know* they are trying to get the theory of primal unconscious out of these essays, to solidify their windy theory of the unconscious.

Huebsch tried to dissuade Lawrence from going to America (where he hoped to lecture). So did Amy Lowell. They feared they might have him on their hands.

Frieda left for Germany alone on 15 October. Lawrence planned to go to Italy. She would join him in Florence. Lawrence had at last found himself a steady publisher in England – Martin Secker. Two of Secker's other novelists, Compton Mackenzie (who owned a third of the shares in Martin Secker Ltd and had persuaded Secker to take on Lawrence) and Francis Brett Young, were living in Capri. The idea of a little colony of Secker novelists appealed to Lawrence. Mackenzie was less sanguine. He wrote to Secker:

Having had your note about one cold novelist [Brett Young] I get a postcard tonight about another cold novelist – to wit D. H. Lawrence. I am not at all sure that a course of 'ice' wouldn't be rather good for *him*. He and his wife are coming here for good. . . . I knew that could happen.

On 14 November Lawrence left Charing Cross, where Kot and the Carswells saw him off. He was out of the cage at last.

11 Pilgrim

Moore 598

Lawrence landed in Italy with £9 in his pocket and drifted south towards Florence, finding Italy much changed by the war. He spent two nights in great luxury at Sir Walter Becker's villa near Turin, argued with the wealthy ship-owner, 'he for security and bank-balance, and power, and I for naked liberty', and put him into *Aaron's Rod* as Sir William Franks.

In Florence Norman Douglas acted as Lawrence's host, and provided him with further material for *Aaron's Rod*, where he appears as Argyle. Waiting for Frieda, Lawrence amused himself observing Douglas (whose robust hedonism and 'wicked whimsicality' charmed even Lawrence) and his friends, particularly the fastidious and patronizing sponger Maurice Magnus, who had been Isadora Duncan's manager, editor and journalist before the war – a cunning little cosmopolitan now totally without means but bent on keeping up appearances at others' cost.

Frieda finally arrived in the early hours of 3 December. Lawrence met her at the station and insisted on taking her for a moonlight drive in an open carriage. Frieda was enchanted:

Look! 13–4

We drove to the Duomo, a heavy, dark, low mass, but near it the Giotto tower rose white in its slender loveliness. The top disappeared in a kind of moon-mist. Then we drove to the Lungarno and over the Ponte Vecchio. Oh, ever since that drive, I have loved Florence better than any other town I know.

Rosalind Popham, a friend from Pangbourne, was planning to take her children to stay in Picinisco, a high remote village in the Abruzzi. Lawrence had made two sheepskin coats for her little girls, and had volunteered to go there ahead of her and see whether the proposed accommodation was suitable. He found it 'staggeringly primitive':

Moore 609

In Picinisco we got right into the wilds, where the ass lived on the doorstep and strolled through the hall, and the cock came to crow on the bent-iron washstand: quite a big, fine-looking house, but lo and behold, one great room was a wine-press, another a corn and oil chamber, and as you went upstairs, half the upstairs was open, a beautiful barn full of maize-cobs, very mellow and warm-looking. The kitchen, a vaulted cave, had never been cleaned since the house was built. One ate one's meals on a settle in front of the great chimney, where the pots swung on the hooks and the green wood sputtered. No one dreamed of a table, let alone a tablecloth. One blew up the fire with a long, long ancient iron tube, with a winged foot to stand in the ashes: and this tube was handed from person to person in the process of blowing up a blaze. Hygienics not yet imagined. Add to this, that all around circled the most brilliant snowy mountain-peaks, glittering like hell: that away below, on our oak-scrub hills, the air had a tang of ice, while the wild river with its great white bed of boulders rushed pale and fizzy from the ice: that there was no road to the house, but everything had to be piled on the ass and forded over the river: that the nearest shop was $1\frac{1}{2}$ hours away, the nearest railway 15 miles of terrific mountain road: and that on the Saturday before Christmas it snowed all day long: and you have it.

The Lawrences endured there for a week, then fled to Capri. Though he found it extremely beautiful and, at first, sympathetic, Lawrence never thought of Capri as other than a stepping-stone. On 16 January he wrote to Martin Secker:

Moore 614–5   Mackenzie and I get on with one-another: also Brett Young. I should like to be with you, because you really care about books. The thought of our being partners all in Secker and Co. pleases me, so long as we are really in sympathy, and so long as we are all friends.

But Capri was too small for three novelists (and their wives). Lawrence, waiting for the manuscript of *The Insurrection of Miss Houghton* to arrive from Germany (where it

Moore 616   had lain inaccessible since before the war), did 'nothing, sweet nothing, except go out to lunch, or walk from one end of the island to the other', and made sure that no one else worked either. Brett Young saw that Lawrence and Mackenzie were reacting on each other 'as a kind of irritating stimulus', and correctly forecast that Lawrence, straining after an earthly nirvana, would not stay more than a month or two on Capri.

On 25 January Lawrence wrote to Lady Cynthia Asquith that he was going to the mainland house-hunting:

Moore 617   To look down the Salernian Gulf, southeast, on a blue day, and see the dim, sheer rocky coast, the clear rock mountains, is so beautiful, so like Ulysses, that one sheds one's avatars, and recovers a lost self, mediterranean, anterior to us. But Capri itself is a gossipy, villa-stricken, two-humped chunk of limestone, a microcosmos that does heaven much credit, but mankind none at all. Truly, humanly, it is a bit impossible for long.

A three-day excursion down the Amalfi coast failed to produce a house. By 5 February the situation on Capri had worsened:

Moore 620   I am very sick of Capri: it is a stew-pot of semi-literary cats – I like Compton Mackenzie as a man – but not as an influence. I can't stand his island. I shall have to risk expense and everything, and clear out: to Sicily, I think.

Later that month, Lawrence escaped for another three-day trip, this time to the Abbey of Monte Cassino.

Maurice Magnus. 'Spruce and youngish in his deportment, very pink-faced and very clean, very natty, very alert, like a sparrow painted to resemble a tom-tit.'

Douglas had led Magnus to believe that Lawrence had plenty of money, which he had not. Magnus wrote to Lawrence obliquely asking for a handout. Lawrence had just received a large cheque from Huebsch, and recklessly sent five pounds of it to Magnus, who claimed it had saved his life. He rewarded Lawrence by appointing him as his guardian angel for the rest of his life, and by inviting him to Monte Cassino, where he was in hiding from the law.

Lawrence had long been fascinated by monastic life. Despite his allegiance to the body, he led a very simple, slightly ascetic life, and his hatred of the human world led him to explore various forms of withdrawal from it. He often spoke of Rananim as a 'monastic' community. Monte Cassino impressed him deeply:

Phoenix 2, 325–6 That hill-top must have been one of man's intense sacred places for three thousand years.

He talked at length with one of the monks from whom he parted 'with real regret', hating the barren world of 'democracy, industrialism, socialism, the red flag of the communists and the red, white and green flag of the fascists' below, but still feeling obliged to keep up the struggle there. Perhaps Lawrence needed to get beyond Europe, but for the moment he would make do with Sicily, the toe-end of Europe and perfect kicking-off point. Sicily had been waiting for Lawrence for centuries, Magnus told him.

On 26 February 1920, Lawrence set off on his house-hunting trip to Sicily, accompanied by the Brett Youngs. He had promised Frieda that he would find a house by the following Thursday, and gave the impression that he had pawned his soul in the undertaking, so furiously did he scour Sicily, insisting on leaving Agrigentum at four in the morning. The Brett Youngs could not keep up with him. By the time they joined him in Taormina, he had already found the splendid Fontana Vecchia.

'We have quite a lovely villa on the green slope high above the sea, looking east over the blueness, with the hills and the snowy, shallow crest of Calabria on the left across the sea, where the straights begin to close in. – The ancient fountain still runs, in a sort of little cave-place down the garden – the Fontana Vecchia.'

Lawrence loved the 'morning world' of Sicily. On 31 March he wrote to John Ellingham Brooks:

Nehls 2, 34   The dawn is so lovely from this house. I open my eye at 5.0, and say Coming; at 5.30, and say yellow; at 6.0, and say pink and smoke blue; at 6.15, and see a lovely orange flare and then the liquid sunlight winking straight in my eye. Then I know it's time to get up. So I dodge the sunlight with a corner of the blanket, and consider the problem of the universe: this I count my sweetest luxury, to consider the problem of the universe while I dodge the dawned sun behind a corner of the sheet; so warm, so first-kiss warm.

But as early as May he was hankering for more distant places:

Kot 211   I am planning next spring to go to the ends of the earth. Sicily is not far enough.

The manuscript of *The Insurrection of Miss Houghton* had finally caught up with Lawrence in Capri, and he had begun to work on it at once. At Taormina he decided to begin the whole thing again, under a new title *Mixed Marriage*. By the time he had finished the novel, on 5 May, it had become *The Lost Girl*. Lawrence assured lady

Moore 628 Cynthia Asquith that the lost girl was 'not morally lost', but to Mackenzie he sounded less sure of his moral bearings:

Mackenzie 178 I'm terrified of my Alvina who marries a Ciccio. I believe neither of us has found a way out of the labyrinth. How we hang on to the marriage clue! Doubt if it's really a way out. But my Alvina, in whom the questing soul is lodged, moves towards reunion with the dark half of humanity.

No sooner had he finished *The Lost Girl* than Lawrence began *Mr Noon*, a novel which he worked on for nine months, in which time he produced 450 pages, before Young 99 abandoning it without a backward look. Simultaneously, 'with ever-diminishing spasms of fitfulness', he worked on *Aaron's Rod*, still nowhere near finished after two Mackenzie 178 and a half years. 'I have to poke myself to be interested in novels,' he wrote to Mackenzie. His soul, at this time, was like a chrysalis writhing in its case, unable to complete its metamorphosis. He seemed to be demanding of his books that they should be ahead of his life:

I feel as if I were victualling my ship, with these damned books. But also somewhere they are the crumpled wings of my soul. They get me free before I get myself free. I mean in my novel I get some sort of wings loose, before I get my feet out of Europe.

Magnus did not remain long at Monte Cassino. As the police closed in to arrest him for an unpaid hotel bill he slipped away to Sicily where he assumed that Lawrence would accept financial responsibility for him. With money 'borrowed' from Lawrence he stayed at the most expensive hotel in Taormina, where the Lawrences had never been able to afford to stay. When they took a trip to Malta, they were amazed to see, from their second-class deck, Magnus lording it on the first. The Lawrences had intended to go to Malta for only two days, but were marooned there by a steamer strike for ten. Moore 631 Lawrence thought it a 'horrible island – stone, and bath-brick dust'.

When Magnus decided to stay in Malta they hoped they had heard the last of him. He wrote saying how fascinating life was there. He was learning Maltese and writing for the newspapers. Would Lawrence go and stay for a month? Lawrence did not reply. Then, in November, he heard from the monk at Monte Cassino that to escape arrest on a fraud charge, Magnus had committed suicide by drinking prussic acid. All his effects had been confiscated except a few worthless manuscripts left in the hands of the two Maltese to whom he had been heavily in debt. They had met Lawrence briefly, and now appealed to him, refusing to give up the manuscripts to Norman Douglas, who was Magnus' literary executor. Lawrence offered to try to get Magnus' *Memoirs of the Foreign Legion* published by writing a long introduction. He scrupulously cleared the project first with Douglas, who replied characteristically:

Whoever wants it may ram it up his exhaust pipe. . . . By all means do what you like with the MS. . . . *Pocket all the cash yourself*.

Lawrence had to hawk the book round several publishers. They all wanted the introduction without the *Memoirs*. Eventually Secker published the *Memoirs*, and

Compton Mackenzie.

Lawrence handed half the proceeds to the Maltese – enough to repay the original debt.

Mackenzie 183   Lawrence had set his heart on a cruise to the South Seas with Mackenzie. 'I'd give my fingers to be off' he wrote to Mackenzie in June. Mackenzie was trying to raise 7,500 guineas to buy an 84 ft ketch, *Lavengro,* in which he and Lawrence were to take a selected group of people to recolonize the Kermadec Islands in the South Fiji Basin. Lawrence bubbled with boyish enthusiasm:

Mackenzie 184   The Lavengro of course thrills me to my marrow. Yes, I'd sail the Spanish Main in her. How big was Drake's ship? Is she steam as well as sails? How many men do you consider you'd want to run her? I pace out her length on the terrace below.

But Secker, who was against the South Seas plan, persuaded Mackenzie to apply instead for a sixty-year lease of Herm and Jethou in the Channel Islands. Lawrence could not conceal his disappointment:

Mackenzie 190   What is this I hear about Channel Isles? The Lord of the Isles. I shall write a skit on you one day.

It was six years before Lawrence wrote 'The Man Who Loved Islands'.

Lawrence had used his departure from England as an excuse to break with Pinker, just at the time when publishers were beginning to compete for his novels. Mountsier became his agent in America. Huebsch, who had already very discreetly published the American edition of *The Rainbow,* and Seltzer both wanted *Women in Love.* It was only through a misunderstanding between Lawrence and Huebsch (caused by Pinker) that Seltzer got it, and published a handsome edition in November 1920. He became Lawrence's exclusive American publisher until his collapse in 1925.

Meanwhile, Secker and Duckworth were competing for the English rights of both novels. When Duckworth demanded cuts, Lawrence went to Secker, and remained with him for the rest of his life. Secker published *The Lost Girl* in November 1920, and *Women in Love* in 1921, but did not get round to republishing *The Rainbow* until 1926. From now on Lawrence had a sufficient income for his modest needs. Never again was he to have to grovel for charity, or devote half his energies to keeping the wolf from the door.

Moore 717   *The Lost Girl* won for Lawrence his first literary prize – £100 – the James Tait Black prize awarded by Rachel Annand Taylor ('with misgivings'). Arnold Bennett, whose *Anna of the Five Towns* had provoked *The Lost Girl,* wrote to Seltzer in June 1921:

I am glad of the opportunity to express my opinion that Mr Lawrence is the foremost of the younger British novelists and beyond question a genius, and that I have a very great admiration for his work. I greatly admire *The Lost Girl,* which, in my opinion, is a novel of great beauty, distinction and force.

Some readers thought less highly of *The Lost Girl.* Katherine Mansfield wrote to Murry:

Mansfield 620–1   Lawrence denies his humanity. He denies the powers of the Imagination. He denies Life – I mean *human* life. His hero and heroine are non-human. They are animals on the prowl. They do not feel: they scarcely speak. There is not one memorable *word*. They submit to the physical response and for the rest go veiled – blind – *faceless* – *mindless*. This is the doctrine of mindlessness.

The letter goes on to become almost hysterical, and tells us more about Katherine Mansfield's sexual problems than about *The Lost Girl*. Nevertheless, it is true that Lawrence's imagination, where human relationships are concerned, had coarsened after *Women in Love*. It could be argued that the best work of these wandering years was the poems in which he recorded his adventures in the world of birds, beasts and flowers, the only world he could still look on with a bright unjaundiced eye.

At the beginning of August Frieda went to Germany, leaving Lawrence to walk round Lake Como with the Whittleys, and then, after a week in Venice, to settle for the whole of September alone in a rambling old explosion-shattered villa at San Gervasio, Florence, where he wrote many of the *Birds, Beasts and Flowers* poems, including the finest, 'Tortoises', of which Carl Van Doren wrote:

Nation 1921   *Tortoises* seems to me as powerful a poem as was ever written about animals and nearly as powerful as was ever written about love.

Two other works written that month at the Villa Canovaia, 'Turkey Cock' and 'America, Listen to Your Own!', turn eagerly towards America and its pre-Columbian heritage:

Phoenix 90–1   Americans must take up life where the Red Indian, the Aztec, the Maya, the Incas left it off. They must pick up the life-thread where the mysterious Red race let it fall. They must catch the pulse of the life which Cortes and Columbus murdered. There lies the real continuity. . . . A great and lovely life-form, unperfected, fell with Montezuma. The responsibility for the producing and the perfecting of this life-form devolves upon the new American. . . . It means a departure from the old European morality, ethic. It means even a departure from the old range of emotions and sensibilities. . . . Montezuma had other emotions, such as we have not known or admitted. We must start from Montezuma, not from St Francis or St Bernard.

The Lawrences' next excursion from Taormina was in early January 1921 to Sardinia. In a mere five days on the island, without making a single note, Lawrence collected enough experiences and impressions for a 200-page book. He had seen nothing before like the Sardinian costumes, or the vegetable market at Cagliari. Lawrence in Sardinia was very much the self-conscious Englishman shrinking from the medieval squalor of Sorgono and the sordid villagers, 'degenerate aborigines' who failed to live up to the promising picturesqueness of the village at a distance. But an hour later, warmed and pacified at the inn, he watched an old man roasting a kid by candlelight 'and it was as if time immemorial were toasting itself another meal'.

The Lawrences had gone to Sardinia to see if they might like to live there, but decided to keep Fontana Vecchia for another year. Shortly after they returned to

Harwood, Achsah and Earl Brewster. 'Let us pitch our tents side by side in the howling wilderness of the christian countries. Let us go from this Sodom of angels like Lot and Abraham, before the fire falls. No, but seriously, let us agree to take a way together into the future.'

Sicily there came the offer of an abandoned farm near Boston, from a Mrs Thrasher, whom Lawrence had met in Florence. 'I want to go to America,' he wrote to Mary Cannan:

Moore 640

> My plan is to go to the Thrasher farm, and write then for America.

Mountsier was appointed to act as Lawrence's agent in the matter, and cabled in the affirmative. But by that time another cable had come, from Else, summoning Frieda to nurse her sick mother, and Frieda had departed.

After a month miserably alone in the rain, finishing *Sea and Sardinia*, Lawrence set off slowly northwards to join Frieda. His first stop was Capri, where he met Earl and Achsah Brewster, Americans, vegetarians and 'budding Buddhists' as Aldington called them. When Lawrence said he had come from Taormina, the Brewsters told him that they had spent their honeymoon in a delightful house there called Fontana Vecchia. The coincidence augured well for the friendship, which was to last the rest of Lawrence's life.

Achsah Brewster recorded her first impressions of him:

Brewster 241

> He did not seem the tormented soul, tortured beyond endurance – as he had been described to us – when suddenly he came lilting along through the poppies under the olives on the upper terrace of Quattro Venti, the sun shining on his warm brown hair, making his beard flicker in red flames on his long chin. His eyes were of a blue to match the sea and sky, wide apart and set low under the dome of his forehead. . . . The nose was blunted and from certain angles together with his great brow suggested the statues of Socrates. His mouth was curiously unmodelled like those the Greeks assigned to Pan and the satyrs. A trick of drooping the head pensively; his gentle expression; the dignity of his pose; the way the beard grew from his delicate, high cheek-bones; the fall of the hair over his forehead; all these made him look like the Christ figure on many a carved crucifix. Again he seemed like Whistler's portrait of Carlyle. In the Paris Salon I have seen a carved wooden head, painted, with blue eyes and red beard, labelled 'the bolshevik'. It might have been done for Lawrence. For me these images merge and shift; but there is left always a brightness of flaming beard and blue eyes, a shine of some fire glowing within. His voice was individual; low, with a reed timbre, flexible, full of variation. He had a silent little laugh when he would just open his mouth and swallow it down. Again he had a short snort of indignation, but mostly a low mirth-provoking laugh. Well, there he stood, laugh and all, debonair and gay, out in the poppies under the olives. Springtime seemed much more springtime because he was there.

When he left Capri a few days later, Lawrence promised to see the Brewsters again before they embarked on their pilgrimage to Ceylon.

⌇

Lawrence, travelling for the sake of travelling, went on to Rome, then Florence. By the end of April he was in Baden-Baden, reunited with Frieda. There, in a fit of work, sitting in the woods, he finished *Aaron's Rod* in May and wrote the first draft of *Fantasia of the Unconscious* in June.

Aaron's Rod is a picaresque novel about the adventures of Aaron Sisson, a Nottinghamshire checkweighman who throws up his job and deserts his wife and children to wander through Europe in search of himself. His rod is his flute, which symbolizes his capacity to grow and blossom. The opening is very similar to the opening of *Pilgrim's Progress*. As Pilgrim flees from the City of Destruction his wife and children cry after him to return:

> But the man put his fingers in his ears and ran on crying, 'Life, life, eternal life'. So he looked not behind him, but fled towards the middle of the plain.

Lawrence is in the direct line of English puritanism characterized by what Birkin calls 'the old effort at serious living', by the conviction that a man's first responsibility in life is to save or rather create his own soul, for without that he is useless to himself, his wife, his country and his race. But for Lawrence blessedness, 'eternal life', is to be found in earthly fulfilment, not in any life-denying otherworldly spirituality.

But Aaron finds that he belongs to the large class of men who are incapable of finding a creative direction unaided. If his life is ever to be more than trial and error, following his own nose, he must give his free submission 'to the heroic soul in a greater man'. The greater man in the novel is the Lawrence-figure Rawdon Lilly. This leadership principle is spelled out all too clearly in *Fantasia*:

> When the leaders assume responsibility they relieve the followers for ever of the burden of finding a way. Relieved of this hateful incubus of responsibility for general affairs, the populace can again become free and happy and spontaneous, leaving matters to their superiors. No newspapers – the mass of the people never learning to read. The evolving once more of the great spontaneous gestures of life.
>
> We can't go on as we are. Poor, nerve-worn creatures, fretting our lives away and hating to die because we have never lived. The secret is, to commit into the hands of the sacred few the responsibility which now lies like torture on the mass. Let the few, the leaders, be increasingly responsible for the whole. And let the mass be free, save for the choice of leaders.
>
> Leaders – this is what mankind is craving for.
>
> But men must be prepared to obey, body and soul, once they have chosen the leader. And let them choose the leader for life's sake only.

Lawrence was forced into this extremity by the depth of his caring. He sought the quickest way out of the City of Destruction, which was Western civilization.

> Let us go from this Sodom of angels like Lot and Abraham, before the fire falls.

He had to be, simultaneously, Pilgrim and Evangelist:

> We've got to rip the old veil of a vision across, and find what the heart really believes in, after all: and what the heart really wants, for the next future. And we've got to put it down in terms of belief and of knowledge. And then go forward again, to the fulfilment in life and art.

He saw that most contemporary 'knowledge' was quite simply wrong because grounded in a sterile mechanical rationalism and not in belief and vision. The clue, he felt, was the unconscious:

> We must discover, if we can, the true unconscious, where our life bubbles up in us, prior to any mentality. The first bubbling life in us, which is innocent of any mental alteration, this is the unconscious. It is pristine, not in any way ideal. It is the spontaneous origin from which it behooves us to live.

And the language of the unconscious is symbolism and mythology, which speaks across time and space and all the artificial divisions of our thinking for the whole man alive. In terms of all this Lawrence tried to formulate a new science which would be simultaneously psychology and religion. He knew that his readers would find it 'bosh and abracadabra', and some of it is, but some of it is also, in Murry's words, 'far in advance of anything the professional psycho-analysts had reached'.

Murry 241

Most of June 1921 was spent at Ebersteinberg. From there, in July, Lawrence walked across the Black Forest to Constance and Zell-am-See. But he found it impossible to work in Austria ('no wits left, all gone loose and scattered') and was glad to get back to Italy in August. In Florence he began a new novel, 'a proper *story* novel – in the Venetian lagoons'. Though he spent most of September on it, no trace of this novel has survived.

Nehls 2, 68
Seltzer 26

Back in Taormina Lawrence's accumulated mail contained both *John Bull's* attack on *Women in Love* ('Loathsome Study of Sex Depravity – Misleading Youth to Unspeakable Disaster') and Heseltine's threat of legal action against Secker for Lawrence's libellous portrait of him as Halliday in that novel.

Lawrence poured his anger into his letters; to the Brewsters:

Moore 669

> It is a world of *canaille*: absolutely. *Canaille, canaglia, Schweinhunderei*, stink-pots. Pfui! pish, pshaw, prrr! They all stink in my nostrils. That's how I feel in Taormina, let the Ionian sea have fits of blueness if it likes, and Calabria twinkle like seven jewels, and the white trumpet-tree under the balcony perfume six heavens with sweetness. That's how I feel. A curse, a murrain, a pox on this crawling, sniffing, spunkless brood of humanity. So, what's it like in Ceylon? I'd much rather go to Mars or the Moon. But Ceylon if there's nothing better. . . . If I hadn't my own stories to amuse myself with I should die, chiefly of spleen.

The stories he was 'pottering with' in these last months of 1921 were 'The Captain's Doll', 'The Fox' for which he wrote a completely new ending (characters he disapproves of are off-handedly killed in fatal 'accidents' in both these stories), 'The Ladybird', and the *England, My England* stories, several of which he revised.

The superiority of 'The Captain's Doll' over 'The Fox' and 'The Ladybird' is a factor of the extent to which the heroine Hannele is given a life of her own and the strength to balance Hepburn in a true relationship. She comes to respect his maleness, but is not, and is never likely to be, subsumed by it. The further Lawrence moves towards wish-fulfilment as dominant male, the thinner his art becomes.

12 Lessons in Disillusion

On 8 October Lawrence had written to Seltzer:

Seltzer 27   I wish I could find a ship that would carry me round the world and land me somewhere in the West – New Mexico or California – and I could have a little house and two goats, somewhere away by myself in the Rocky Mountains.

There must have been real power in that wish, for on 5 November Lawrence received, out of the blue, a potent package. It contained a letter several feet long, rolled like papyrus, and charms, a few leaves of *desachey* whose perfume the Indians say makes the heart light, a little *osha*, the root that is a strong medicine, and a necklace with Indian magic in it, all from a white witch called Mabel Dodge Sterne, designed to draw Lawrence to Taos, New Mexico.

Mabel's three husbands had been Carl Evans, a Buffalo socialite, Edwin Dodge, a Boston architect, and Maurice Sterne, an artist (whom Lawrence had just met in Anticoli). She also collected artists and writers, playing the patroness at the Big House in Taos. At the time she was living with Tony Luhan, a Taos Indian, whom she later married. She had read the first of the *Sea and Sardinia* chapters in *The Dial* and felt that Lawrence was the only writer who could really *see* the Taos country and the Indians and put them, alive, between the covers of a book.

Mabel put all the right things in her letter:

Luhan 4   I told him all I could about Taos and the Indians – and about Tony and me. I told him how much I wanted him to come and know that country before it became exploited and spoiled, before good roads would let in the crowds. I tried to tell him every single thing I could think of that I felt would draw him – simple things as well as strange ones. I remember I described it as a lofty, pastoral land far from railroads, full of time and ease, where the high, clear air seemed full of an almost heard but not quite heard music, and where the plainest tasks took on a beauty and significance they had not in other places.

Lawrence smelt the scent and nibbled the medicine and wrote the same day that he would like to come. To Earl Brewster he wrote:

Moore 677   The Indian, the Aztec, old Mexico – all that fascinates me and has fascinated me for years. *There* is glamour and magic for me. Not Buddha. Buddha is so finished and perfected and fulfilled and *vollendet*, and without new possibilities – to me I mean. The glamour for me is in the West, not in the fulfilled East. It seems to me my fate.

But when it came to booking his passage, he wavered. Stubbornly Lawrence held on to the idea that he must at all costs avoid New York, and approach the New World from the West, across the Pacific. Also he feared the intensity of his own hopes for America. It is almost as though he wanted to fool both America and himself that he was really going somewhere else entirely, and then creep up on her from behind. So the first step was to be Ceylon. Though he had no deep hope in the old world, he wanted to see it and speak with it. Perhaps a withdrawal from the world towards 'the inner realities that *are* real' would fortify him to return later to the raw world he felt America to be:

Brewster 27   I will go east, intending ultimately to go west.

Waiting for his passage Lawrence was on thorns. He filled his time by translating *Mastro-don Gesualdo* by Giovanni Verga, a Sicilian writer who had died the previous month. He finished it on shipboard. As the *Osterley* steamed south, Etna hovered in the air for hours behind him, calling him back, but he hardened his heart and denied her.

The Lawrences arrived in Kandy on 13 March 1922. Earl Brewster was studying
Unpub.   Pali and Buddhism at the monastery of the Tooth ('perhaps I shall study in that same molar monastery' Lawrence had written to Lady Cynthia Asquith). He had a huge ramshackle bungalow:

Moore 696   It is about a mile or mile and a half from Kandy, looking down on the lake: very lovely. It stands uphill among a sort of half wild estate – cocoa-nut palms and cocoa – and jungle trees – almost like the jungle. We sit on the verandahs and watch the chipmunks and chameleons and lizards and tropical birds among the trees and bamboos – there's only a clear space of about three yards round the house.

Achsah Brewster gives a delightful description of Lawrence at work there:

Brewster 250   Lawrence sat curled up with a school-boy's copy-book in his hand, writing away. He was translating Giovanni Verga's short stories from the Sicilian. Across the pages of the copy-book his hand moved rhythmically, steadily, unhesitatingly, leaving a trail of exquisite, small writing as legible as print. No blots, no scratchings marred its beauty. . . . All of this went on in the family circle. Frieda would come for consultation as to whether the rabbit's legs should be embroidered in yellow or white. The pen would be lifted a moment then go on across the page. Sometimes Lawrence would stop and consult us about the meaning of a word; considering seriously whatever comments were offered. He listened gravely and intently to everyone.

The highlight of the Lawrences' stay in Ceylon was undoubtedly the Perahera on 23 March:

Moore 697

We were at the Perahera here for the Prince of Wales. It was wonderful, gorgeous and barbaric with all the elephants and flames and devil dances in the night. One realizes how very barbaric the substratum of Buddhism is. I shrewdly suspect that high-flownness of Buddhism altogether exists mostly on paper: and that its denial of the soul makes it always rather barren, even if philosophically, etc., more perfect. In short, after a slight contact, I draw back and don't like it.

The heat was very bad for Lawrence (it was exceptional that year even for Ceylon); he was ill all the time, and of course blamed 'nauseous' Ceylon, 'the silly dark people' and Buddha, with his temples 'like decked up pigsties'. In reaction his thoughts turned back to England, whose virtues shone brighter in strict ratio to his distance from it:

Moore 698

I do think, still more now I am out here, that we make a mistake forsaking England and moving out into the periphery of life. After all, Taormina, Ceylon, Africa, America – as far as *we* go, they are only the negation of what we ourselves stand for and are: and we're rather like Jonahs running away from the place we belong. . . . So I am making up my mind to return to England during the course of the summer. I really think that the most living clue of life is in us Englishmen in England, and the great mistake we make is in not uniting together in the strength of this real living clue – religious in the most vital sense – uniting together in England and so carrying the vital spark through. Because as far as we are concerned it is in danger of being quenched. I know now it is a shirking of the issue to look to Buddha or the Hindu or to our own working men, for the impulse to carry through. It is in ourselves or nowhere. . . . The responsibility for England, the living England, rests on men like you [Robert Pratt Barlow] and me and Cunard – probably even the Prince of Wales – and to leave it all to Bottomleys, etc., is a worse sin than any sin of commission.

Lawrence had intended to stay in Ceylon two or three months, but by the end of March he had had enough:

Moore 699

No, the East doesn't get me at all. Its boneless suavity, and the thick, choky feel of tropical forest, and the metallic sense of palms and the horrid noises of the birds and creatures, who hammer and clang and rattle and cackle and explode all the livelong day, and run little machines all the livelong night; and the scents that made me feel sick . . . the undertaste of blood and sweat in the nauseous tropical fruits; the nasty faces and yellow robes of the Buddhist monks, the little vulgar dens of the temples: all this makes up Ceylon to me, and all this I cannot bear. *Je m'en vais. Me ne vo.* I am going away. Moving on.

Lawrence's first letter from Australia, to Earl Brewster, was about leaving it, and his next stopping place. He had invented a new disillusion-proof philosophy of travel:

Moore 703

I'm determined to *try* the South Sea Isles. Don't expect to catch on there either. But I love trying things and discovering how I hate them. How I *hated* a great deal of my time in Ceylon: never felt so sick in my life. Yet it is now a very precious memory, invaluable. Not wild horses would drag me back. But neither time nor eternity will take away what I have of it: Ceylon and the East.

Many of the passengers on the *Osterley* had been 'simple Australians', and they had made a favourable impression on Lawrence:

Huxley 540   I believe Australia is a good country, full of life and energy.

One, a Mrs Jenkins, had made an even more favourable impression than her compatriots by having with her a copy of *Sons and Lovers*. Mrs Jenkins met the *Orsova* at Freemantle and arranged for the Lawrences to stay at Leithdale, a guest house in Darlington which belonged to two Quaker nurses, Nellie Beakbane and Mollie Skinner. The Lawrences were placed at the same table as their fellow guests Eustace and Maudie Cohen. Maudie, who had read *The White Peacock*, told Lawrence with typical Australian tact that she didn't think much of it, and would lend him a book just as good by Mollie Skinner. Lawrence liked *Letters of a V.A.D.* and sought out Mollie Skinner in the wash house. They talked long about the seasons and wildlife of the bush. He told her to drop *Black Swans* and write a book about the first settlers, with her own brother as hero:

Skinner 113   The settlers – men and women with their children arriving here, dumped on the sand with the surf behind them, a few merchants, a few soldiers, a few packing cases into which they crept for shelter after chucking out the pianos; building camp ovens, burning their hands, looking for fresh water, longing for

Mollie Skinner about 1922.

THE
BOY
IN
THE
BUSH

BY

D.H. LAWRENCE
AND M.L. SKINNER

DHL

achievement, hungry for land, their cattle starving, their women scolding, homesick but full of courage, courage carrying them forward. What kept them?

Skinner 116 Mollie Skinner asked him who would publish such a book. 'Send it to me,' said Lawrence. 'I'll look after that.' During the next year Mollie Skinner wrote *The House of Ellis* and sent it to Lawrence. He completely rewrote it, with her reluctant approval (she wept at the new ending), and published it as *The Boy in the Bush*. *The Boy in the Bush* perhaps gives us Lawrence's response to Australia more purely than his own Australian novel *Kangaroo*:

> 'What would my father mean, out here?' he said to himself. And it seemed as if his father and his father's world and his father's gods withered and went to dust at the thought of this bush. And when he saw one of the men on a red sorrel horse galloping like a phantom away through the dim, red-trunked, silent trees, followed by another man on a black horse; and when he heard their far, far-off yelling Coo-ee! or a shot as they fired at a dingo or a kangaroo, he felt as if the old world had given him up from the womb, and put him into a new weird grey-blue paradise, where man has to begin all over again.

Lawrence at Wyewurk. 'There it crouched, with its long windows and its wide veranda and its various slopes of low, red-tiled roofs. Perfect! . . . A little front all of grass, with loose hedges on either side – and the sea, the great Pacific right there and rolling in huge white thunderous rollers not forty yards away.' (Kangaroo)

Lawrence's jacket design for The Boy in the Bush. *'I made it, and I think it's rather nice.' It was not used.*

The Lawrences stayed a fortnight at Darlington, then sailed to Sydney, just for the sake of rolling on. They took a train along the coast, looking out of the window for somewhere nice. At four they got out at Thirroul, and two hours later were settled in a beautiful bungalow on the Pacific – 'Wyewurk'. The place was a sordid mess, so they set to work scrubbing and polishing. But they had a whole world to themselves and revelled in it. They took long walks along the shore gathering shells, or drove in a pony cart into the bush, with its golden woods of mimosa. They saw no one but a few traders and farmers, and two English couples they had met on the boat who came for a weekend.

Lawrence loved the dream-like pristine bush, but couldn't stand the people (it seems Lawrence never saw, or showed any interest in, the Aborigines):

Moore 707–8   This is the most democratic place I have *ever* been in. And the more I see of democracy the more I dislike it. It just brings everything down to the mere vulgar level of wages and prices, electric light and water closets, and nothing else. You *never* knew anything so nothing, *nichts, nullus, niente,* as the life here. They have good wages, they wear smart boots, and the girls all have silk stockings; they fly around on ponies and in buggies . . . and in motorcars. They are always vaguely and meaninglessly on the go. And it all seems so empty, so *nothing*, it almost makes you sick. They are healthy, and to my thinking almost imbecile. That's what life in

The Lawrences with Mr and Mrs Arthur Denis Forrester and Mr and Mrs William L. Marchbanks (behind). 'D.H. took us for a drive in a hired car on Sunday, and he seemed to get real pleasure from showing us the beauty of the Australian scenery in these parts. We had our lunch at some falls – I think it may have been Fitzroy Falls, which is quite some distance from Thirroul. Anyhow, it was a long and expensive drive.' (Arthur Denis Forrester)

a new country does to you: it makes you so material, so *outward*, that your real inner life and your inner self dies out, and you clatter round like so many mechanical animals. . . . I feel if I lived in Australia for ever I should never open my mouth once to say one word that meant anything. . . . Yet the weird, unawakened country is wonderful and if one could have a dozen people, perhaps, and a big piece of land of one's own – But there, one can't.

This letter reveals, perhaps unwittingly, the deep connection between Lawrence's unkillable dream of Rananim and his compulsive talking. When he tries to imagine what it would be like if his inner life died, he thinks of losing the capacity to say meaningful things. Lawrence insisted that the inner life can only sustain itself in relationships; and within human relationships he insisted on the primacy of the sexual. What he does not normally insist on, but affirms nevertheless in his art and his life, is the importance of conversation as a fundamental human relationship. The importance he attaches to it is masked by the fact that he hates trivial conversation, cocktail conversation, or the urbane sort that goes round with the port in senior common rooms, even more than blank dumbness. But it seemed to him natural, necessary even, that if you have an active inner life it should express itself in a verbal exchange of ideas and interests, hates and enthusiasms, hopes and fears, with those around you. So that it was simultaneously a relief and a torment to Lawrence to be driven into marital isolation, relief from the company of those who would not or could not understand and be sympathetic and talk in good faith, but torment to have no one to talk to but Frieda, and an intolerable burden on her. Hence the stream of letters which flowed from Lawrence's pen, trying to keep conversations going at long range. And hence the hortatory tone into which the novels of his exile so frequently lapse:

He preached, and the record was taken down for this gramophone of a novel.

In the early pages of *Kangaroo* Lawrence describes himself pining for England, even for London:

He longed for Europe with hungry longing: Florence, with Giotto's pale tower: or the Pincio at Rome: or the woods in Berkshire – heavens, the English spring with primroses under the bare hazel bushes, and thatched cottages among plum blossom. He felt he would have given anything on earth to be in England. It was May – end of May – almost bluebell time, and the green leaves coming out on the hedges. Or the tall corn under the olives in Sicily. Or London Bridge, with all the traffic on the river. Or Bavaria with gentian and yellow globe flowers, and the Alps still icy. Oh God, to be in Europe, lovely, lovely Europe that he had hated so thoroughly and abused so vehemently, saying it was moribund and stale and finished. The fool was himself. He had got out of temper, and so had called Europe moribund: assuming that he himself, of course, was not moribund, but sprightly and chirpy and too vital, as the Americans would say, for Europe. Well, if a man wants to make a fool of himself, it is as well to let him.

But before returning to England there was America to confront, and before that, this Australian novel to write. Lawrence went 'full tilt' at *Kangaroo*, which he aimed to finish in three months, and finished in two.

As Lawrence well knew, the novel is not fundamentally about Australia at all. In it Lawrence is 'struggling with the problem of himself and calling it Australia' – and the same could be said of every place he wrote about. Nevertheless, the novel's plot, the surface description of political activity in Sydney in 1922, is extraordinarily, mysteriously, accurate. Lawrence had no time to do any research beyond reading the *Sydney Bulletin* and the old newspapers he found lying around at Wyewurk; yet he was in possession of detailed information about the right-wing secret army which had just come into existence in Sydney, made up almost entirely of ex-servicemen and dedicated to resisting the spread of communism. This information was unknown to the Australians themselves until some years later. It seems that someone, perhaps a returning officer he had met on the boat, had confided in him, perhaps even tried to enlist his support. We know that Lawrence never invented material when he could draw on reality. That Lawrence had a real and not a fictitious political situation in mind is clear from his question to Seltzer when revising the novel in New Mexico in October:

Seltzer 43 Do you think the Australian Govt. or the Diggers might resent anything?

Had Lawrence published *Kangaroo* before leaving Australia, he might well have been in some danger.

By July Australia was beginning to exert an insidious grip on Lawrence, which his puritanism made him fear as if it were a Lotus Land:

Moore 712 If I stayed here six months I should have to stay for ever – there is something so remote and far off and utterly indifferent to our European world, in the very air. I should go a bit further away from Sydney, and go 'bush'. . . . But my conscience tells me not yet.

Lawrence could justify to himself a state of private happiness and atonement with nature and the gods only as preparatory to a further effort in the world of men, not as a permanent condition. Then there was Mabel Luhan willing Lawrence to come to Taos, every night commanding him with her whole being, and enlisting Tony's powerful influence to help her.

The Lawrences embarked on the *Tahiti* on 10 August 1922 and arrived at Raratonga ten days later. They spent a day there and two days in Tahiti, and that was enough for Lawrence. He found the South Sea Islands 'beautiful to look at', but:

Moore 713 There is a sort of sickliness about them, smell of cocoa-nut oil and sort of palm-tree, reptile nausea. . . . These are supposed to be the earthly paradises: these South Sea Isles. You can have 'em. . . . Travel seems to me a splendid lesson in disillusion – chiefly that. . . . I wonder how long we shall stay in America.

13 The New World

It took Mabel and Tony all day to drive the ninety miles of dirt road to Lamy Junction to meet the evening train. Of course Mabel had already decided to dislike Frieda:

Luhan 36   Lawrence and Frieda came hurrying along the platform, she tall and full-fleshed in a suit of pale pongee, an eager look on her pink face, with green, unfocused eyes, and her half-open mouth with the lower jaw pulled a little sideways. Frieda always had a mouth rather like a gunman. Lawrence ran with short, quick steps at her side. . . . I had an impression of his slim fragility beside Frieda's solidity, of a red beard that was somehow too old for him, and of a nervous incompetence. He was agitated, fussy, distraught, and giggling with nervous grimaces. Tony and I felt curiously inexpressive and stolid confronting them.

They had a meal at the station, and Mabel decided that Lawrence was ready to break with Frieda, and that she, Mabel, was just the woman he now needed:

The womb in me roused to reach out to take him.

On the way to Santa Fe the car broke down. Tony's explanation was that there must be a snake near by. When, at last, they reached Santa Fe, it was too late to get the Lawrences into a boarding-house. But Mabel's friends, Witter Bynner, a poet, and Willard Johnson, his secretary, were still up, and glad to provide a room. They sat up late talking, and Bynner decided that Frieda was exactly the right woman for Lawrence:

Bynner 6–7   For all his flares at her, usually over trifles, he knew that she was his mate. Lion-chasers and neurotic women, who tried to disparage Frieda and to attract him by substituting their ambitions and vanities for her fond, amused, understanding, creative patience found presently that a real lion would have been tamer in drawing-room or boudoir than this odd simian cat whose interest in them was finally a puzzled, tolerant curiosity.

'Tolerant curiosity' also describes Frieda's attitude to the Bynner–Johnson menage. 'The young thin one seems rather nice,' she said to Mabel. Lawrence liked Johnson too, and immediately renamed him Spoodle. Everyone else, throughout his life, called him Spud. Spud was co-editor of a little magazine called *The Laughing Horse*.

'*You have asked about Mabel Dodge: American, rich, only child, from Buffalo on Lake Erie, bankers, forty-two years old, has had three husbands — one Evans (dead), one Dodge (divorced), and one Maurice Sterne (a Jew, Russian, painter, young, also divorced). Now she has an Indian, Tony, stout chap. She has lived much in Europe — Paris, Nice, Florence — is a little famous in New York and little loved, very intelligent as a woman, another "culture-carrier", likes to play the patroness, hates the white world and loves the Indian out of hate, is very 'generous', wants to be 'good' and is very wicked, has a terrible will-to-power, you know — she wants to be a witch and at the same time a Mary of Bethany at Jesus's feet — a big, white crow, a cooing raven of ill-omen, a little buffalo.*'

Willard Johnson, Witter Bynner and Lawrence at Bynner's home in Santa Fe. Photo probably by Frieda.

He showed Lawrence a copy in the hope that he might contribute, as he did several times in the next few years.

Bynner got up early next morning only to find that Lawrence had already washed the supper things and prepared an ample breakfast.

Soon Mabel and Tony arrived, and in the clear morning sun they set off over the high desert, through the Rio Grande canyon, towards the Taos plateau in the foothills of the Rockies. Years later Lawrence remembered it:

Phoenix 142   The moment I saw the brilliant, proud morning shine high up over the deserts of Santa Fe, something stood still in my soul, and I started to attend. There was a certain magnificence in the high-up day, a certain eagle-like royalty, so different from the equally pure, equally pristine and lovely morning of Australia, which is so soft, so utterly pure in its softness, and betrayed by green parrots flying. But in the lovely morning of Australia one went into a dream. In the magnificent fierce morning of New Mexico one sprang awake, a new part of the soul woke up suddenly and the old world gave way to a new.

It was Lawrence's thirty-seventh birthday.

Mabel took the Lawrences to the Big House in Mabeltown, as Lawrence called it, a mile out of Taos on the edge of the desert towards the Pueblo. Tony had built a lovely little adobe house nearby, especially for them. Next day they settled in happily. A

'Taos village is a Mexican sort of plaza – piazza – with trees and shops and horses tied up.'

Mabel's house in Taos.

day or two later Tony was leaving to drive 120 miles to an Apache feast at the Jicarilla Reservation, and Mabel made him take Lawrence. Immediately on his return, Lawrence wrote up his reactions in 'Indians and an Englishman'. He had found himself bemused, as if he had been dropped on the moon. It had all seemed to him too much like a comic opera, or the sort of thing he had seen as a lad, done by circus troupers. He could find no 'common purpose' or 'common sympathy' with the Indians, whose dances and songs seemed to him to deny the individual:

Phoenix 95   Listening, an acute sadness, and a nostalgia, unbearably yearning for something, and a sickness of the soul came over me. The gobble-gobble chuckle in the whoop surprised me in my very tissues. Then I got used to it, and could hear in it the humanness, the playfulness, and then, beyond that, the mockery and the diabolical, pre-human, pine-tree fun of cutting dusky throats and letting the blood spurt out unconfined.

When Lawrence thought he saw what he had hailed at a distance made manifest, he was appalled, and recanted:

Phoenix 99   The voice out of the far-off time was not for my ears. Its language was unknown to me. And I did not wish to know. . . . Our darkest tissues are twisted in this old tribal experience, our warmest blood came out of the old tribal fire. And they vibrate still in answer, our blood, our tissue. But me, the conscious me, I have gone a long road since then. And as I look back, like memory terrible as bloodshed, the

'At the foot of the sacred Taos mountain, three miles off, the Indians have their pueblo, *like a pile of earth-coloured cube-boxes in a heap.'*

dark faces round the fire in the night, and one blood beating in me and them. But I don't want to go back to them, ah, never. I never want to deny them or break with them. But there is no going back. Always onward, still further. The great devious onward-flowing stream of conscious human blood. From them to me, and from me on. . . . My way is my own, old red father; I can't cluster to the drum any more.

Moore 716　On 20 September Lawrence wrote to Forster of the Indians: 'I haven't got the hang of them yet', and indeed his second article on them, 'Taos', with its incident of a white woman attempting to enter an Indian church, is sadly imperceptive in comparison with the opening chapter of *A Passage to India*, which Forster was then writing.

Lawrence's first response to the Indians was to debunk them. Perhaps this was partly a reaction against Mabel's excessive claims and expectations. She had even laid on Indian dances at the Big House, and bullied her guests, including Lawrence, into silly attempts to copy the impossibly subtle steps. The talk at her house was all about the Bursum Bill, whereby the government sought powers to break up the Indian reservations and allow the commercial exploitation of their lands:

Moore 727　It has been the Bursum Bill till we're sick of it.

Nevertheless, the sheer bare-faced injustice of it stung Lawrence to write his article 'Certain Americans and an Englishman' which was published in the *New York Times* in December:

Phoenix 2, 243　Let us have the grace and dignity to shelter these ancient centres of life, so that, if die they must, they die a natural death. And at the same time, let us try to adjust ourselves again to the Indian outlook, to take up an old dark thread from their vision, and see again as they see, without forgetting we are ourselves.

Perhaps the article made some contribution to the defeat of the bill.

Mabel also expected Lawrence to write the Great American Novel, which would be the story of her life:

Luhan 52　Of course it was for this I had called him from across the world – to give him the truth about America: the false, new, external America in the east, and the true, primordial, undiscovered America that was preserved, living, in the Indian

70　bloodstream. . . . I wanted Lawrence to understand things for me. To take *my* experience, *my* material, *my* Taos, and to formulate it all into a magnificent creation.

On the morning after his return from the Apache trip, Lawrence and Mabel began their work in her bedroom. Lawrence's first words were inauspicious:

59　I don't know how Frieda's going to feel about this.

Which meant that he knew only too well. The next day he said that they had better
60　work at his house; but Mabel could not recapture the 'complete, stark approximation of spiritual union, a seeing of each other in a luminous vision of reality' with Frieda stamping round sweeping and singing. Still, Lawrence had enough material to make a start, and a very promising start, in a new style, sardonic and spiky. But the first

chapter was all Frieda allowed him to write. Mabel had met her match.

Whenever Frieda felt Lawrence's attention straying she would deliberately provoke him, often with some vulgarity uttered with a cigaratte dangling from her mouth. Lawrence would explode against her, but she had his attention, and minutes later they would be thick as thieves.

Lawrence was always busy. If there was no housework to do, he would sit under a bush and write. In the evening there would be social gatherings for conversation and games, with Lawrence giving a passionate harangue, or a brilliant impersonation in charades. Learning to ride was a great pleasure to Lawrence and Frieda. Though Lawrence never looked comfortable on horseback, he rode fast and fearlessly, and never fell off.

Luhan 78   Mabel's twenty-year-old son, John Evans, was about to marry the fifteen-year-old Alice Henderson. Mabel asked Lawrence to give him some advice. They were left alone for an hour. John later told his mother that Lawrence had advised him to be 'always separate', never to let his wife know his thoughts, to be gentle with her when

Frieda and Lawrence

she was gentle, and to beat her when she opposed him. Frieda's bruises testified to the fact that Lawrence practised what he preached.

The spirit of debunking persisted in Lawrence's next undertaking, the final rewriting of his *Studies in Classic American Literature*. Here it is not so much America and the American writers he is debunking, as the extravagant and over-earnest claims he had made for them when the scenario for the book had been not the real America, but the mythic America of his childhood reading and equally romantic adult yearnings. The personal application is evident in the introductory chapter:

> Men are free when they are in a living homeland, not when they are straying and breaking away. Men are free when they are obeying some deep, inward voice of religious belief. Obeying from within. Men are free when they belong to a living, organic, *believing* community, active in fulfilling some unfulfilled, perhaps unrealized purpose. Not when they are escaping to some wild west.

In the first version of the Crèvecoeur essay, written in 1917, Lawrence had been already sceptical about the romanticization of Nature. In the final version, written actually in that 'wild and noble America' Lawrence had pined for ever since reading Fenimore Cooper as a boy, there is a new note of personal disenchantment:

> Hazlitt, Godwin, Shelley, Coleridge, the English romanticists, were, of course, thrilled by the *Letters from an American Farmer*. A new world, a world of the Noble Savage and Pristine Nature and Paradisal Simplicity and all that gorgeousness that flows out of the unsullied fount of the ink-bottle. Lucky Coleridge, who got no farther than Bristol. Some of us have gone all the way.

Lawrence takes up the point again in the Fenimore Cooper essay:

> It is perhaps easier to love America passionately, when you look at it through the wrong end of the telescope, across the Atlantic water, as Cooper did so often, than when you are right there. When you are actually *in* America, America hurts, because it has a powerful disintegrative influence upon the white psyche. It is full of grinning, unappeased aboriginal demons, too, ghosts, and it persecutes the white men, like some Eumenides, until the white men give up their absolute whiteness.

And again in the Melville:

> We can't go back. We can't go back to the savages: not a stride. We can be in sympathy with them. We can take a great curve in their direction, onwards. But we cannot turn the current of our life backwards, back towards their soft warm twilight and uncreate mud. Not for a moment. If we do it for a moment, it makes us sick. We can only do it when we are renegade. The renegade hates life itself. He wants the death of life. So these many 'reformers' and 'idealists' who glorify the savages in America. They are death-birds, life-haters. Renegades.

The renegade Lawrence had most in mind was, of course, Mabel Luhan. Mabel later recognized herself as 'The Woman Who Rode Away' – 'that story where Lorenzo thought he finished me up'. But by 1924, when that story was written, Lawrence's attitude towards America and the Indian had acquired a much deeper understanding, and its tone is very far from debunking.

It was obvious that Lawrence could not stay long under the wing of the padrona. When the situation at the Lawrence house became intolerable, each would seek support from Mabel, who occasionally, to her own surprise, found herself on Frieda's side. Lawrence felt he was in a witches' brew and had to make a bid to escape.

Despite his declared intention of keeping clear of the Taos artists' colony, Lawrence had in fact got to know several of them, including their president Walter Ufer, who had introduced him to two itinerant young Danish artists, just arrived in town, Knud Merrild and Kai Gótzsche. The Lawrences and the Danes found they liked each other's company. They made no demands on each other, and an easy friendship developed spontaneously. In November the Lawrences and the Danes camped out for a few days on an abandoned ranch on Lobo mountain, seventeen miles from Taos, which belonged to Mabel's son John. One evening Lawrence told the Danes that Mabel had offered the ranch for the winter, and invited the Danes to join him and Frieda there. The Danes found the invitation very attractive, but felt unable to accept because, being unable to sell their work in Taos, they felt they could not support themselves up there for the whole winter. Lawrence, knowing they would have refused anything that looked like charity, tactfully suggested that they could earn their keep by designing book-jackets for him and helping with the heavy work. And Lawrence would commission Gótzsche to paint his portrait.

Del Monte ranch. 'The last foothills of the Rocky Mts. – with forest and snow mountains behind – and below, the desert, with other mountains very far off, west.'

The Danes went out into the night to discuss the invitation. The air was incredibly pure and cold. The alfalfa fields under snow sparkled in the moonlight. The majestic mountains were silhouetted against endless starry space. An owl hooted and coyotes howled. How could they turn their backs on all that and Lawrence too. It was agreed. But next day Mabel, whose plans held no place for these insignificant Danes, sent a messenger to tell Lawrence that he could have only one of the two cabins. Lawrence fulminated against the venomous Mable. That afternoon he and Gótzsche went scouting, and came back triumphant: they had rented two cabins from William Hawk on the lower ranch, the Del Monte. On 1 December they moved in.

The cabins had not been lived in for many years and there was much work to be done – roofing, carpentering, plastering, glazing, paperhanging, painting, whitewashing . . . Then there were several days of woodcutting and hauling to stock up for the winter. Lawrence always insisted on doing his share of work even when it was obviously too heavy for him. Any job within his physical capacity he did well and with enjoyment. The Danes, fortunately, were athletic and fit and used to heavy work, which they were glad to do. Conditions were primitive. Water was so precious that none could be spared for bathing; they had to take rub-downs in the snow or drive twenty miles to Manby Hot Springs in the Danes' faithful Lizzie. Food was of the simplest, though once or twice a week Lawrence would cook a special meal, such as roast beef and Yorkshire pudding. He also baked excellent bread and cakes. Frieda had by this time become a good cook, but Lawrence could not bear to leave her alone in the kitchen. She mothered the Danes, making them curtains, sheets, pillows and woollen caps. Their continual presence removed a great weight from Frieda.

The Danes lived very close to the Lawrences for four months, and, according to Frieda, knew them more intimately than anyone else before or after; yet the Danes recalled no serious quarrels between Lawrence and Frieda, except, perhaps, for one incident when Lawrence had tried to knock Frieda's cigarette out of her mouth. He had missed; but subsequently Frieda had to hide her hoard of cigarettes in the Danes' cabin. When she wrote to England for news of her children, she still had to do that secretly.

One moment of strain between Lawrence and the Danes came when Lawrence was outraged to hear that a woman friend of the Danes, a broadminded artist and composer Meta Lehmann, having taken most of the day to hitch-hike from Taos, was

Lawrence and Frieda with Bibbles.
'Little black snub-nosed bitch with a shoved-out jaw
And a wrinkled reproachful look . . .

Self-conscious little bitch,
Aiming again at being loved . . .
All humanity is jam to you.'

proposing to spend the night in their cabin. Lawrence ordered that she should be thrown out into the snow. What worried him was not so much the fact of her staying as the gossip to which it would certainly give rise. The Danes insisted firmly that it was their business, and Meta stayed.

Another near-quarrel came when Lawrence completely lost his temper with his pup Bibbles and viciously kicked her in sight of the angry Danes. Normally, of course, Lawrence hated any kind of cruelty. He hadn't quite the conviction to be a vegetarian, but he was upset when the Danes shot rabbits near his house. Better, he said, to go out and kill some people – that he could enjoy – bankers, industrialists, lawyers, war-makers, schemers of all kinds – starting with Mabel.

Lawrence at last had sympathetic listeners, and would talk to the Danes for hours every day:

Merrild 85   Since he felt this sympathy in his listeners, he would, without the slightest self-consciousness, talk and talk at great length; and he talked as brilliantly and frankly as he wrote. He had the 'gift of interest' and could make one interested in almost anything. . . . Sometimes he would brood, but more often he was gay, even to playfulness. He could be bitter and sometimes exploded in a fury of hatred toward the humbug and rottenness of present-day civilization, its society and people. He hated bullying, people trying to alter one into an approximation of themselves. He had no social, moral or intellectual affectations and was free from any kind of snobbery. He had his fits once in a while, but on the whole, in everyday life he was easy-going. A man of strong personality and character, almost overpowering and absolutely fearless.

Merrild did jacket designs for *The Captain's Doll, Kangaroo, Studies in Classic American Literature* and *Birds, Beasts and Flowers*, but Lawrence was able to persuade Seltzer to use only the first of these, though he authorized Seltzer to pay for them out of his own royalties. Seltzer put appallingly inappropriate commercial covers on *Women in Love* and *Kangaroo*, and used Lawrence's own design for *Birds, Beasts and Flowers*. He did not have the interest in the appearance of his books that might have been expected in a small publisher. Seltzer did, however, go to great pains to publicize *Sea and Sardinia*; and when three of his books, including *Women in Love*, were seized by John S. Sumner of the New York Society for the Suppression of Vice, he put up a courageous fight and was thoroughly vindicated when Judge George W. Simpson congratulated him on the high literary quality of the three books and dismissed the charges. The three titles rapidly sold out.

The Seltzers almost worshipped Lawrence. Thomas would not let his wife touch Lawrence's letters without washing her hands. Adele thought Lawrence was
Seltzer 185   'Chaucer, Piers Ploughman, John Bunyan, Fielding, Shakespeare, Goethe, Schopenhauer, Nietzsche rolled into one, modernized and added to'. The Seltzers stayed at Del Monte for the week between Christmas and New Year. Seltzer remembered most vividly the 'small but sweet' voice of Lawrence singing English Christmas carols. Later he wrote to Merrild:

Merrild 125   Follow him in the kitchen when he cooks, when he washes and irons his own

underwear, when he does chores for Frieda, observe him when he walks with you in the country, when he is in the company of people whom he likes and to a certain extent respects – how natural he is in every movement and yet how distinguished, how satisfying because he is natural; and in his conversation he is almost always inspiring and interesting because of his extraordinary ability to create a flow, a current between himself and the other person.

Lawrence decided that he could trust Seltzer. Though Seltzer was trustworthy as a man, as a businessman he was not, and Lawrence had to watch helplessly as he stumbled towards ruin over the next two years, in spite of the excellent sales of several of his Lawrence titles. It was, of course, a bad time for publishers, and better businessmen than Seltzer went under.

From Taos Seltzer went straight to Hollywood to negotiate the film rights of *Women in Love*. Warner Brothers had offered $10,000, which Lawrence would gladly have accepted, but Seltzer was holding out for $20,000. The Lawrences and the Danes Merrild 126 spent the anticipated fortune many times over. One of their schemes was to 'buy a small ship in which to cruise the southern seas in search of a place where we could live off and in Nature, starting a new life'. By the time Seltzer reached Hollywood, Warner Brothers' interest had cooled, and he left empty-handed.

Lawrence could console himself that 1922 had been his most successful year so far, financially, his gross income from America alone being $5,439.67.

Despite the severity of the winter (the temperature often dropped to 25°F. below freezing point at night), it was a happy time for Lawrence, perhaps the nearest he ever came to his Rananim – working and riding and hiking and chatting with the friendly Danes. Outwardly it seemed ideal, yet still he resisted the spirit of the place, even the landscape, calling it great and beautiful, but empty and dead and hostile. Neither it nor the Indians inspired him to write anything more at Del Monte than a few more poems for *Birds, Beasts and Flowers*, and his letters speak of returning to Europe via Greenland, or spending a few months in Russia.

From Wellington, her birthplace, Lawrence had sent a card to Katherine Mansfield. In December he had written to Mary Cannan:

Unpub.   I see Murry boosts me a bit – patronizingly.

Someone must have sent him Murry's enthusiastic review of *Aaron's Rod* in the *Nation and Athenaeum*:

Draper 177   To read *Aaron's Rod* is to drink of a fountain of life. . . . *Aaron's Rod* is the most important thing that has happened to English literature since the war. To my mind it is much more important than *Ulysses*.

Later that month, after a three-year estrangement, Lawrence had received a cordial letter from Murry and had replied cordially. Murry's next letter, which Lawrence received on 2 February, was to tell him of the death of Katherine of tuberculosis at the age of thirty-five in a sanatorium at Fontainebleau. Now Lawrence, who had shown the worst of himself two years earlier when he wrote to Katherine:

Moore 620   You revolt me stewing in your consumption.

showed how sensitive he could be in his condolence:

Moore 736   The dead don't die. They look on and help.

That same day Lawrence asked Seltzer to send Murry the two psychoanalysis books. Moore 104–6 Murry thought the *Fantasia* was 'a wonderful book' and 'the pinnacle of Lawrence's achievement':

It clinched my half-formed determination to found the *Adelphi*. He was willing to 'unite up again'; he was in the throes of a revulsion from America. Then let him

come back, and we would begin. In the meantime, I would prepare the place for him. I would make a new magazine, and begin by publishing the essential chapters of the *Fantasia*. We (that is Koteliansky and I) cabled to him in New Mexico; he agreed to the publication. And the *Adelphi* began. I neither desired, nor intended, to remain editor of it. I was, in my own eyes, simply *locum tenens*, literally lieutenant, for Lawrence; and I waited eagerly for his coming.

But Lawrence was not so eager to play Christ to Murry's John the Baptist. He knew

Kot 252 Murry to be more suited to the role of Judas. Also Lawrence had a 'deep mistrust of England':

I have not much faith in literary ventures, either!

In any case, Lawrence had decided that he wanted next to see Old Mexico, perhaps even settle there and start his colony, first with the Danes, then adding one or two friends at a time. They would have a small ranch and grow bananas. So, in mid-March, the Lawrences set off for Mexico City.

Lawrence at Bynner's house on the way to Mexico. Photo by Witter Bynner.

14 Paradise Lost and Found

In Mexico City Lawrence found a homely little Italian hotel, the Monte Carlo. Speaking Italian and drinking chianti, it is not surprising that he found Mexico rather like southern Italy. A week later the Lawrences were joined by Bynner and Spud. Together they set out to visit all the museums, cathedrals, and other tourist attractions.

'Isn't this a nice photograph – in the cloisters of Cuernavaca cathedral.' Photo by Witter Bynner.

Teotihuacan

11 April 1923

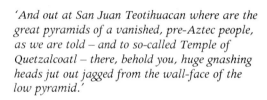

'And out at San Juan Teotihuacan where are the great pyramids of a vanished, pre-Aztec people, as we are told – and to so-called Temple of Quetzalcoatl – there, behold you, huge gnashing heads jut out jagged from the wall-face of the low pyramid.'

Lawrence knew little about pre-Columbian Mexico, but learned fast. He had brought with him a letter of introduction from Dr Lyster to the famous English anthropologist and archaeologist Zelia Nuttall, who lived in the city. He lunched at her house three times. She gave him a copy of her book *Fundamental Principles of Old and New World Civilizations*, in which he found the Aztec bird-serpent god Quetzalcoatl interpreted as symbolizing the fertilizing contact of sky and earth (as his own rainbow had done), together with a host of associated gods and symbols, many of which he was to use in his Mexican novel at first called *Quetzalcoatl*, later *The Plumed Serpent*. Mrs Nuttall also lent Lawrence, or put him on to, several other books he was able to draw on, such as Prescott's *Conquest of Mexico*.

   The Plumed Serpent opens with a very accurate account of a bull-fight the party visited at the beginning of April. Lawrence had seen at once how despicably everything was stacked against the bull – 'the only one among them with heart or

Bynner 50 brain' – and wanted to leave. The others pleaded to stay for at least the first round, so that they would know exactly what they were condemning. Lawrence remained to see the bull disembowel an old blindfolded horse, leapt to his feet howling his disgust at the crowd in Spanish, and stumbled out, followed by Frieda. In the novel Bynner and Spud, there called Owen and Villiers, are pilloried for staying, yet five months later Lawrence sat through another bullfight, in Tepic, and saw two bulls killed.

   These were very privileged tourists. Through the American Embassy they met

'We saw this bullfighting – pretty disgusting.' Photo by Witter Bynner.

Roberto Haberman and Fred Leighton, who were in charge of the teaching of English in the Mexico City schools, and through them they met several artists, writers and labour leaders. Lawrence had little sympathy with any of them. He thought the new murals by such artists as Diego Rivera were hideous caricatures. Nevertheless, he expressed a desire to meet Jose Vasconcelos, the Minister of Education, and a lunch was arranged. At the last moment the Minister was called to an emergency cabinet meeting and invited the waiting group to lunch with him the following day. Lawrence stalked out in a fury and refused to attend on the pretext of being ill. This was not the only occasion on which Lawrence was bad-tempered and ill-mannered, and he created a bad impression on several of the people he met in Mexico City.

Lawrence had already decided that Vasconcelos and all the other Mexican socialists and reformers were 'ninnies' doing as much harm as good:

Seltzer 80   Criminal to want to educate these peons with our education.

The whole post-Columbian superstructure seemed to Lawrence to be mere rickety overlay. Underneath were the Aztec and pre-Aztec realities, the fanged, reptilian
Phoenix 105   gods he had glimpsed at Teotihuacan. It was not really like Italy – 'none of the phallic preoccupation of the old Mediterranean'.

Lawrence was torn between returning to England or looking for a house somewhere outside Mexico City where he could settle down to write his Mexican novel. Frieda wanted to stay, so on 12 April they set off for Puebla, leaving Spud in the American hospital suffering from acute lumbago. Trains were favourite targets for rebels and bandits. Armed guards rode on top. The train stopped for half a day with no explanation and all blinds drawn. When it finally moved on, they saw bodies by the line a few miles ahead. Many of the fine haciendas had been ruined in the Zapata uprising.

Lawrence was not impressed by Puebla. By the time they reached Orizaba he had a bad cold, and sensed evil everywhere, and just wanted to get back to England. By now he knew a good deal of Mexican history, and every town reminded him of some atrocity committed there, as though the spirit of Mexico itself demanded cruelty and blood. Atlixco was better, and they spent several happy, lazy days there; but
Bynner 43   Lawrence did not want to stay. He wanted 'a place with water'. He would give Mexico one last chance. If Lake Chapala did not live up to the description in *Terry's Guide to Mexico*, he would book his passage home. Lawrence went alone to see.

⁓

Bynner 79   'CHAPALA PARADISE. TAKE EVENING TRAIN,' said the telegram Frieda received next day, 1 May. Spud and Bynner took Frieda as far as Guadalajara, put her on the camion for Chapala, and stayed for a few days with the Purnells. Idella Purnell was a former student of Bynner's, and editor of a little poetry magazine called *Palms* for which she was later to extract some poems from Lawrence in exchange for a pot of home-made marmalade. Her father was a dentist. The following day Lawrence wrote to Bynner:

Huxley 566   Chapala very pleasant – just enough of a watering place to be *easy*. We can bathe from the house.

'We are already in our house – pleasant – near lake but not looking on it, on our own little garden.'

Later he told Bynner it was the place they had been waiting for. After a few days, Bynner and Spud joined the Lawrences there.

Lawrence and Bynner fundamentally disliked and disapproved of each other and only just maintained an edgy companionship. Bynner thought Lawrence was egotistic, overbearing and, at times, satanic. He had read little of Lawrence and understood less. To Lawrence it seemed that Bynner was incapable of 'serious living'.

Nehls 2, 239   He called him a Playboy of the Western World, 'taking life as a cocktail before dinner'. As for Spud, he was so mild, so non-committal, that it was difficult to have any feelings about him at all, beyond the feeling that he was rather too nice to go through life as Bynner's side-kick. Yet Lawrence wanted them with him, not just in Chapala, but in his house. Bynner wisely insisted on a hotel.

Bynner admired Frieda, and advised her to spike Lawrence's guns by always attacking him first, even quite unreasonably, whenever she suspected that he was about to turn on her. Frieda tried the gambit with some success.

Lawrence feared that the peace of Chapala, of Mexico, might be that of a sleeping volcano. He had heard rumours from his *criada*, Isabel, of impending reprisals by the peons against the employers and against foreigners:

Merrild 301   We have a man to sleep on the verandah with a pistol: and we may not walk outside the village for fear of being robbed or carried off by bandits.

But nothing could spoil, even for someone as irritable and nervous as Lawrence, the immediate calm, the abundance of exotic bird life, and the splendour of sunsets over

Idella Purnell, Lawrence, Frieda, Spud and Dr Purnell on Spud's twenty-sixth birthday. Photo by Witter Bynner.

the lake. In the mornings they would work, in the evenings talk. It was idyllic, dreamlike, as Spud recalled:

Nehls 2, 240   And through it all, like a chorus to our song, were amicable birthday dinners and pleasant visits from Guadalajara friends and tropical moonlight nights when guitars and wandering singers from across the lake and love-lorn couples made music all night long. Woven into the pattern of our days were motor-trips to this town and that in search of an old church, or a fiesta, or an ancient Indian dance combined with a Spanish miracle-play, or to purchase *serapes* or Toltec idols.

Lawrence wanted to stay in Chapala as long as it took him to write his Mexican novel, which he began at once. By the end of May he had written ten chapters. He would sit under a willow on the waterfront with an exercise-book on his knees, writing swiftly, often with an audience of donkeys. From there he could watch the whole life of the lakeside, which was transmuted at once into the background of his novel:

Nehls 2, 236   There were the little boys who sold idols from the lake; the women who washed cloths at the water's edge and dried them on the sands; there were the lone fishermen, white *calzones* pulled to their hips, bronze legs wading deep in the waters, fine nets catching the hundreds of tiny *charales*: boatmen steering their clumsy, beautiful craft around the peninsula; men and women going to market with baskets of *pitahayas* on their heads; lovers, even, wandering along the windy shore; goatherds; mothers bathing babies; sometimes a group of Mexican boys swimming nude offshore . . .

It was a place where the writing flowed. As Frieda knew:

Frieda 156   Lawrence could only write in places where one's imagination could have space and free play, where the door was not closed to the future, where one's vision could people it with new souls to be born, who would live a new life.

The new life Lawrence envisioned there he outlined in a letter to his mother-in-law:

Moore 744   But Mexico is very interesting: a foreign people. They are mostly pure Indians, dark like the people in Ceylon but much stronger. The men have the strongest backbones in the world, I believe. They are half-civilized, half wild. If they only had a new faith they might be a new, young, beautiful people. But as Christians they don't get any further, are melancholy inside, live without hope, are suddenly wicked, and don't like to work.

His hero, Don Ramon, sweeps away Christianity and gives them a new faith, first, in himself, as leader, as a natural aristocrat of the spirit, then in the gods he serves, principally Quetzalcoatl, the ancient Toltec god of the reconciliation of opposites who had laid the foundations of Mexican culture, now resurrected and renewed as the gleaming son of the morning who steps from the waters of Lake Chapala to redeem his people.

In June Lawrence's flickering desire to return to England was almost extinguished when he received from Murry the first number of the *Adelphi*:

Dr Purnell, Bynner, Spud, Idella, Frieda and Lawrence on a canoa – 'a fairly large primitive half-enclosed vessel, like a Chinese junk, with one enormous rounded sail' (Bynner).

Moore 747   It seemed to me so weak, apologetic, knock-kneed, with really nothing to justify its existence. A sort of beggar's whine through it all. . . . No really! Is this the best possible in England?

They had already decided to give up the house at the end of the month. In a last gesture Lawrence and Frieda sailed up the lake to Ocotlan to see about renting a little farm. Lawrence reported to Merrild:

Moore 747–8   We were away two days travelling on the lake and looking at haciendas. One could easily get a little place. But now they are expecting more revolution, and it is so risky. Besides, why should one work to build up a place and make it nice, only to have it destroyed. So, for the present at least, I give it up. . . . It is no good, I know I am European, so I may as well go back and try it once more.

Lawrence at the mast of the canoa. Photo by Witter Bynner.

For his last week in Chapala, Lawrence proposed that they should invite the Purnells, hire a *canoa*, and sail around the lake (which was ninety miles long) for a few days. During the first night a storm broke, lashing the lake into a tossing sea. The rain poured in. Everyone was seasick, especially Idella. Bynner became very ill with an infected fistula. Next morning he and Idella left the *Esmeralda*, and Bynner was rushed off to hospital in Guadalajara for an operation. The care and kindness he received from Lawrence during his illness caused him to revise his opinion of Lawrence's character a good deal. The rest of the party sailed on for three more days without further mishaps on the milky lake, the three Mexicans singing to the guitar, Lawrence singing his English ballads . . . Spud recalled:

Nehls 2, 240   Our craft moved when the wind moved, and lay becalmed under myriad stars whole nights. She was poled into quaint old ports where we bought fruit and chickens, eggs and tortillas. She glided magnificently over gentle, choppy waves to islands where mangos and goats' milk replenished our larder – where sometimes a shepherd would kill a kid for our pirate appetites. We cooked most of the food ourselves over a charcoal stove made of an oil can.

Idella welcomed them back.

Nehls 2, 251   How unkempt and unshaven and happy they looked! And how filled they were with delight of their adventure.

So, with the maximum of regret, on 9 July, the Lawrences left Chapala:

Seltzer 99   I don't really want to go back to Europe. But Frieda wants to see her mother. Perhaps I shall have to go, this once. But feel sure I shan't stay. – Perhaps round the world again, and try to do a novel in India or China: the East. Then to America, and perhaps back to Mexico. So far, I think I like Mexico best of all the places, to live in. . . . I'm sad to go. But I suppose it's best, for the moment.

So Lawrence tried to shift the responsibility for leaving on to Frieda, but at the station Frieda blew her nose noisily into a huge handkerchief several times saying, 'I *like* Chapala, I *like* Chapala!'.

⌇

The Lawrences took ten days to get from Chapala to New York, via Laredo, San Antonio, New Orleans and Washington. Seltzer had rented a country cottage for them in New Jersey, and Lawrence invited the Seltzers to join them there. The four lived together for a month, while Lawrence did a proof-reading marathon – *Kangaroo*, *Birds, Beasts and Flowers*, and *Mastro-don Gesualdo*. But it was not like Del Monte, and was slightly spoiled for the Seltzers by the constant bickering of the Lawrences.

Lawrence found New York wearing. He longed for the west, the mountains and the desert. When the time came to book passages to England, he could not go through with it:

Moore 750   I find my soul doesn't want to come to Europe, it is like Balaam's ass and can't come any further.

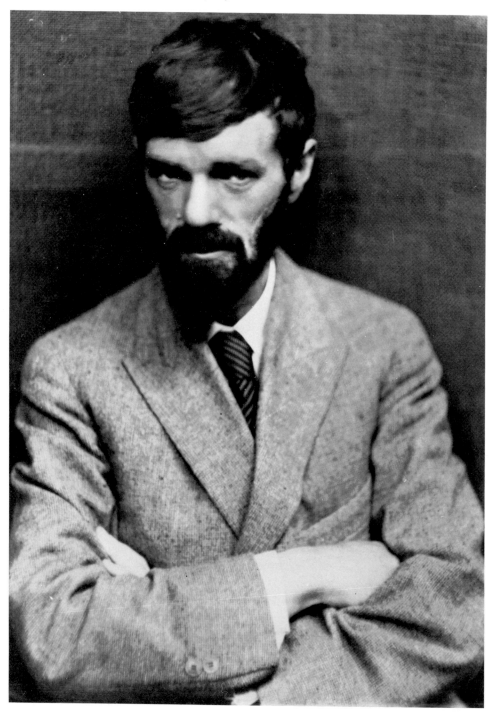

Photo by Nickolas Muray.

Moore 749   Frieda would go alone to see her children. 'Wrong or not,' Lawrence wrote to Murry, 'I can't stomach the chasing of those Weekley children.' He would join up with the Danes in Los Angeles. To Merrild he wrote:

Huxley 573–4   We might like to spend the winter at Palm Springs or among the hills. Or we might go again to Mexico. And I should like to see you and Gótzsche and have a talk about the future. If there was nothing else to do, we might take a donkey and go packing among the mountains. Or we might find some boat, some sailing ship that would take us to the islands: you as sailors, myself as cook: nominal.

Lawrence saw Frieda off on 18 August. To all his correspondents he wrote of her rejoining him in October, but Frieda had other ideas:

Seltzer 105   I am glad to be alone and I will *not* go back to him and his eternal hounding me, it's too ignominious! I will *not* stand his bad temper any more if I never see him again – I wrote him so – He can go to blazes, I have had enough – The worm that turns.

This rebellious spirit lasted until Frieda reached England, when she invited Murry, whom Lawrence had asked to look after her, to become her lover. Murry took her on a trip to the Continent, was sorely tempted, but declined out of loyalty to Lawrence.

Lawrence set off west. His first stop was Buffalo, where he stayed four days, lunched with Mabel's mother, and visited all the 'blue blood' on his best behaviour:

Seltzer 105   The town is like Manchester sixty years ago – or Nottingham – very easy and sort of nice middle-class, BOURgeois.

Knud Merrild, Kai Gótzsche, J. Winchell Bøttern and Lawrence in Los Angeles.

On 30 August Lawrence arrived in Los Angeles to be met at the station by the
Seltzer 107 Danes in 'that ancient Lizzie of Del Monte fame'. On the way he had read the manuscript
of Mollie Skinner's novel *The House of Ellis*, and he wrote at once to her that there was
no chance of getting it published as it stood, but that he would be glad to 'recast' it if she
would give him a free hand. He began work on it at once, changing the title to *The Boy in
the Bush*.

Despite picnics and motor-trips Lawrence was bored and lonely in Los Angeles,
especially in the mornings, when the Danes had to work. He went to the docks, trying
to get himself hired as a cook on a boat, with the Danes as deckhands, but with no
success. Every evening they discussed possibilities. Lawrence was for returning to
Mexico to look for a farm. Merrild was for saving up to pay their way to the South
Seas, for a Gaugin pilgrimage.

Though he believed in Lawrence, Merrild wanted to make his own way, not live
through Lawrence. Nor could be believe that Lawrence would last long without
Frieda. Such objections did not deflect Gótzsche:

Merrild 329   I feel fortunate to be able to go to Mexico with Lawrence no matter how it turns
out, and I am willing to spend my last penny with him.

On 25 September Lawrence and Gótzsche set off on the Southern Pacific for
Guaymas. There Lawrence was offered free land for his commune, but declined
because of the wildness and isolation of the place. It would have been like living on
Mars. Navojoa was no improvement. From there Lawrence wrote to Bynner:

Moore 755–6   This West is much wilder, emptier, more hopeless than Chapala. It makes one feel
the door is shut on one. There is a blazing sun, a vast hot sky, big lonely inhuman
green hills and mountains, a flat blazing *littoral* with a few palms, sometimes a dark
blue sea which is not quite of this earth – then little towns that seem to be slipping
down an abyss – and the door of life shut on it all, only the sun burning, the clouds
of birds passing, the *zopilotes* like flies, the lost lonely palm-trees, the deep dust of
the roads, the donkeys moving in a gold-dust-cloud. In the mountains, lost,
motionless silver-mines. . . . There seems a sentence of extinction written over it
all. – In the middle of the little covered market at Alamos, between the meat and
the vegetables, a dead dog lay stretched as if asleep. The meat vendor said to the
vegetable man: 'You'd better throw it out'. The veg.-man looked at the dead dog
and saw no reason for throwing it out. So no doubt it still lies there. We went also
to *haciendas* – a cattle *hacienda*: wild, weird, brutal, with a devastating brutality.

They travelled by train as far as Tepic, then by car over impossible roads and by
muleback for nine hours to Ixtlan; next day another six hours on mule-back to
Estlatlan, where they could catch a train again to Guadalajara.

There was a letter waiting from Frieda:

Moore 757–8   Frieda says she likes England now, and it is my place, and I must come back. I
wonder. . . . Mexico has a certain mystery of beauty for me, as if the gods were
here. Now, in this October, the days are so pure and lovely, like an enchantment,
as if some dark-faced gods were still young. I wish it could be that I *could* start a

little centre – a ranch – where we could have our little adobe houses and make a life.

The same vague invitation went to both the Carswells and the Brewsters. Lawrence wrote to Seltzer from Chapala:

Seltzer 117   The lake *so* beautiful. And yet the lake I knew was gone – something gone, and it was alien to me. I think I shall go to Europe soon . . .

What had gone was Frieda. He could not conceive a new life, or any life, without her. Suddenly he became aware of practical difficulties of farming in Chapala he had been quite oblivious of before. 'So you see,' Gótzsche wrote to Merrild, 'even the plan is already beginning to disintegrate':

Merrild 341   I am absolutely sure that he would feel happier and live more happily if he could go out for a few hours a day, and have some work to do, milk a cow or plow a field. As he lives now, he only writes a little in the morning and the rest of the day he just hangs around on a bench or drifts over to the market place, hands in pocket, perhaps buying some candy, fruit, or something. If he could only have access to a kitchen, so he could make our food, that would occupy him for a couple of hours.

The little work he was doing was on *The Boy in the Bush*.

Lawrence wrote to Murry that he would probably come back by the beginning of December and work a while with him on the *Adelphi*. A day or two later came another letter from Frieda saying that she would on no account come back to Mexico. On 2 Seltzer 121   November came a cable from Frieda with the one word 'COME'. Frieda had 'had a great time' with her children but realized that they had no more need of her. She had liked Murry very much. She imagined Murry and Kot bearing Lawrence in triumph to his 'reception feast'. Lawrence knew there was a conspiracy to drag him back. By the middle of the month he had finished *The Boy in the Bush*. He wanted to rewrite *Quetzalcoatl*, but that could wait. There was nothing to hold him:

Moore 761   Frieda and everybody insist on my going to England. And I, I shall give in once more, in the long fight. I may as well go and settle finally with England. But I shall not stay long. A short time only. And directly or indirectly I shall come back here, this side, Mexico.

So, with a heavy heart and the deepest misgivings, Lawrence embarked on 22 November at Vera Cruz for England.

15 Resurrection

Frieda, Murry and Kot met Lawrence at Waterloo. Murry recalled that he looked 'positively ill':

Murry 1, 110 His face had a greenish pallor. Almost the first words he spoke were: 'I can't bear it.' He looked, and I suppose he felt, as though the nightmare were upon him again. All he had to suggest was that the *Adelphi* should attack everything, everything; and explode in one blaze of denunciation.

Lawrence's spirits were not raised by his instant realization, on the station platform, that the relationship between Frieda and Murry had become far more 'chummy' than ever before. Already Lawrence knew that it had been a mistake to come:

Seltzer 124 Am here – loathe London – hate England – feel like an animal in a trap. It all seems so dead and dark and buried – even *buried*. I want to get back west – Taos is heaven in comparison, even if Mexico for the time is impossible. It's good to see Frieda again, but then I can take her with me, out of this cold stew.

'God get me out of here,' he cried in his next letter to Seltzer three days later.

Despite Murry's drivelling parish magazine editorials, the *Adelphi* had been much more successful than Murry had dared to hope. As for his championship of Lawrence, he certainly had published something of Lawrence in each issue, but otherwise the spirit of the magazine, reflecting Murry's ('a pale yellow *cri de l'âme*'), was quite alien to Lawrence's. Lawrence offered to stay for four months and edit the *Adelphi*. Murry refused, believing Lawrence would only destroy it; and he could not allow the destruction of so perfect a vehicle for his own ego.

Lawrence booked a private room at the Café Royal for a party of his special friends. His guests were Murry, Kot and Gertler, the Carswells, Mary Cannan and Dorothy Brett. Much claret and port was drunk, far more than most of them were used to. Kot made an emotional declaration of admiration for Lawrence, punctuated by the breaking of several glasses. Then Lawrence made the invitation he had called them together for, asking them, one by one, if they would go with him back to New Mexico and start a new life. Catherine Carswell recalled their replies:

Mary Cannan was the only one to return a flat negative to Lawrence's question. . . .
Carswell 211 'No', said she hardily. 'I like you, Lawrence, but not so much as all that, and I think

you are asking what no human being has a right to ask of another'. Lawrence accepted this without cavil or offence. It was a clear, hard honest answer. What Gertler said, I can't remember. I rather think it was a humouring but dry affirmative, which we all understood to mean nothing. Kot and Donald both said they would go, less drily, but so that any listener guessed they were speaking from goodwill rather than from deep intention. Dorothy Brett said quietly that she would go, and I, knowing that she would, envied her. Murry promised emotionally that he would, and one felt that he wouldn't. I said yes, I would go. And I meant it, though I didn't see how on earth it could be, anyhow for a long time. Unlike Mary and Dorothy Brett, I had neither money of my own nor freedom from responsibility.

Murry kissed Lawrence, who said 'Do not betray me!' Murry replied: 'I love you, Lorenzo, but I won't promise not to betray you'. Shortly afterwards, Lawrence slumped forward, vomiting, lost consciousness, and was carried home.

On Christmas Day Lawrence stuffed and cooked a goose for dinner at Brett's house. Afterwards, between the songs, Murry and Kot repeatedly urged Lawrence to stay in England. When they all went to see *The Covered Wagon* and several real Indians came on to the stage, Lawrence sighed deeply; never before had he felt so much affection for them: they were from his world.

On New Year's Eve Lawrence wrote to Seltzer that he was thinking of coming to America in the early spring:

Seltzer 127   Murry talks of coming with us: says he too wants to break away. The idea is, if we get the *Adelphi* planted in America, after about six months or a year, to publish it from that side and get more American contributors: but to keep it if possible a little 'world' magazine. One can only try. – Dorothy Brett, an old friend, wants to come too. She is deaf – and paints pictures – and is a daughter of Viscount Esher.

But to Mabel he confessed:

Moore 766   Apparently Murry does want to come, but I don't altogether trust him. Can't rely on him *at all*.

Lawrence's mistrust was well-founded. Murry had already decided, wisely enough, that, though he might have gone with Lawrence and Frieda, or with a larger party, he could not make up a four with Brett. He had only just extricated himself from an affair with her. But he felt unable to tell Lawrence that, and even went through the motions of asking Lawrence what new clothing he would need to buy for Taos.

Lawrence 'celebrated' the New Year with his people in the Midlands and saw his father for the last time. He felt there the dead hand of the past even more clammily.

From there Lawrence went to Shropshire to visit Frederick Carter. They tramped the border hills discussing dragons, Lawrence storming against St John the Divine for his blasphemies against the great life symbols. He was also storing up impressions of that area for use in his story 'St Mawr' some months hence.

On 23 January, stupefied by London, the Lawrences set off to Paris and Baden-
Moore 777   Baden. Lawrence found Paris, 'agreeably soulless'. In Germany he sensed 'the old

Lawrence's father in retirement at Ripley. 'Lawrence said he had come to understand and respect his father much more than when he wrote Sons and Lovers. *He grieved over the hostile portrait. His father was a piece of the old gay England that had gone.' (Rhys Davies)*

fierceness coming back', and welcomed it, fearfully. In his 'Letter from Germany' to the *New Statesman*, he predicted another Attila. The *New Statesman* waited ten years to publish the piece. By then its predictions had already been fulfilled.

Moore 789 The Lawrences returned to London at the end of February, and within a week embarked on the *Aquitania* for New York, taking with them Dorothy Brett. Murry was supposed to be following in a few weeks, but wrote to say that rather than 'wild-goose-chasing in other continents', he had decided to stay at home, marry Violet le Maistre, an infatuated twenty-three-year-old contributor to the *Adelphi*, and devote himself to turning her into a replica of Katherine Mansfield, a process so thoroughly accomplished that Violet became fatally consumptive within two years.

During Lawrence's absence from Taos there had been a partial reconciliation with Mabel, who claimed to have come to a better understanding of herself, and indeed seemed 'wiser' to Lawrence when the Lawrences stayed with her on their return. As a gesture of renewed friendship Mabel gave Frieda the Flying Heart ranch, the ranch they would have lived in all along but for Mabel's jealousy of the Danes. Frieda reciprocated by giving Mabel the manuscript of *Sons and Lovers*, which was worth a good deal more than the ranch. Mabel later used it to pay her psychiatrist.

Lawrence's drawing of corn dancers at Santo Domingo Pueblo, April 1924. 'You become aware of the ripple of bells on the knee-garters of the dancers . . . of the seed-like shudder of the gourd-rattles, as the dance changes, and the swaying of the tufts of green pine-twigs stuck behind the arms of all the dancing men, in the broad green arm-bands. Gradually come through to you the black, stable solidity of the dancing women, who poise like solid shadow, one woman behind each rippling, leaping male. The long, silky black hair of the women streaming down their backs, and the equally long, streaming, gleaming hair of the males, loose over broad, naked, orange-brown shoulders. Then the faces, the impassive, rather fat, golden-brown faces of the women, with eyes cast down, crowned above with the green tablets, like a flat tiara. Something strange and noble about the impassive, barefoot women in the short black cassocks, as they subtly tread the dance, scarcely moving, and yet edging rhythmically along, swaying from each hand the green spray of pine-twig out – out – out, to the thud of the drum'. ('Dance of the Sprouting Corn')

'Latest of Brett — doesn't she dress up?'

Lawrence and Frieda with Candido, Trinidad, and the Mexican carpenter. 'With three Indians and a Mexican carpenter we have built up the 3-room log cabin – and very good little house – and made adobes for the chimney. . . . I hope in the coming weeks to get the houses all finished, roofs shingled and all. . . . And naturally I don't write when I slave building the house – my arms feel so heavy, like a navvy's, though they look as thin as ever.'

April they spent lazily in Taos, riding out to the hot springs, visiting the Santo Domingo dances, playing mah jongg and charades in the evenings. Taos soothed Lawrence; the big spaces, the smell of sagebrush, the sound of the Indian drums. Brett was 'blissfully happy on an old horse', which she rode like an Amazon in a cowboy hat. But when Lawrence and Brett were riding or painting together, Mabel felt out of it, and conceived a strong dislike of Brett. And Brett's large brass ear-trumpet, Toby, inhibited conversation. But Frieda said that Brett didn't count.

When spring came, it was time to move out to the ranch and make it habitable. Lawrence changed its name to Lobo, the name of the mountain. They went up to the ranch on 5 May. A fortnight later Lawrence wrote to the Seltzers:

Moore 786

We have only one little spring of water - pure water - that will fill a pail in about 3 minutes: it runs the same summer & winter. If we want to grow anything, we must water, irrigate. Maclure used to bring the water in a made ditch, over deep places by a wooden runnel bridges, for nearly 3 miles: from the Gallina Canyon. Then, from the home canyon, he brought it down two miles. It's very difficult, though, in a dry country with dry gravelly soil. You can't bring much flow, so far: & in summer very often none. So we leave the ranch quite wild - only there's abundant feed for the five horses. And if we wanted to take the trouble, we could bring the water here as Maclure did, & have a little farm. - There's quite a lot of land, really - it says 160 acres. but it takes a terrible long time to go round the fence, through the wild forest. - We got lots of wild strawberries - & we still get gallons of wild raspberries, up our own little Canyon, where no soul ever goes. If we ride ten miles, we can get no further. Beyond, all savage, unbroken mountains.

We get our things from Taos - 17 miles - either by wagon or when someone is coming in a car. Our road is no road - a breaking through the forest - but people come to see us. Every evening, just after tea, we saddle up and ride down to Del Monte Ranch, for the milk, butter, eggs, & letters. The old trail passes this gate, & the mailman, on horseback, leaves all the mail in a box nailed on a tree. Usually we get back just at dark. Yesterday we rode down to San Cristobal, where there is a cross-roads, a blacksmith, & a tiny village with no shop no anything, save the blacksmith - only a handful of Mexicans who speak Spanish. We went to get Frieda's grey horse - the Azul - shod. They call him in Spanish el Azul - the Blue. - During the day there's always plenty to do - chopping wood, carrying water - & our own work: Sometimes we all paint pictures. Next week the Indian Geronimo is coming up to help me mend the corral, & build a porch over my door,

Lawrence's letter to his niece Margaret.

'The big cabin is finished and you have spent the morning decorating the apple-green dresser with plates and cups and saucers. It is amazing how well the old tin plates look and the odd assortment of cups. You are immensely proud of the job and call us in to admire.' (Brett)

Seltzer 135–7   Taos is looking very lovely, full spring, plum-blossom like wild snow up the trails, and green, green alfalfa, apple orchards in bloom, the dobe houses almost pink in the sun. It is almost arcadian. But of course, the under spirit in this country is never arcady.

On the same day he wrote to invite the Carswells:

Moore 790   I hope you'll scrape the money together and come for a whole summer, perhaps next year, and try it. Anyway it would make a break, and there is something in looking out on to a new landscape altogether.

The Frederick Carters were also invited:

Moore 792   You could have one of the houses, and Mrs Carter could start a little farm.

And so were Bynner and Spud . . . But the Lawrences were landed with just Brett and Toby.

Brett had to live in a cabin so tiny it would only just hold her cot bed, a small table and chair, and her trunk. She became Lawrence's self-appointed handmaiden. When he hammered, she held the nails.

Moore 794   The Brett is a little simple but harmless, and likes to help.

Frieda once offered Brett half-a-crown to contradict Lawrence, but she never earned it.

Despite his aching arms, Lawrence did begin 'Pan in America'. The essays he had written on the Indians the previous month had been still debunking:

'Indians and   You can perform the mental trick, and fool yourself and others into believing that
Entertainment'   the befeathered and bedaubed darling is nearer to the true ideal gods than we are. This last is just bunk, and a lie.

Perhaps living with Indians at the ranch brought him a deeper understanding:

Phoenix 31   And still, in America, among the Indians, the oldest Pan is alive.

The Indians had rituals to enable them to handle the potent, potentially destructive, energies of Pan. For the white man there must be a death to the old consciousness (symbolized by a ritual sacrifice of the heroine in 'The Woman Who Rode Away') followed by a resurrection, equally painful, to a new reality – the stark, sordid, beautiful, awe-inspiring reality of Pan, which Lawrence himself was now wrestling with on that pack-rat infested, lightning-scarred, but certainly not god-forsaken ranch. The life there inspired Lawrence to write that summer his finest story since the war – 'St Mawr' – fine because it finds such perfect shape and symbolism to
Moore 789   explore Lawrence's deepest preoccupations: the deadness of England ('England is as unreal as a book one read long ago'), the need to find another reality, the claims of the monastic or hermit life, the consequences of exposure to Pan. The stallion, St Mawr, offers Lou a choice 'between two worlds'. He is a messenger from the ancient world of the gods, and from those fastnesses where the gods are still remembered, as in Wales,

or are not yet dead, as in New Mexico. Lou accepts the message, and goes, like Brett, to Lobo ranch. She accepts the gods of that place, 'grim and invidious and relentless, huger than man, and lower than man'. Whether she can live with them, and whether doing so will bring her fulfilment, remains, at the end, in question.

Lawrence himself was certainly happy that summer; but the peace was punctuated by several quarrels and sulks which continuing contact with Mabel invariably caused.

Secker 58   We sit here very quietly, with the sun and the thunderstorms, the trees and the horses. I go on slowly with my second long-short story – a queer story. Frieda of course admires her 'place' all the time.

'Meantime Mabel is twisting long creepers into wreathes. You are already crowned with one and you look like Pan. You feel like him, too: there is a gleam in your eye, a joyousness about you. . . . Snapshots are taken; and thus adorned, you pile back into the car.' (Brett)

In August Mabel and Tony took the Lawrences to see the Hopi Snake Dance in Arizona. In Santa Fe on the way back Lawrence wrote another of his debunking pieces, 'Just Back from the Snake Dance – Tired Out' – debunking not the Hopi, about whom Lawrence had little to say, but those whites who had flocked to see the show:

Moore 804   Good old Hopi, he sure is cute with a rattler between his teeth.

Mabel was outraged:

Luhan 267   He had written a dreary terre à terre account of the long road to the Hopi village and of the dance, a mere realistic recital that might have been done by a tired, disgruntled business man. It had no vision, no insight, no appreciation of any kind.

Lawrence meekly agreed to try again, and produced what is perhaps the finest of his writings about the Indians, 'The Hopi Snake Dance':

We dam the Nile and take the railway across America. The Hopi smooths the rattlesnake and carries him in his mouth, to send him back into the dark places of the earth, an emissary to the inner powers.

Suddenly it was autumn, with its ephemeral beauty and frosty nights:

Moore 812   The country here is very lovely at the moment. Aspens high on the mountains like a fleece of gold. Ubi est ille Jason? The scrub oak is dark red, and the wild birds are coming down to the desert. It is time to go south. – Did I tell you my father died on Sept. 10th, the day before my birthday? – The autumn always gets me badly, as it breaks into colours. I want to go south, where there is no autumn, where the cold doesn't crouch over one like a snow-leopard waiting to pounce. The heart of the North is dead, and the fingers of cold are corpse fingers. . . . But I want to go south again to Oaxaca, to the Zapotecas and the Maya.

So the ranch was boarded up for the winter, and the Lawrences and Brett headed for Oaxaca.

Moore 816   They found little to do in Mexico City ('this city no go'), but Lawrence dined with the PEN club, met Somerset Maugham ('a bit rancid'), and got to know the British Vice-Consul, whose brother, Padre Edward A. Rickards was a priest in the Cathedral Chapter in Oaxaca, and had a house to let there.

On 8 November the Lawrences left Mexico City for Oaxaca, pottering along on the narrow railway with twenty guards guarding forty passengers. First impressions were very favourable:

Moore 817   Oaxaca is a very quiet little town, with small but proud Indians – Zapotecas. The climate is perfect – cotton dresses, yet not too hot. It is very peaceful, and has a remote beauty of its own.

Moore 818 He felt that the 'soft warm air' at an altitude of 5,000 feet was good for his chest and

Mrs Conway, Lawrence, Eduardo Rendon and Frieda. Photo by G. R. G. Conway in the garden of his home in Mexico City.

throat. A major purpose in coming to Mexico was 'to get them sound this winter, and next year stay on much later at the ranch'.

After ten days the Lawrences moved into Padre Rickards' house, leaving Brett at the Hotel Francia. The floors were scrubbed, chairs painted white, mattresses and blinds sewn, charcoal fires lit. Furniture was borrowed from the American community; smaller items were bought in the market. A young mozo, Rosalino, came with the house. Lawrence, seeing the threadbare serape under which he slept, immediately took him off to the market to buy him a new one, of his own choice. Every morning Lawrence spent an hour helping him with his reading and writing, despite finding him a 'dumb-bell'. Rosalino, who had known much cruelty and little kindness, adored Lawrence.

PEN club dinner at the Oriental Cafe, Mexico City, 31 October 1924. Louis Quintanilla is on Lawrence's left. 'I said: here we are together, some of us English, some Mexicans and Americans, writers and painters and business men and so on, but before all and above all we are men together

tonight. That was about what I said. But a young Mexican jumped up: "It's all very well for an Englishman to say I am a man first and foremost, but a Mexican cannot say so, he must be a Mexican above everything." '

Oaxaca

'This is F. and me in the garden, with the Padre who owns the house, and the dog Corasmin and the parrots.'

'The boy in the picture is our mozo Rosalino – marketing with us.'

Lawrence and Frieda on the steps of the Church of Soledad, 18 December 1924. Photos by Brett

Immediately Lawrence got down to work. He reread the first draft of *Quetzalcoatl* and realized that he would have to rewrite it:

Brett 181   Chapala has not really the spirit of Mexico, it is too tamed, too touristy. This place is more untouched.

But despite its loveliness and the perfect climate, the quietness of Oaxaca came gradually to seem oppressive, like the quiet of a prison. It made Lawrence feel like buying huge revolvers and knives and killing somebody. Soon he was hankering for

Skinner 151   the Mediterranean or Western Australia and planning to sail away from this 'hard and jolting' continent if he found he could not work in Oaxaca. But the novel went well, and by the end of December he had written almost half of it, despite taking time off to write the four sketches of life in Oaxaca for *Mornings in Mexico* – those

'But the First Street of the Mines was just a track between the stiff living fence of organ cactus, with pointsettia trees holding up scarlet mops of flowers.' ('Walk to Huayapa')

delightful vignettes of the green parrots giving their mocking imitations of Rosalino, or of somebody calling Corasmin in Spanish, or of Corasmin himself barking, all perfect 'only a little more so'; of Lawrence's almost fruitless attempts to buy oranges in the orange-filled village of Huayapa; of the desperate nostalgia for his own village that the walk to Huayapa had aroused in Rosalino; of the peasants and Indians dashing into town for the market, with their piled donkeys and lumbering ox-carts, in clouds of dust; of Lawrence turning up his nose at the huaraches which had been tanned with human excrement, to the great amusement of the vendors.

Just before Christmas Lawrence and Brett had gone out on the road to Mitla on two consecutive days, Brett to paint, Lawrence to write his sketches, when he was not 'improving' Brett's paintings. Frieda was sullen when they returned. She was no longer so sure of Brett's harmlessness. According to Brett, Frieda told her that she resented the curate-and-spinster relationship of Lawrence and Brett, and would Brett 208 rather they made love, except that Lawrence could never love such an 'asparagus stick'. In the New Year friction built up to the point where Lawrence had to write to Brett:

Moore 836 You, Frieda and I don't make a happy combination now. The best is that we should prepare to separate: that you should go your own way.

Padre Rickards with Corasmin, Frieda, Lawrence and Maximiliano Salinas, walking to San Filipe del Agua. Photo by Brett.

'The picture is Mitla: top of my head. Miss Brett has taken to photography. The other man is José Garcia.' 'The carved courts of Mitla, with a hard, sharp-angled, intricate fascination of fear and repellance. Hard, four-square, sharp-edged, cutting, zig-zagging Mitla, like continual blows of a stone axe.' (The Plumed Serpent)

So Brett was packed off back to the ranch. A week later Lawrence wrote to her:

Moore 828–9   Friendship between a man and a woman, as a thing of first importance to either, is impossible: and I know it. We are creatures of two halves, spiritual and sensual – and each half is as important as the other. Any relation based on the one half – say the delicate spiritual half alone – *inevitably* brings revulsion and betrayal. Your friendship for Murry was spiritual – you dragged sex in and he hated you. He'd have hated you anyhow. The halfness of your friendship I also hate, and between you and me there is no sensual correspondence. . . . You're not superior to sex, and you never will be. Only too often you are inferior to it. You like the excitation of sex in the eye, sex in the head. It is an evil and destructive thing. . . . You make me ill, by dragging at one half at the expense of the other half. And I am so much better now you have gone. . . . So sit under your tree, or by your fire, and try, try, try to get a real kindliness and a wholeness. . . . Don't still go looking for men with strange eyes, who know life from A to Z. Maybe they do, missing out all the rest of the letters, like the meat from the empty eggshell. Look for a little flame of warm kindness. It's more than the Alpha and Omega.

By mid-January Lawrence could see his way to finishing *Quetzalcoatl* and was planning to sail to England in time for the spring. He felt a great longing for the English spring, which he had not seen for five years. And Frieda's mother was pleading for a visit. Lawrence vowed that he would avoid seeing anyone in England

Moore 830   except his agent and his sisters. Particularly he would avoid Murry – 'last time was once too many'. Lawrence finished *Quetzalcoatl* on 29 January. They were to leave for Mexico City the following week. But Lawrence, who had been suffering from influenza since Christmas, was struck down with malaria, which the soldiers had brought into the town. The local doctor prescribed quinine injections, then stayed away, being afraid of foreigners. Frieda put hot sandbags on Lawrence, which eased him. But he got rapidly worse and for several days was more dead than alive. He

Irvine 2, 44   looked 'like the shadow of a white rose-leaf', said Frieda. One night he said to her:

Frieda 165   But if I die, nothing has mattered but you, nothing at all.

Frieda herself became ill. An earthquake shook the house. It was decided to move Lawrence to the Hotel Francia. The American community, mine-owners and engineers mainly, rallied round spendidly. Slowly he pulled through, and on 24 February the Lawrences left Oaxaca for Mexico City. There Lawrence booked cabins to sail for England on 17 March, intending to recuperate on the Devonshire coast.

Nehls 2, 396   'Struggling through the days with some difficulty, feeling done in by this dirty sickness', Lawrence did not want to see anyone. But a friend from his earlier visits, Louis Quintanilla, Professor of English at the University of Mexico, poet and diplomat, hearing that Lawrence was at the Hotel Imperial, sent him a note and was invited to call with his brother. They were so appalled by his condition that they persuaded him to see a doctor of their acquaintance. After blood tests, Dr Uhlfelder told Frieda:

Frieda 167   Take him to the ranch; it's his only chance. He has T.B. in the third degree. A year or two at the most.

Lawrence was told that he had tuberculosis, but not how badly, and that the voyage to England would be bad for him.

The berths were cancelled, and on 25 March the Lawrences left Mexico City for the ranch. But Lawrence looked so ill that the immigration officers at El Paso would not let him enter the U.S.A. He was detained there for two days. It was only with the help of the American Embassy in Mexico City, and by putting rouge on his cheeks, that Lawrence was able at last to get through. It was during this journey that he began his beautiful story 'The Flying Fish', dictating the first pages to Frieda. He never finished it:

Brewster 288   It was written so near the borderline of death, that I never have been able to carry it through; in the cold light of day.

After a few days with the Hawks at Del Monte, the Lawrences moved up to their own ranch, which Lawrence had now decided to call Kiowa after the local Indians. Brett was to remain at Del Monte. Trinidad and his wife Ruffina helped Frieda with the work while Lawrence rested, read *Arabia Deserta*, and played with the cat, Timsy Wemyss. He even allowed Frieda to do the cooking.

Lawrence and Timsy. Photo by Brett.

The high clear air, sunbaths, and the spring, gradually brought Lawrence back to life. It was a real resurrection, as Frieda saw:

Frieda 168   How thrilling it was to feel the inrush of new vitality in him; it was like a living miracle. A wonder before one's eyes. How grateful he was inside him! 'I can do things again. I can live and do as I like, no longer held down by the devouring illness.' How he loved every minute of life at the ranch. The morning, the squirrels, every flower that came in its turn, the big trees, chopping the wood, the chickens, making bread, all our hard work and the people and all assumed the radiance of new life.

Soon he was able to start 'ranching' again. In a letter of 30 May he gave his sister Emily a picture of life on the ranch:

Moore 842   It is a terribly dry spring – everything burnt up. I go out every morning to the field, to turn the water over a new patch. So the long 15-acre field is very green, but the ranges are dry as dry sand, and nothing hardly grows. Only the wild strawberries are flowering full, and the wild gooseberries were thick with blossoms, and little flocks of humming birds came for them. – We are now building a new corral for the four horses – and we are having a black cow on Monday – and we've got white hens and brown ones, and a white cock – and Trinidad caught a little wild rabbit which is alive and very cheerful.

That cow, Susan, proved to be a handful, and there were other problems:

Secker 63   I milk the cow – black-eyed-Susan – and F. collects the eggs. Sounds idyllic, but the cow escapes into the mountains, we hunt her on horseback, and curse her blacker than she is, an eagle strikes one of the hens, a skunk fetches the eggs, the half wild cows break in the pasture, that is drying up as dry as pepper – no rain, no rain, no rain. It's tough country.

Lightning struck and split the pine tree just outside the cabin. The porcupines were gnawing the pine trees again. One night Frieda rushed in thinking she had seen a bear. Lawrence went out with the .22 with which he had been practising against the

Lawrence with Prince, building a shed for Susan. July 1925. Photo by Brett.

'And when she is safely in her milking place, still she watches with her great black eyes as I dismount. And she has to smell my hand before the cowy peace of being milked enters her blood. Till then, there is something roaring in the chaos of her universe. When her cowy peace comes, then her universe is silent, and like the sea with an even tide, without sail or smoke: nothing. That is Susan, my black cow.' ('. . . Love Was Once a Little Boy') Photo by Brett.

'You let the fire die down and rake out the hot ashes. In goes one of our precious chickens and the bread. The board that serves as a door is quickly closed, and the large stone put against it. Then you sit down and wait. While waiting, you tell me how when quite tiny, only just able to see over the edge of the table, you would watch your mother making the bread. I run for my Kodak and take a photo of you sitting on the shed step, near the oven.' (Brett)

toilet door, and shot it, to his mingled pride and regret. But he would not let Trinidad shoot the deer which were glimpsed occasionally above the cabin.

Though Brett was now banished to Del Monte, she defeated the purpose of that by going up to Kiowa every day. Frieda's hints went unheeded. At last Frieda wrote to her asking her to 'go away quietly and with dignity. . . . You are just a beastly nuisance'. Lawrence himself called her 'a born separator'. Brett decided this time to fight back, telling Lawrence, 'If Frieda starts her spinster and curate and asparagus nonsense again, I will rope her to a tree and hit her on the nose until she has really got something to yell about'. Brett now regarded this as her home, but to Frieda she was just a guest overstaying her welcome. Frieda's irritability was partly caused by her arguments with Lawrence over her wish to invite her daughters to the ranch. Brett had no desire to return to the old life, from which Lawrence had lifted her. Her deafness made travel difficult. Where was she to go? In any case, the Lawrences themselves were planning to return to Europe in September, perhaps for a whole year. But Lawrence did not like the idea of leaving Brett alone on the ranch all winter, and persuaded her to have a look at Italy, promising her a letter of introduction to the Brewsters in Capri.

So the ranch was shuttered up again. After tearful farewells, Bill Hawk drove the Lawrences down the familiar dusty trail for the last time. It was Lawrence's fortieth birthday. From New York Lawrence wrote to Brett:

Of course one is a fool to leave the ranch, but perhaps Europe will be good for us, for the winter. . . . I just refrain from thinking about the Azul and Timsy and Moses and all of them – à la guerre comme à la guerre.

The following day Frieda wrote:

Lawr already doesn't look so well!

On 22 September they embarked on the S.S. *Resolute* for Southampton.

Two months later, in Italy, Lawrence was to write in an article, 'A Little Moonshine with Lemon' for the *Laughing Horse*:

I wonder if I am here, or if I am just going to bed at the ranch. Perhaps looking in Montgomery Ward's catalogue for something for Christmas, and drinking moonshine and hot water, since it is cold. Go out and look if the chickens are shut up warm: if the horses are in sight: if Susan, the black cow, has gone to her nest among the trees, for the night. . . . In a cold like this, the stars snap like distant coyotes, beyond the moon. And you'll see the shadow of actual coyotes, going across the alfalfa field. And the pine trees make little noises, sudden and stealthy, as if they were walking about. And the place heaves with ghosts. That place, the ranch, heaves with ghosts. But when one has got used to one's own home ghosts, be they never so many, and so potent, they are like one's own family, but nearer than the blood. It is the ghosts one misses most, the ghosts there, of the Rocky Mountains, that never go beyond the timber and that linger, like the animals, round the water-spring. I know them, they know me: we go well together. But they reproach me for going away. They are resentful too.

Irvine 2, 50

Brett 228

Moore 837

Moore 853

Lawrence and Frieda embark on the S.S. Resolute, *leaving America for the last time.*

16 Insouciance

The Lawrences stayed a week in London. Despite all his protestations, the first letter Lawrence wrote from Garland's Hotel was to Murry, asking if he would be in town. Murry replied offering the Lawrences an adjacent cottage at Abbotsbury in Dorset:

Moore 858
> But . . . he's got Jesus, badly and nastily. The *Nation* compares Murry, in detail, to Mr Pecksniff. Anyhow it all sounds sloppy and nasty. I shan't go down.

Moore 858
He preferred to spend a weekend with the Carswells, who were 'buried alive in a horrid little cottage in damp and dismal Bucks'.

Barby brought her fiancé to dinner at Garland's, and afterwards they all went to
Moore 863
see *The Gold Rush*. Lawrence did not approve of the fiancé, 'an absolute nothingness of a fellow, 35, would-be artist, born failure, sponger on a woman's emotions', and decided that he and Frieda would have to laugh her out of it, which they did. But Lawrence was far from reconciled to Frieda's children:

Moore 863
> Privately, I can't stand Frieda's children. They have a sort of suburban bounce and suffisance which puts me off. When they appear, I shall disappear. The boy kept his loftiness to the Vic. and Albert Museum, and soon, very probably, will sit in one of the glass cases, as a specimen of the perfect young Englishman.

Moore 857
Lawrence also visited the Seckers at Bridgefoot, and saw the Eders, but 'no more of the old crowd – not Kot', before going north to visit his sisters. Immediately Lawrence went down with a cold. After a few days, Ada and Eddie took him
Moore 859
motoring all over Derbyshire – 'one of the most interesting counties in England. But I can't look at the body of my past, the spirit seems to have flown'. He felt smothered
Carswell 229
by childhood memories, and would have been glad if the place 'were puffed off the face of the earth'.

The last night before he left London for Baden-Baden Lawrence invited Murry to stay the night. They talked about Jesus and Judas. Lawrence invited the Murrys to join him in Ragusa, or somewhere in Italy. Murry accepted, perhaps intending to go for a short holiday merely, but in the event the doctor forbade his wife, who was expecting their second child, to go. Next morning, as Murry was waiting for his taxi, Lawrence rushed out to buy him a bag of fruit, telling Murry to direct the taxi to the fruit shop if it came before he got back. The taxi went the wrong way. It was too late to turn back; Murry had a train to catch. He never saw Lawrence again. Three years later Lawrence wrote:

Poems 603

> A man wrote to me: We missed it, you and I.
> We were meant to mean a great deal to one another;
> but we missed it.
> And I could only reply:
> A miss is as good as a mile
> mister!

In Baden-Baden Lawrence found his mother-in-law noticeably older, though still very lively, amid the 'departed grandeur' of the Ludwig Wilhelmstift. He would run *Centaur 24* away into the Black Forest to escape yet another round of whist 'with ancient Barons, *Carswell 231* Baronesses, Counts and Excellencies' – 'ghosts from the Turgenev period'.

Martin Secker's wife Rina came from Spotorno, and the Seckers recommended it to the Lawrences. They arrived there on 15 November, and a week later moved into the Villa Bernarda.

'It's a nice old house sticking up from the little hill, under the castle, just above the village and the sea. The sun shines, the eternal Mediterranean is blue and young, the last leaves are falling from the vines in the garden. The peasant people are nice. I've got my little stock of red and white wine – from the garden of this house – we eat fried chicken and pasta and smell rosemary and basilica in the cooking once more – and somebody's always roasting coffee – and the oranges are already yellow on the orange trees. It's Italy, the same forever.'

The Villa Bernarda belonged to the wife of a smart lieutenant in the Bersaglieri, Angelo Ravagli, destined to become Frieda's third husband.

Lawrence did not intend to stay long in Spotorno, but was vague about his plans. He wrote to Brett, now in Capri:

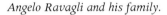

We might all make some sort of excursion, with light luggage: perhaps to Amalfi and Paestum (where I've never stopped) and Sicily. I wish we weren't always poor. I wanted to go to Dalmatia and the Isles of Greece. Why doesn't anybody ever have a yacht and sail the coasts of the Mediterranean – Greece and Constantinople and Damascus and Jaffa and Egypt and Tunis and Morocco – or at least Algiers. How nice it would be! . . . But even if all of us, and Earl and Achsah, put our money together, we'd never afford a little ship.

In Capri, the following March, Lawrence commissioned a nautical friend to find him a cheap lugger, but nothing turned up.

Angelo Ravagli and his family.

Meanwhile, Lawrence found in Italy, after the tenseness of America, a refreshing insouciance:

Phoenix 118   I've been a fool myself, saying: Europe is finished for me. It wasn't Europe at all, it was myself, keeping a strangle-hold on myself. . . . No. it's a relief to be by the Mediterranean, and gradually let the tight coils inside oneself come slack. There is much more life in a deep insouciance, which really is the clue to faith, than in this frenzied, keyed-up care, which is characteristic of our civilization, but which is at its worst, or at least its intensest, in America.

Moore 876   That nearness to death a year ago had had a permanent effect on Lawrence. All he wanted now was to be well and easy. He refused to take himself so seriously 'except between 8.0 and 10.0 a.m., and at the stroke of midnight'. Enemies were not to be hated but forgotten. There were many blessings to be counted, not least the sun and the sea:

Moore 878   The sun means a *lot*. It's almost the grace of God in itself. May a mackerel swallow the larvae of all Words!

Moore 881   The sea goes in and out its bays, and glitters very bright. There is something forever cheerful and happy about the Mediterranean: I feel at home beside it.

In December Lawrence produced three stories, 'Smile', 'Sun' and 'Glad Ghosts'. 'Sun' was clearly suggested to Lawrence by the situation of the Seckers: Rina and her little boy of twenty months, Adrian, sunbathing in the lemon groves at Spotorno, and Martin coming to visit them when he could. On 30 November Lawrence had written to Secker:

Secker 68   Today is superbly sunny and warm – so was yesterday. Rina usually comes with Adrian in the afternoon. She is much better now, was very nervosa at first, and a bit trying, no doubt, to her parents. But she gets better now every day. Adrian is not 'in the pink' but the scarlet. He is very bonny, and growing fast, and perfectly happy and chirpy here.

But whereas, in the story, Lawrence mocks the husband, in real life his sympathy was for Secker:

Moore 873   He's a nice gentle soul, without a thrill: his wife a living block of discontent – why, I don't know, for she's not so perfect.

'Glad Ghosts' was written for Lady Cynthia Asquith's *Ghost Book*. But Lawrence's combination of sex and the supernatural (not to mention the thinly disguised pairing of himself and Lady Cynthia) was not to her taste, and he patiently wrote 'The Rocking Horse Winner' for her instead.

When the winter set in, Lawrence would have preferred to move south to Capri or Sicily, but Frieda had invited her daughters, and Lawrence, to balance them, his sister Ada and a friend; and he was still expecting the Murrys in January. Barby was

Lawrence and Rina Secker at the Villa Bernarda.

living at Alassio, only twenty-five miles away, and so was able to make several visits. She had quite fallen for Lawrence, but he still resented her as part of Frieda's life in which he had no share. Once he flung wine in Frieda's face in front of Barby, who sprang to her mother's defence. But soon Lawrence could no longer overcome his liking for Barby. He encouraged her with her paintings, adding figures to some of them. He felt the Slade, 'a criminal institution', had taken all the life out of her work. Barby told him what it had been like growing up in a house where her mother's name could not be mentioned, a household dominated by her aunt and grandmother. Lawrence recreated that household in his next story 'The Virgin and the Gipsy'.

Moore 873

But if Lawrence was stuck in Spotorno for the winter, at least he could begin to make plans for the spring. On 9 January he wrote to the Brewsters:

Barbara Weekley.

Moore 879 Now then, let's do something. The ship for preference. Or Spain in March –
Balearic Isles, Majorca and Minorca – or central Sicily, that place, is it
Castelvetrano, in the centre, where the flowers are really, really a wonder, in
March. It's where Persephone rose from hell, each spring. Or Calabria – though
most people get typhoid there, with the filthy water. Or Tunis, and to Kairowan, to
the edge of the desert. Or across Italy to Dalmatia. Spoleto and Ragusa, very lovely;
and Montenegro. But with a ship we could do all that to a marvel. I could put £100
sterling to the ship.

Moore 884 But Earl Brewster's reply, which Lawrence found 'very old-maidish and mimping-
pimping', announced that they were preparing for a second journey to India in the
spring.

Lawrence's next plan was to go to Russia with Kot, who was back in favour now
that Murry had cried off. He began at once to learn his Russian ABC, and to reread

Kot 278 *The Brothers Karamazov*, 'not as fiction, but as life'. He invited Witter Bynner to Russia also. But Russian grammar he soon abandoned in despair.

Ada and her friend Mrs Booth arrived on 10 February to find Lawrence in bed with flu, which had given him a haemorrhage. It was pouring with rain, very cold, and there were no fires in the Villa Bernarda. Ada and Frieda quarrelled about who should nurse Lawrence. Ada adored Lawrence and felt that she had rights to him which overruled those of any mere wife. Ada told Frieda that she hated her from the bottom of her heart. One night, when Frieda went to Lawrence's room, she found it locked: Ada had the key. Frieda had never been so deeply hurt. She and her daughters moved out to the hotel. Lawrence's idea of balancing his own past against Frieda's had been disastrous. A few days later he took Ada to Monte Carlo, and then saw her off to England from Nice. Then, unable to face Frieda and her daughters, he fled to Capri.

It was to be six weeks before he returned home. The first two were spent on Capri with Brett and the Brewsters, meeting such old friends as the Brett Youngs, Mary Cannan (grown intolerably garrulous) and Faith Mackenzie, whose husband was on one of his islands. One evening, after much wine, she confided in Lawrence, and he used much of what she told him in 'The Man Who Loved Islands' a few months later.

Brett found Lawrence weary, hurt and hopeless:

Brett 271   My life is unbearable. I feel I cannot stand it any longer. Chopping and changing is not my way, as you know; but I get so tired of it all. It makes me ill, too. I don't know what to do. I just don't know what will happen.

Brett encouraged Lawrence to break permanently with Frieda, or, if he could not bring himself to do that, at least to 'make hay while the sun shines'. When the Brewsters left for India, Lawrence took Brett to Ravello, ostensibly to visit Millicent Beveridge and Mabel Harrison, who lived there. They had adjacent rooms in the Hotel Palumbo. Brett has recorded what happened:

Brett III   Lawrence suddenly walked into my room in his dressing gown. 'I do not believe in a relationship unless there is a physical relationship as well,' he said. I was frightened as well as excited. He got into my bed, turned, and kissed me. I can still feel the softness of his beard, still feel the tension, still feel the overwhelming desire to be adequate. I was passionately eager to be successful, but I had no idea what to do. Nothing happened. Suddenly Lawrence got up. 'It's no good,' he said, and stalked out of the room. I was devastated, helpless, bewildered.

All the next day Lawrence was a bit glum. Nothing was said. And I was too tense and nervous to say anything, even if I had known what to say. That night, he walked into my room and said, 'Let's try it again.' So again he got into my bed, and there we lay. I felt desperate. All the love I had for him, all the closeness to him spiritually, the passionate desire to give what I felt I should be giving, was frustrated by fear and not knowing what to do. I tried to be loving and warm and female. He was, I think, struggling to be successfully male. It was hopeless, a hopeless horrible failure.

They decided that it would be best to part for the time being. Brett would return to Capri. Lawrence took her to the boat. He was, she said, 'kind, worried, and upset'. Lawrence in his carriage driving up the hill, Brett standing on the deck, waved to each other for a long time. They never saw each other again. A few days later Lawrence wrote to Brett:

Moore 893

One has just to forget, and to accept what is good. We can't help being more or less damaged. What we have to do is to stick to the good part of ourselves, and of each other, and continue an understanding on that. I don't see why we shouldn't be *better* friends, instead of worse. But one must not try to force anything.

In May Brett returned to Kiowa ranch.

Shortly after Brett's departure there came a much milder letter from Frieda. Lawrence made his way slowly north in the company of Millie Beveridge and Mabel Harrison, spending a few days in Rome, Perugia, Assisi, Florence and Ravenna. He arrived back in Spotorno at the beginning of April to find three women waiting at the station resplendent in their Easter bonnets:

Irvine 2, 63

All very quiet and welcoming here – quite a change.

He now found that Barby and Elsa could even be enlisted on his side:

Moore 898

I find Frieda very much softened. Her daughters are very fierce with her. They simply will not stand her overbearing, and fly at her very much in her own way, which abashes and nonplusses her considerably. I am rather amused. Finding her own daughters so very much more brutal and uncompromising with her than I am, she seems to change her mind about a good many matters.

The change was not all on Frieda's side. Lawrence himself was somewhat chastened:

Moore 894
896

For the moment I am the Easter-lamb. When I went away, I was very cross, but one must be able to forget a lot and go on. . . . I shall be glad when this stupid and muddled winter is at last over.

Lawrence had no sympathy with rising Italian Fascism. On 7 April the Hon. Violet Gibson shot at Mussolini. The bullet passed through his nose. 'Put a ring through it,' Lawrence advised Ravagli next day. In Florence he had heard dreary tales about Russia, and his enthusiasm for that had evaporated. But the University Museum in Perugia had fired him to want to write about the Etruscans:

Secker 72

We might go to Perugia, and I might do a book on Umbria and the Etruscan remains. It would be half a travel book . . . and half a book about the Etruscan things, which interest me very much.

On 20 April the Lawrences, still with Barby and Elsa, left Spotorno for Florence.

Moore 904

Frieda enjoyed herself with her 'long-legged daughters'. She wanted to settle for a while in a villa somewhere near Florence. Lawrence didn't know what he wanted, beyond a bho tree somewhere to sit under. On the day the girls left, 28 April, the Lawrences went out to look at a vacant apartment in the Villa Mirenda, San Paolo Mosciano, Vingone, about seven miles from Florence in the Tuscan Hills. They rented the upper floor for a year:

Frieda 203–4   We painted the shutters of the Mirenda, and the chairs, green; we put 'stuoie', thick pale grass matting, on the red-tiled floor in the big sitting-room. We had a few Vallombrosa chairs, a round table, a piano, hired, a couch and an old seat. The walls were syringed white . . . That was done fast, and the sun poured into the big room so still and hot. The only noises came from the peasants, calling or singing at their work, or the water being drawn at the well. Or best, and almost too fierce, were the nightingales singing away from early dawn, almost the clock round . . . The spring that first year was a revelation of flowers, from the first violets in the woods . . . We took joyful possession of the unspoiled, almost medieval, country around us.

Moore 908   Lawrence immediately settled down to work, writing 'Two Blue Birds' and 'reading up about my precious Etruschi':

Frieda 223   The bronzes and terracottas are fascinating, so alive with physical life, with a powerful physicality which surely is as great, or sacred, ultimately, as the *ideal* of the Greeks and Germans.

Next door, at the Villa Poggi, were the Wilkinsons:

Moore 909   We have one family of English neighbours, who would send you into fits if you saw them: he's got the wildest red beard, sticking out all round – and wife and daughter and son, all with sandals and knapsacks. But they're jolly and very clever: paint, and play guitar and things. They used to have a very fine puppet show, puppets they made themselves, going with a caravan and giving shows in all the villages in England. Rather fun!

The Wilkinsons were great walkers and nature-lovers, concert and theatre-goers, strenuously pursuing health and culture simultaneously, trying to make each day a work of art unsullied by care, by the 'unpleasant' doings of other people in the world beyond the Tuscan Hills. They rather patronized Lawrence for his commitment to that world and exasperation with it:

Wilkinsons 63   Poor chap – what a nightmare he does suffer.

'Village-arty people', Lawrence called them. Nevertheless, the Lawrences and the Wilkinsons formed a warm and lasting friendship. Lawrence soon learned not to ride his hobby-horses too much in their company, and his lack of sympathy for their way of life found expression only in the lightest and most genial banter. Almost every day some time would be spent with the 'Wilkses' – tea or supper parties, sing-songs, walks, picnics . . .

San Paolo Mosciano with Florence beyond. The largest building is the Villa Mirenda. 'On the top of one of those Tuscan little hills stood a villa. My heart went out to it. I wanted that villa. It was rather large, but so perfectly placed, with a panorama of the Valdarno in front, Florence on the left, and the umbrella-pine woods behind.' (Frieda Lawrence) From a painting by Arthur Wilkinson.

On a typical June day Lawrence would get up about six and walk to Vingone with a basket for the day's provisions. Then he would spend the rest of the morning sitting among the olive trees near the Mirenda writing his latest story 'The Man Who Loved Islands'. After lunch and a siesta, he would sit on the verandah typing out Frieda's translation of *David* into German. After supper the Wilkses might come round 'as there is a cake and the promised Kummel, and, let us hope, a tune or two going.'

On 12 July the Lawrences left the Mirenda for Baden (for the Baroness's seventy-fifth birthday) and England. Lawrence found Germany soothing; he drank the hot waters for his 'miserable bronchi' and walked in the intensely green forests. By the end of the month the Lawrences were in Chelsea. There Lawrence met Montagu Weekley for the first time since the elopement, and made an immediate impact on him. Frieda was surprised and delighted by their 'loving kindness' for each other 'all of a heap!'

Another young man who came to visit Lawrence at Rossetti Gardens was Rolf Gardiner. Gardiner had found Cambridge uncongenial, and had chosen Lawrence as his alternative beacon, his hero-poet. Gardiner had been involved with John Hargrave's Kibbo Kift movement, but, sensing the drift of that movement towards Fascism, had recently broken away, and was trying to start his own international youth movement on more Lawrentian lines – dedicated to the destruction of industrialism, rational humanism and democracy in favour of individualism and

Wilkinsons 64

Luhan 307

Rolf Gardiner, May 1928. From a painting by Maxwell Armfield.

natural aristocracy. Gardiner wanted Lawrence to come in with him. Lawrence was attracted but wary:

Moore 928   But I should like to come to Yorkshire. I should like even to try to dance a sword-dance with iron-stone miners above Whitby. I should love to be connected with something, with some few people, in something. As far as anything *matters*, I have always been very much alone, and regretted it. But I can't belong to clubs, or societies, or Freemasons, or any other damn thing. So if there is, with you, an activity I *can* belong to, I shall thank my stars. But, of course, I shall be wary beyond words of committing myself.

At their meeting Lawrence questioned Gardiner closely. Gardiner was the only man Lawrence ever met who responded fully to his challenge, who came more than halfway to meet him, who was prepared to devote his whole life to the great cause. His very intensity probably scared Lawrence, and his insistence on camping, walking, dancing and other strenuous activities was not quite Lawrence's style. Lawrence advised him to drop all that and to try to found 'flexible monasteries ' – Rananim by proxy. On his return to Italy he wrote to Gardiner:

Moore 951   We'll have to establish some spot on earth, that will be the fissure into the underworld, like the oracle at Delphos, where one can always come to. I will try to do it myself. I will try to come to England and make a place – some quiet house in the country – where one can begin – and from which the hiker, maybe, can branch out. Some place with a big barn and a bit of land – if one has enough money.

Gardiner replied:

Nehls 3, 122   Your idea of a *centre* has been in my mind for a long while. We must have dominion with the earth again and woo it truly and masterly. We must get back the real power again; without it all else is futile. . . . We want farmsteads, and castles, and monasteries again, as the Church and the Chivalry had them in the Dark Ages. Many such nuclei, and perhaps a State within the State, growing up like the new burgeon under the rotting fruit. . . . A State within a State from the Adriatic to the Arctic, from the Weichsel to Atlantis. I believe it is possible. That's why I think one must first stir up the people in disciplined activity, getting groups going in every corner of northern Europe. But no hard and fast organization yet. Only the methods and perhaps the symbol: Yggdrasil.

Lawrence did not answer this letter for several months. The answer, when it came, was revealing:

Huxley 684   But don't forget you yourself want to be too suddenly and completely a leader – spring ready-armed from the head of Jove. The English will never follow – not even a handful – you see if they do. . . . But go ahead – there's nothing without trying. . . . I shall be interested to know what you make of your 'centre' when you've got it. It seems to me the most important – the world sails on towards a debacle – camps and wanderings won't help that – but a little ark somewhere in a quiet place will be valuable. So make it if you can.

But there is no more talk of Lawrence joining the venture.

Gardiner acquired Gore Farm in Dorset from his uncle, built a large barn there, and started Springhead, his centre for rural reconstruction. But he had called Lawrence's bluff. Or rather, he was a year too late. Lawrence was being subtly modified by Europe. In America 'something in the soul perished: the softness, the floweriness, the natural tenderness'. Europe revived these qualities in him. In his Christmas 1926 letter Gardiner had written:

Phoenix 267

Nehls 3, 122

> I take it you meant *The Plumed Serpent* absolutely seriously. For me, it was a most wonderfully courageous essay to think out the course of action that must be taken somewhere.

In 1925 Lawrence would have answered, as he wrote to Secker:

Moore 859

> I *do* mean what Ramon means – for all of us.

But by the end of 1926 Lawrence was well on the way towards his repudiation of Don Ramon:

Moore 1045

> The hero is obsolete, and the leader of men is a back number. After all, at the back of the hero is the militant ideal: and the militant ideal, or the ideal militant, seems to me also a cold egg. We're sort of sick of all forms of militarism and militantism, and Miles is a name no more, for a man. . . . The leader-cum-follower relationship is a bore. And the new relationship will be some sort of tenderness, sensitive, between men and men and men and women, and not the one up one down, lead on I follow, ich dien sort of business.

Huxley 705

Lawrence continued to advise Gardiner, but insisted that leadership must be based not on power but on a 'reciprocity of tenderness'. Gardiner became a pioneer of ecology and conservation, a field in which he believed Lawrence would have been very active had he survived into the second half of the century. Gardiner had some lasting influence on Lawrence, who was to put into *Lady Chatterley's Lover* and 'A Dream of Life' and 'Nottingham and the Mining Countryside' something of Gardiner's utopianism and enthusiasm for communal singing and dancing.

Two friends had invited Lawrence to Scotland, Compton Mackenzie, to an island off Lewis in the outer Hebrides, and Millicent Beveridge, to her home at Newtonmore, Inverness. Lawrence accepted the latter, and, leaving Frieda in London, arrived at Newtonmore on 11 August. From there he made an excursion to Skye, which, he felt, restored the Old Adam in him:

Moore 931

> There is still something of an Odyssey up there, in among the islands and the silent lochs: like the twilight morning of the world, the herons fishing undisturbed by the water, and the sea running far in, for miles, between the wet, trickling hills, where the cottages are low and almost invisible, built into the earth.

The man who loved islands was not only Compton Mackenzie, but Lawrence himself. From Scotland Lawrence went straight to Mablethorpe on the Lincolnshire coast, where his sisters had taken a bungalow for a month. Frieda joined him a few days later, and they took a bungalow for a fortnight at Sutton-on-Sea, two miles away.

Lawrence was much less bitter about England and his home district on this trip:

Moore 933   Curiously, I like England again, now I am up in my own regions. It braces me up: and there seems a queer, odd sort of potentiality in the people, especially the common people. One feels in them some odd, unaccustomed sort of plasm twinkling and nascent. They are not finished. And they have a funny sort of purity and gentleness, and at the same time, unbreakableness, that attracts one.

But the effects of the coal strike upset him:

Moore 937   This strike has done a lot of damage – and there is a lot of misery – families living on bread and margerine and potatoes – nothing more.

What was keeping Lawrence in England was his desire to attend the first rehearsals of his play *David*, which was due to be given two performances by the Stage Society at the end of October. But when Lawrence returned to London on 16 September, he found that they had postponed the production until December, and felt that he could hang about no longer. He had promised to return to Baden for an inhalation cure, but decided he had had enough travelling, and would get back to the Mirenda in time for the grape harvest. The Lawrences left England on 28 September. Lawrence had seen the last of his native land.

Lawrence and his sister Ada at Mablethorpe. 'I like this flat coast, it's where I first knew the sea.'

17 Tenderness

What Lawrence had seen in England had convinced him that the country was on the brink of a class war. In mid-October he began a story about how two people through their sensitivity and awareness and respect for life above all else might bridge that fatal class-chasm, and build their own little ark against the coming flood; a story to be called *Lady Chatterley's Lover*.

Lawrence and Frieda with Millicent Beveridge at her Villa near Florence.

Lawrence photographed by Millicent Beveridge.

The previous June the Lawrences had visited Sir George and Lady Ida Sitwell at their medieval castle at Montegufoni, near Florence. When Sir George showed Frieda his vast collection of seventeenth-century beds, she amazed him by trying them all. Sir George and Lawrence had in common a thorough knowledge of Derbyshire. Probably Sir George told Lawrence about the trouble his son Osbert was having to save Sutton Scarsdale, an eighteenth-century hall very near his own Renishaw. The Arkwright family, so prominent in the industrial revolution, had occupied Sutton Scarsdale for over a hundred years, but had sold it in 1920. The last of the Arkwright occupants, William Arkwright, had died in 1925. Sir George must have told Lawrence his strange story. Born in 1857, educated at Eton and Christchurch, William Arkwright had suffered terrible injuries when thrown from his horse at the age of twenty. He lay unconscious for six weeks, and had a silver plate inserted in his head. He recovered sufficiently to write three books and become an expert linguist, but the accident had left him impotent. Seven years later, against the advice of his family, he married a beautiful young woman from an aristocratic family, Agnes Mary Summers-Cox. The marriage was unhappy, and they lived apart for most of their lives.

It was suggested that Lawrence, during his visit to England, should call on Osbert and Edith at Renishaw. He did call there during a tour of Derbyshire in his sister's car, but the Sitwells had left for Italy. Nevertheless, he saw enough of the hall and its surroundings to use it as the model for Wragby in *Lady C*. Lawrence met Osbert Sitwell for the first time the following May, by which time the first two versions of *Lady Chatterley's Lover* had been written. Though he did incorporate some features of Osbert into Sir Clifford Chatterley in the third version, Sir Clifford was in no sense, as Edith Sitwell later claimed, a 'portrait' of Osbert; and the Arkwrights, not the Sitwells, had probably inspired the story.

In London the Lawrences had renewed their friendship with the Aldingtons, Richard and Arabella, and invited them to the Mirenda for the grape harvest. They found the house festooned with bunches of small sweet grapes, with great vats of them on the lower floor waiting to be trodden. They found the Lawrences equally mellow. It was the beginning of a golden interlude in Lawrence's life, the next nine months at the Mirenda.

The next visitors were Aldous and Maria Huxley, whom the Lawrences had also seen in London. Huxley had a similar background to Murry, similar wishy-washy opinions, and had been pithed by Bloomsbury; but he was altogether more intelligent, open-minded, affectionate and trustworthy than Murry, and, since Lawrence had now learned to demand rather less of his friends, the friendship blossomed.

The Huxleys had just bought a big new Italian car, and tried to persuade Lawrence to buy their old one – ideal for his Etruscan tour:

Moore 944   But I won't bother myself learning to drive, and struggling with a machine. I've no desire to scud about the face of the country myself. It is much pleasanter to go

Lawrence and Aldous Huxley at the Villa Mirenda, 28 October 1926. Photo by Maria Huxley.

quietly into the pinewoods and sit and do there what bit of work I do. Why rush from place to place?

The Huxleys did manage to unload on to Lawrence four unwanted canvasses which had been abandoned in their house. Lawrence, fed up with painting doors, windows and drawers, could not resist them:

Phoenix 2 603   I sat on the floor with the canvas propped against a chair – and with my house-paint brushes and colours in little casseroles, I disappeared into that canvas.

The first picture which came he called his *Unholy Family*

Moore 945   because the bambino – with a nimbus – is just watching anxiously to see the young man give the semi-nude young woman un gros baiser. Molto moderno!

For his third picture, a fortnight later, Lawrence borrowed an easel from the Wilkinsons, for he was now taking his painting very seriously:

Unpub.   I pretend to write a novel – scene in England – but am much more of a *Maestro* painting a picture of Boccaccio's story of the nuns who find their gardener asleep in the garden on a hot afternoon, with his shirt blown back from what other people are pleased to call his *pudenda* and which the nuns named his *glorietta*. Very nice picture!

Lawrence and Frieda at the Mirenda. Photo by Arthur Wilkinson.

Irvine 2, 72   It is indeed a beautiful painting. The nuns 'in frocks like lavender crocuses' and bobbing honey-coloured bonnets tiptoe across a ploughed field bordered by spurting silvery olives towards the sprawling gardener with glowing limbs who is only pretending to be asleep.

        Painting became a real passion for Lawrence:

Kot 304   Think I'll turn into a painter, it costs one less, and probably would pay better than writing.

His method, lacking any technique to fall back on, was hit-or-miss. But there are many successes – the stately biblicals, *Resurrection* and *The Finding of Moses*, the amusing mock-biblical *Throwing Back the Apple*, the radiant *Summer Dawn*, the finely modelled *Contadini*, the sensuous *Leda*; *Red Willow Trees* in which Lawrence merges his naked men into a landscape reminiscent of Fra Angelico; *Dance Sketch* in which man, woman, goat and grove seem caught up in the same rhythm; and *Renascence of Men* where the two naked men glow as if indeed new-born, with flesh like mother-of-pearl. Lawrence put life into his paintings as he did into everything he touched:

Moore 1037   Some people very shocked – worse than my writing. But *I* think they're rather lovely and almost holy.

Lawrence had intended to return to England in December to help with the production of *David*, but that was now postponed until March. *The Widowing of Mrs Holroyd* was to be performed instead in December, and Lawrence did not feel so strongly that his presence would be needed for that. Nevertheless, he anxiously begged his friends to send him reports of the production. On 13 December Rolf Gardiner wrote to him:

Nehls 3, 121   I have just come back from seeing *Mrs Holroyd*. It was a very good performance and Esme Percy had produced it in the right way. Mrs Holroyd [Marda Vanne] herself was perfect, and Blackmore [Colin Keith-Johnston] and the children and all the subsidiary characters, quite splendid. But the man who played Holroyd wasn't fine or big enough, I thought; not that touch of fire and physical splendour that I feel was the hidden ore in the body of him as you meant him perhaps. The atmosphere was right and you were in the play right through; only of course they couldn't talk the Derby vernacular. Bernard Shaw, who was there, said the dialogue was the most magnificent he had ever heard, and his own stuff was *The Barber of Fleet Street* in comparison! The actors loved the play; one felt that. The bulk of the audience? I can't tell. But anyway the audiences at these shows are mostly bloody.

After Lawrence's death Shaw himself wrote:

Time and Tide   In my ignorance, I attached no importance to Lawrence until one afternoon at the
6.8.32   Stage Society, when I saw a play by him which rushed through in such a torrent of profuse yet vividly effective dialogue, making my own seem archaic in comparison, that I was strongly interested technically.

Shaw was never lavish in his praise of other dramatists. However, the production attracted on the whole little attention.

There were three families of peasants on the Mirenda estate, the Orsinis, the Bandellis and the Pinis, twenty-seven in all. Lawrence had an excellent relationship with them, especially the children:

Ada 145–6   We are busy getting ready a Christmas tree for our peasants. There will be about twelve children, and I expect their parents will have to come to look. So many people work on this little estate. And the children are wild little things. They've never seen a Christmas tree, but they heard of some other English people who made one for the peasants, so they all had fits hoping we'd do one. We've got all kinds of little wooden toys from Florence, and with a few glittering things and some sweets and dates, and the candles, it'll do for them. They never get sweets or anything like that from year's end to year's end. They're very much poorer than even the really poor in England.

Lawrence provided free milk for all the peasant women when they were nursing babies. The Pini's eldest daughter, Giulia, aged sixteen, they took into service:

Frieda 202   We loved Giulia . . . never was anything too much for her, gay and amusing and wise, she was.

When they left the Mirenda, Lawrence wrote regularly to Giulia for the rest of his life.

Lawrence's concern for others was also evidenced by the frequent delightful letters he sent to his Eastwood friend and former next-door-neighbour Gertie Cooper, now languishing with one lung in a sanatorium. Lawrence did what he could to cheer her up, and offered to pay £1 a week to keep her in the sanatorium, should her own funds run out.

In February Lawrence finished the second version of *Lady Chatterley's Lover*:

Moore 972   It's what the world would call very improper. But you know it's not really improper – I always labour at the same thing, to make the sex relation valid and precious, instead of shameful. And this novel is the furthest I've gone. To me it is beautiful and tender and frail as the naked self is, and I shrink very much even from having it typed.

The production of *David* had been postponed yet again, so Lawrence proposed to Earl Brewster, who had just moved to Ravello, that they should go together on the long-planned tour of the Etruscan sites, while Frieda went to Baden.

After a week at Ravello, Lawrence and Earl Brewster set out at the beginning of April, taking in Rome, Cerveteri, Tarquinia, Vulci, Grosseto and Volterra. Lawrence

Centaur 29   found the tombs 'far more twinkling and alive than the houses of men':

Frieda 238   The Etruscan tombs are very interesting and so nice and lovable. They were a living, fresh, jolly people, lived their own lives without wanting to dominate the lives of others.

Lawrence identified very closely with the Etruscans. In doing so he had to ignore some of the things he perfectly well knew – that the Etruscans were a colonizing and trading people who used slave labour in the mines of Populonia and did not spend their whole lives 'dancing and fluting along through the little olive trees'.

All the books Lawrence had read on the Etruscans could not provide answers to the questions which really interested him – the meaning of their language, their art,

*Tomb of the Lionesses, Tarquinia. 'All round the room the dolphins are leaping, leaping all downwards into the rippling sea, while birds fly between the fishes. On the right wall reclines a very impressive dark red man wearing a curious cap, or head-dress, that has long tails like long plaits. In his right hand he holds up an egg, and in his left is the shallow wine-bowl of the feast. The scarf or stole of his human office hangs from a tree before him, and the garland of his human delight hangs at his side. He holds up the egg of resurrection, within which the germ sleeps and the soul sleeps in the tomb, before it breaks the shell and emerges again.' (*Etruscan Places*)

their smiles, and the quality of their religion and their daily lives. He felt free to interpret the surviving artefacts imaginatively, resurrecting a race of which he felt himself to be a lost survivor:

> There is a simplicity, combined with a most peculiar, free-breasted naturalness and spontaneity, in the shapes and movements of the underworld walls and spaces, that at once reassures the spirit. . . . They leave the breast breathing freely and pleasantly, with a certain fullness of life. Even the tombs. And that is the true

Etruscan quality: ease, naturalness, and an abundance of life, no need to force the mind or the soul in any direction.

His long pilgrimage had brought him at last to these tombs, and in them he found the vivid human life he had been seeking, a life of perfect awareness and relatedness, without the crippling dualism of mind versus body, human versus non-human, physical versus metaphysical, life versus death. All these had been resolved, easily and joyfully, if only for a century or two, before the Romans trod Etruscan culture underfoot.

It is interesting that Lawrence's image for this human perfection is also an image of his own good health – 'breathing freely and pleasantly'. Had Lawrence caught malaria in the Maremma, we might have had no *Etruscan Places*.

If a perfect human society had once existed, then it might again. In 'A Dream of Life', which Lawrence wrote a few months later, he was to combine these qualities of the Etruscans with those of his own Derbyshire people to create his only Utopia. But he could not finish that story, for the same reason that he could never in real life found his Rananim – he could not reconcile the claims and aspirations of the individual with the uniformity of the community. His primary image for an ideal community is a shoal of dolphins or flock of birds, where the individuals are indistinguishable. But the uniqueness of every individual was also one of his most fundamental beliefs.

‌‌‌*℘*

Etruscan Places was not the first thing Lawrence wrote after his return from the Etruscan tour. In Volterra, on Easter morning, Lawrence and Earl Brewster had passed a shop in the window of which was a toy rooster escaping from an egg. Brewster had suggested a resurrection story called 'The Escaped Cock'. On 3 May Lawrence wrote to him:

Moore 975

I wrote a story of the Resurrection, where Jesus gets up and feels very sick about everything, and can't stand the old crowd any more – so cuts out – and as he heals up, he begins to find what an astonishing place the phenomenal world is, far more marvellous than any salvation or heaven – and thanks his stars he needn't have a 'mission' any more. It's called 'The Escaped Cock' from that toy in Volterra.

By the end of April Lawrence had also written 'Flowery Tuscany' and begun *Etruscan Places*. Frieda has described the spot in the hills above the Mirenda where Lawrence would sit under a large umbrella pine:

The First Lady Chatterley

It was an enchanting place where Lawrence went to write every day, especially in spring. He had to walk a little way by the olive trees to get to his umbrella pine. Thyme and mint tufts grew along the path and purple anemones and wild gladioli and carpets of violets and myrtle shrubs. White, calm oxen were ploughing. There he would sit, almost motionless except for his swift writing. He would be so still that the lizards would run over him and the birds hop close around him. An occasional hunter would start at his silent figure.

At last Lawrence got a definite date for a production of *David* at the end of May, and reluctantly began to make plans to go, fearing that they would make a mess of it without him. But on 4 May he was struck down by another attack of malaria. His letter of 19 May to his sister Ada is the first in which his declining health seems really to be getting him down:

Ada 156–7   I wish really I felt more solid. When one turns forty it seems as if ones old ailments attack one with a double fury. I never seem to get really free. And then one gets sort of disillusioned. I feel like turning hermit and hiding away the rest of my days away from everybody.

The attraction of the hermit life is mentioned several times in letters of this period. But with improving health, and by satirizing both himself and Earl Brewster in his story 'The Man Who was Through with the World', Lawrence managed to exorcise the temptation:

Moore 980   It's no good my thinking of retreat: I rouse up, and feel I don't want to. My business is a fight, and I've got to keep it up.

Lawrence then swung to the opposite extreme, telling Trigant Burrow that his illness was nothing but chagrin caused by 'the absolute frustration of my primeval societal instinct'. Of course the positions are not really opposite:

Moore 993   Myself, I suffer badly from being so cut off. But what is one to do? One can't link up with the social unconscious. At times, one is *forced* to be essentially a hermit. I don't want to be. But anything else is either a personal tussle, or a money tussle: sickening: except, of course, just for ordinary acquaintance, which remains acquaintance. One has no real human relations – that is so devastating.

The Huxleys had taken a villa at Forte dei Marmi and invited the Lawrences for a few days in mid-June. Lawrence intended, when he got back, to do another Etruscan tour, this time with Frieda, to Arezzo, Cortona, Chiusi, Orvieto and Perugia. His intention was that *Etruscan Places* should have a dozen or fourteen essays and about a hundred photographs, which he had been assiduously collecting. Lawrence hated Forte, and sea-bathing there brought on haemorrhages after his return to the Mirenda:

Nehls 3, 146   One hot afternoon Lawrence had gathered peaches in the garden and came in with a basket of wonderful fruit – he showed them to me – a very little while after he called from his room in a strange gurgling voice; I ran and found him lying on his bed; he looked at me with shocked eyes while a slow stream of blood came from his mouth. 'Be quiet, be still', I said. I held his head, but slowly and terribly the blood flowed from his mouth. I could do nothing but hold him and try to make him still and calm and send for Dr Giglioli. He came, and anxious days and nights followed. In this great heat of July nursing was difficult – Giulia, all the peasants – helped in every possible way. . . . The Huxleys came to see him, Maria with a great bunch of fantastically beautiful lotus, and Giglioli every day, and Orioli came and helped. But I nursed him alone night and day for six weeks, till he was strong enough to take the night train to the Tyrol.

The doctor had ordered Lawrence 'into the pines' at about 800 m. But the decline in Lawrence's health could not, this time, be halted.

The Lawrences left the Villa Mirenda for Villach, Austria, on 4 August. At the end of the month they moved to the Villa Jaffe at Irschenhausen, which belonged to Frieda's sister Else, whose husband, Edgar Jaffe, had died in 1921. It was a relief to Lawrence, after the drought of Tuscany, to be in a wetter, cooler and greener land. Irschenhausen was one of the stillest places he knew. He rested, drank goat's milk and malt beer, was fattened up on trout and partridges and venison, wandered in the forest, translated Verga . . .

Lawrence with Johanna and Emil Krug, Villach, August 1927. 'I like it all right — we make little excursions in the motor-buses, to the various lakes, which are quite beautiful. Frieda's sister is on the Ossiachersee, just near — we see them a good deal — but she, my cognata, *is not very contented, having got a newish bourgeois banker husband, ten years older than herself, instead of a ne'er-do-well ex-army officer — she changed them four years ago — the husbands, I mean, and the good bourgeois bores her and oppresses her, and she is in a bad humour, having always lived a gay life; and altogether I think the female of the species is a trial nowadays.'*

To the Wilkinsons he wrote, in high spirits:

Wilkinsons 71   The woods are simply uncanny with mushrooms, all sorts and sizes and shapes and smells, in camps and circles and odd ones – the brightest red, the blackest black, and the sea-weediest green – and we pick the little orange-yellow ones and eat them fried in butter. – The dark blue Autumn gentian is out – and the deer are about – little roe-buck – they fly across the paths just like a Persian picture – and then they stop fascinated by my famous little white jacket. The jays are so cheeky they almost steal the tears out of your eyes. I really like it here – but when it's dark and rainy then you sing: 'A little ship was on the sea' – for the oceans of old Time seem to sweep over you.

At the beginning of October the Lawrences went to Baden for a fortnight. Lawrence began hot-air inhalation treatment; but Hans Carossa examined him and advised against it, so he took the cold radium air inhalations instead. Carossa was both a creative writer and a leading tuberculosis specialist:

Nehls 3, 159   If a poet who is a doctor can't tell me what to do with myself, then who can?

But Carossa later told a friend that Lawrence was beyond treatment:

160   An average man with those lungs would have died long ago.

He recommended two months in a sanatorium, but Lawrence instinctively shied away from that:

Moore 1008   Doctors and sanatoriums only lower my spirits.

Baden itself lowered his spirits:

Moore 1011   Really, in Baden one ought to be at least 75 years old, and at least an Excellenz, at the very least a Generälchen. This place is such a back number, such a chapter in faded history, one hardly dares exist at all. I efface every possible bit of my manhood, and go around as much as possible like a paper silhouette of myself.

Lawrence had turned against Italy, as he had turned against Mexico, blaming it for his illness, and was not cheered by the prospect of returning, except for the likelihood of real sunshine, for it was getting wintry in Baden. He would have gone back to live in England, in Devonshire, but for the thought of perpetual rain and damp. He began to pine again for the space and freedom of the ranch.

Back at the Mirenda Lawrence began work revising his *Collected Poems* for Secker:

Moore 1020   We sit here rather vaguely, and I still haven't been to Florence. . . . I do bits of
Luhan 334–5   things – darn my underclothes and try to type out poems – old ones. . . . My word, what ghosts come rising up! But I just tidy their clothes for them and refuse to be drawn.

Secker was also publishing a new collection of short stories *The Woman Who Rode Away*. One of the stories was to be 'The Man Who Loved Islands'. But Compton Mackenzie, having read the story in the *London Mercury* in August, had objected to Secker, assuming Cathcart to be a defamatory portrait of himself. Lawrence felt that Mackenzie should be flattered, since Cathcart was worth taking a good deal more seriously than Mackenzie himself. Lawrence had put into Cathcart all his own love of islands and longing for the hermit life, as well as a few superficial aspects of Mackenzie. But that was the end of that friendship:

Moore 1188   Aren't these little authors beyond belief, with their vanity!

Through Norman Douglas Lawrence had become friendly with the Florentine bookseller and publisher Pino Orioli. Now he conceived the idea of getting Orioli to publish *Lady Chatterley's Lover* privately, as he had done some of Douglas's novels. This way Lawrence hoped to make enough money for the trip back to the ranch. But first the novel had to be rewritten. The final version, which Lawrence thought of calling *Tenderness*, was begun on 3 December and finished on 8 January. The first hint of trouble came that very day, when Lawrence received a letter from Nelly Morrison, who had volunteered to type it, saying that she found it distasteful –

Pino Orioli, Frieda and Lawrence on the Santa Trinita bridge, just across the road from Orioli's bookshop on the Lungarno.

Moore 1032 pandering to a pornographic taste. Lawrence insisted gently, as he was to have to insist more and more militantly, that 'although you are on the side of the angels and the vast majority, I consider mine is the truly moral and religious position.' Catherine Carswell arranged for the typing of the first half, and Maria Huxley undertook the second.

The Lawrences had spent Christmas with the Huxleys, who had then gone off to Switzerland, inviting the Lawrences to join them there. The doctor had told Lawrence that Les Diablerets (4,000 ft) was just right for his lungs, whereas the ranch would be too high. Lawrence overcame his hatred of snow and, at the end of January, struggled up to Les Diablerets, hoping to get his lungs strong enough to go later to the ranch.

Frieda 269 I must say, I don't like it. I am no snow-bird, I hate the stark and shroudy whiteness, white and black. It offends the painter in one – it is so uniform – only sometimes lovely contours, and pale blue gleams. But against life.

At Les Diablerets Lawrence finished his work on the *Collected Poems* and prepared an expurgated version of *Lady C.*:

Lawrence and Aldous Huxley at Les Diablerets. 'We drove in a sledge, tinkletinkle, to the top of the pass yesterday, F and I – the others came on skis – and we picknicked on the pass, very high, very sparkling and bright and sort of marvellous – and some men did some fine ski-running. I liked it very much – and it sort of puts life into one.'

Moore 1041 I did a fair amount of blanking out and changing, then I sort of got colour-blind, and didn't know any more what was supposed to be proper and what not.

Lawrence felt the word 'penis' had to go, but hardly improved matters by substituting for it, in a single speech, 'tilter', 'jouster' and 'little Lancelot'. 'Fucking' became, in a single page, 'making love', 'loving a woman up', 'love-practice', 'taking', 'sensation' and 'sensation-rousing'. He must have been thoroughly colour-blind when he suggested to the publishers, as a title for the *expurgated* edition, *John Thomas and Lady Jane*. In any case, he was wasting his labour, since both Knopf and Secker rejected his expurgated version.

The Lawrences returned to the Mirenda at the beginning of March. On 9 March
Moore 1043 Lawrence delivered the complete typescript of *Lady C.* to Orioli – 'great moment'. For the next two months he did nothing but paint and see *Lady C.* through the press:

Irvine 2, 82 I'm very busy with my novel – buying paper, hand-made – correcting proofs – making a phoenix from a nest in flames, like the seal I gave Murry, for the cover stamp – getting cover-paper – etc.

The proof correcting was a headache, since the printer knew no English:

Moore 1052 He writes dind't did'nt, dnid't, dind't, din'dt, didn't like a Bach fugue.

Lawrence had felt that it was only fair to tell the printer what the book contained:

Phoenix 2 515 And when told, he said, with the short indifference of a Florentine: 'O! ma! but we do it every day!'

❧

At the end of February Lawrence received a letter from the American playboy poet and publisher Harry Crosby asking if he had for sale any manuscripts, preferably having some connection with the sun. Crosby had adopted the sun as his private symbol. He sent Lawrence his collection of poems *Chariot of the Sun*; his press was the Black Sun Press, his house the Moulin du Soleil, his racehorse Sunstroke . . . He offered to pay Lawrence in pure gold. His letter had been written floating down the Nile, and had begun its journey to Lawrence by camel. The promised gold arrived by an even more unorthodox route. First it had to be smuggled from Boston to Paris in a friend's shoes. As soon as it arrived, Harry Crosby parcelled it, rushed off to the Gare de l'Est, and thrust his parcel into the hands of the first honest-looking man he saw on
Nehls 3, 200 the Florence train, asking him to mail it in Florence. 'Glad to – not a bomb, I trust,' said the Englishman as the train pulled out. 'No, it's gold,' shouted Crosby, 'gold for a poet.' Crosby had chosen well. The gold was delivered in person by the Duke of Argyll.

Moore 1051 That was very nice of you, to send me that little pseudo-book full of red gold. How beautiful the gold is! such a pity it ever became currency. One should love it for its yellow life, answering the sun.

Unfortunately, Lawrence was unable to deliver the goods. He wrote in a panic to Nancy Pearn in Curtis Brown's office:

Huxley 717 Have you got by any chance the manuscript of 'Sun' in the office? An American asks me for it particularly, and offers $100. So there's a windfall, if it exists. If it doesn't, povero me! for I haven't got it, the MS.

Nancy Pearn replied:

Here is the list of recent manuscripts we have been holding for you, and how I regret that 'Sun' is one of those we previously returned! Are you sure you burnt them all; and tell me, would it be cheating to write out the story again in your own fair handwriting to sell to the eager Yank? If not, why not?

Lawrence took her advice, but Crosby got good value, for Lawrence could not resist the opportunity to revise the story as he wrote it out. The Black Sun Press subsequently published it.

In April there was another visit from Barby. Frieda went back with her to Alassio, and then, alone, to see Angelo Ravagli in Spotorno. Lawrence turned a blind eye, saying to Frieda:

Nehls 3, 189 Every heart has a right to its own secrets.

Lawrence had now had enough of Italy, but was kept in Florence by the slowness of the printers, who had not enough type to set up the whole novel. Finally, on 7 June, he signed the last sheets and was free. Three days later the Lawrences left for Switzerland to look for a place at about 3,000 feet where Lawrence could strengthen his lungs. His plan was, in the autumn, to sail round the world on the *Messageries Maritimes* for £120, ending up in San Francisco:

Brewster 168 Otherwise we might go straight to the ranch. But it would be so nice, just for a bit, to be drifting out of reach of mail and malice, no letters, no literature, no publishers or agents or anything – what a paradise! I'm awfully tired of all that side of the world.

Little did Lawrence suspect what a hell that side of the world was stoking up for him.

Lawrence photographed by Robert H. Davis in Orioli's bookshop, May 1928. '"Select a spot on the opposite bank of the river and show some concern in it. Project your mind and the eye will record interest. Anyhow, that's my theory about portrait photography." "I've got it," replied Lawrence, his face lighting up. "A bit of rare architecture. Beautiful lines." Illuminated by the spring sunshine, the little book shop, glowing with an old ivory tone reflected from the ancient parchment bindings, became an ideal studio.' (Robert H. Davis)

18 Autos-da-fé

The Brewsters decided to accompany the Lawrences to the Alps. They found Lawrence much weaker, but on the train to Turin he lead the singing of Nonconformist and Salvation Army hymns, of which he seemed to know every word.

Brewster 284 The party stopped at Chambéry, Aix-les-Bains and Grenoble, and eventually found 'the floweriest spot of all', the Hotel des Touristes at St Nizier de Pariset, where they intended to stay for a while. Lawrence retired in high spirits. But next morning the proprietor told Earl Brewster that Lawrence had been coughing in the night and would have to leave. Lawrence was outraged. They moved on to the Grand Hotel at Chexbres-sur-Vevey, where the Brewsters were well known. Here, by the waters of Leman, Lawrence wrote the last works of fiction he was ever to write, the second half of *The Escaped Cock*, and 'Blue Moccasins'. From this time forth he had the strength or the will to produce only short newspaper articles, essays, poems, paintings, and the unfinished *Apocalypse*.

At the beginning of July the Lawrences found the Chalet Kasselmatte on the hillside above Gsteig, surrounded by flowery meadows, pine forests, and snow-capped mountains. Almost at once Lawrence had a slight haemorrhage, but made light of it. Here, sitting at a rustic table among the pines, he wrote most of the newspaper articles later collected as *Assorted Articles*. He could not walk as far as Gsteig, a mile away, because of the climb back. The Brewsters, staying at a hotel in the village, came up almost every day, sometimes with their Hindu friends Dhan Gopal Mukerji and Boshi Sen, who massaged Lawrence. His health did not improve, and by the end of July he was writing to the Huxleys that he had made a design for his tombstone in Gsteig churchyard: 'Departed this life, etc., etc., – *He was fed up!*'

Lawrence had received his copy of *Lady Chatterley's Lover* on 28 June. He wrote at once to Orioli:

Moore 1065 *Lady Chatterley* came this morning, to our great excitement, and everybody thinks she looks most beautiful, outwardly. I do really think it is a handsome and dignified volume – a fine shape and proportion, and I like the *terra cotta* very much, and I think my phoenix is just the right bird for the cover. Now let us hope she will find her way safely and quickly to all her destinations.

The edition was of 1,000 signed copies at £2 each. Thanks to many dedicated helpers, particularly Kot (despite the fact that he disapproved of the book), Enid Hilton and Richard Aldington, who distributed the books themselves when faint-hearted booksellers cancelled their orders, the books did reach most of their destinations in England. It proved more difficult to get copies into the U.S.A., and only 140 were shipped there. The many difficulties encountered in distributing the book, and the mass of correspondence Lawrence undertook in connection with it, must have taxed him severely.

Of course the publication of *Lady C.* cost Lawrence a lot of friends, or rather helped him to discover who his friends were:

Priest 448   Oh I am so glad to lose the fag end of my friends! especially the old maidy sort.

Several galleries had expressed an interest in exhibiting Lawrence's paintings. He hesitated for a while between the Warren Gallery and Claridge's. Finally he decided

Moore 1066 on Dorothy Warren, though he thought her so unreliable that it was like 'riding to the moon on a soap-bubble'. Dorothy Warren was Lady Ottoline's niece, and Lawrence had met her back in the Garsington days. Before opening the Warren Gallery in 1927 she had already achieved some fame as an interior decorator and designer, and had had a brief flirtation with the film industry. Now, at thirty-two, she was about to marry Philip Trotter. One of her first exhibitions at the gallery had been of carvings and drawings by an unknown Yorkshire miner's son called Henry Moore. Lawrence's exhibition was scheduled for October.

So many people having been 'mortally offended' by *Lady C.*, Lawrence warned

Nehls 3, 237 Dorothy Warren that the show 'might only carry the offence further':

Personally, I think such skunks should be offended to the last inch.

Despite being ill and overworked, Dorothy Warren replied, courageously:

Nehls 3, 239   Of course I anticipate prudish objections and attacks on myself and my Gallery. All that will have to be faced and it won't be a very new experience, although it is one to which I am not absolutely hardened! But I think your pictures fine and free and individual so that I want to show them.

By the end of August Lawrence had had enough of Switzerland and its eternal mountains, but he had to stay a little longer, having invited his sister Emily, who had never been out of England, and her daughter Margaret, aged nineteen, to spend a fortnight at Kesselmatte. He had to hide *Lady C.* like a skeleton in his cupboard. He was in bed with a cold for much of the time, and his relations depressed him further. Lawrence very much wanted to see his pictures:

Moore 1084   I'm *pining* to see them framed and hung. But whether I shall have the strength to put my nose into that stink-pot of an island, I don't know. I very much doubt it.

A visit to Baden was owing. Accompanied by the Brewsters, the Lawrences left Gsteig on 18 September.

Nothing ever changed in Baden:

Moore 1092   We go to the *Kurhaus* and drink hot waters and listen to music and – eat, of course.

To celebrate Earl Brewster's fiftieth birthday Lawrence hired two two-horse landaus and they all drove through the forest for three hours in stately bliss. But on all their short excursions on foot, Lawrence, for all his enthusiasm, was soon exhausted and dragging behind.

❧

Lawrence left Baden-Baden on 1 October in search of the sun. The Brewsters accompanied him as far as the French Riviera, on their way to Italy. They stopped in Strasbourg to look at Lawrence's favourite Gothic cathedral, but the cold drove them into a cinema where *Ben Hur* was showing. The lack of any human content nauseated Lawrence, and he had to be taken out. He went to La Lavandou to wait for Frieda, who had gone to close up the Mirenda (and to visit her lover Angelo Ravagli in Trieste).

Lawrence felt pleasant and easy and well lounging on the sands in the sun. When Frieda arrived, they went over to Port-Cros, the island where the Aldingtons had invited them to stay in their fortress, La Vigie. But Frieda brought a raging Italian cold and gave it to Lawrence, so that once he had struggled a mile up to the Vigie, he could not go down again to join the others at their bathing, but stayed in his tower, Moore 1093–4 looking down over 'the green island, all umbrella pines, and the blue sea and the other isles, and the mainland ten miles off'. The following week he had haemorrhages and stayed in bed, reading Aldous Huxley's much-acclaimed new novel *Point Counter Point*, in which he found himself portrayed, admiringly, as Mark Rampion, whom Lawrence thought a boring 'gas-bag'.

Two days later came news of the reception of his own novel in England. Under the heading 'FAMOUS NOVELIST'S SHAMEFUL BOOK, A Landmark in Evil', *Lady Chatterley's Lover* was described in *John Bull* as

Draper 278 the most evil outpouring that has ever besmirched the literature of our country. The sewers of French pornography would be dragged in vain to find a parallel in beastliness.

Lawrence was called 'a bearded satyr' (with a retouched photograph to prove it), and a 'sex-sodden genius', who ought to be put away for 'a good stiff spell'. The irony was that this was about to happen to Horatio Bottomley, editor of *John Bull*, on several charges of fraud. Lawrence's friends laughed at the reviews, but they hurt Lawrence deeply.

Ostensibly, it was bad weather which drove the Lawrences back to the mainland, but Lawrence had probably sensed that Aldington and Brigit Patmore were having an affair, and strongly objected to the ménage à trois. He never wrote to Aldington again. ❧

Frieda wanted a house, but could not make up her mind between Lago di Garda, Taormina, and the ranch. Lawrence himself wanted to go back to Italy to finish the

Lawrence and his sister Emily at the Chalet Kasselmatte. Photo by Margaret Needham. 'I am not really "our Bert". Come to that, I never was. And the gulf between their outlook and mine is always yawning, horribly obvious to me.'

Etruscan essays, or to Spain, or to Zululand ('Climate supposed to be perfect'). In the event he got no further than Bandol, and 'blank indecision' kept him there:

Huxley 762   It is incredibly lovely weather, and the place very lovely, swimming with milky gold light at sunset, and white boats half melted on the white twilight sea, and palm trees frizzing their tops in the rosy west, and their thick dark columns down in the dark where we are, with shadowy boys running and calling, and tiny orange lamps under foliage, in the under dusk.

Huxley 776   As December advanced, Lawrence was getting bored with Bandol, 'a dull little place, apart from the sun'. He wanted to go to Spain, but Barby and Elsa were expected for Christmas. He amused himself with his poems:

Huxley 766   I have been doing a book of Pensées, which I call pansies, a sort of loose little poem form; Frieda says with joy: real doggerel.

Rhys Davies, who stayed with the Lawrences for a few days just before Christmas, was particularly impressed by the life he put into his paintings:

Nehls 3, 274   For all his fury and rages, he got immense fun out of writing *Pansies*. He would write them in bed in the mornings, cheerful and chirpy, the meek sea air blowing in from the enchanting little bay outside his window . . . But it was out of his painting he seemed to get the most joy, turning to it with relief and a sense of escape. . . . He was almost pathetic in his absorption in these paintings; he said that words bored him now.

Davies was a young Welsh novelist who had recently come to live in Nice. Lawrence was put in touch with him by the London bookseller Charles Lahr, editor of *New Coterie* and publisher of Lawrence's *Sun* and, later, the unexpurgated *Pansies*. Lahr had sent Lawrence Davies's recent first novel *The Withered Root* which Lawrence had found good and real:

Moore 1083   I was glad to have the book, and so feel that weird, depressing Welsh flavour of dark slate subsoil.

Lahr had also confirmed the rumours that a pirated edition of *Lady C.* had appeared in America. Several more appeared in its wake. Lawrence immediately released the 200 ordinary-paper copies already printed, at one guinea, in an attempt to undersell the pirates, but the edition was far too small, and he began to search for a publisher to bring out a popular edition.

Lawrence's paintings were still sitting in Dorothy Warren's gallery with no definite opening date. But now Lawrence was approached by an enthusiastic young Australian, P. R. Stephensen, who wanted to produce a book of reproductions of the paintings. Stephensen had been collaborating with Jack Lindsay with the Fanfrolico Press and the *London Aphrodite*, but was in the process of breaking away from Lindsay to start his own press, the Mandrake, and Lawrence's paintings would be the

Kot 370   first publication. The project excited Lawrence, who offered to write 'a good peppery foreword *against* all that significant form piffle'.

In *Lady Chatterley's Lover* Lawrence had claimed for the novel:

It can inform and lead into new places the flow of our sympathetic consciousness, and it can lead our sympathy away in recoil from things gone dead.

He believed that by modifying the sympathetic awareness of individuals, not only in his novels, but in his paintings and even the little Pansies, he was making his contribution to the revolution he felt must come. He sent a New Year message to the Durham miners' leader Charles Wilson:

Moore 1110   It's time there was an *enormous* revolution – not to install Soviets, but to give life itself a chance. What's the good of an industrial system piling up rubbish, while nobody lives.

Lawrence's health had improved. He had not spent a single day in bed since coming to Bandol. He was now reconciled to spending the whole winter there. Life was very pleasant and easy as Frieda remembered it:

Frieda 211   A sunny hotel by the sea, friendly and easy as only Provence can be. . . . Lawrence wrote *Pansies* in his room in the morning, then we went to have our aperitif before lunch in a café on the sea-front. . . . We knew all the dogs of the small place, we saw the boats come in, their silvery loads of sardines glittering on the sand of the shores. Lawrence . . . watched the men playing 'boccia' on the shore, after lunch. We seemed to share the life of the little town, running along so easily. We went with the bus to Toulon. We saw the coloured soldiers. We went to a beautiful circus. Yes, easy and sunny was this winter in Bandol.

Belatedly, in mid-January, the police began to confiscate copies of *Lady C.* entering England. This scarcely mattered, since they were the last few copies. More important, they also seized a typescript of *Pansies* addressed to Curtis Brown. Aldous Huxley, who visited the Lawrences at Bandol, wrote to his friend St John Hutchinson, a barrister and parliamentary candidate with contacts in the House of Commons, who already knew Lawrence from the war years. Hutchinson reported that he had several members willing to raise the matter in the House, and that they might even get Ramsay MacDonald (shortly to be Prime Minister) to do it. In the event a question to the Home Secretary was tabled by Ellen Wilkinson. Sir William Joynson-Hicks ('Jix') said that he had ordered the MSS. to be kept for two months to give the author an opportunity to establish that they did not contain indecent matter. He assured the House that they did. Lawrence decided to struggle no more; it was not the only copy. Also, rather than quarrel with Secker about proposed omissions and deletions, he would let Secker do as he liked, and bring out his own unexpurgated edition privately with Charlie Lahr. He was shortly to be cheered by the victory of the Labour Party at the General Election, which meant, of course, the departure of the hated 'Jix' to the House of Lords as Lord Brentford.

In February Ada came for a holiday. Despite Lawrence's fondness for her, she depressed him:

Huxley 786   I feel all those Midlands behind her, with their sort of despair. I want to put my pansies in the fire, and myself with them – oh, dear!

It was so cold in Bandol that all the palms and eucalyptus trees froze to death. Lawrence was determined to move on soon, but where to? They decided to risk Spain after all. But a last minute change of plan saw Lawrence off to Paris, accompanied by Rhys Davies, to see if he could arrange for a popular edition of *Lady C*. He felt that a new outfit was appropriate:

Moore 1137   I shall bloom out in my new grey suit and even a pair of Toulon gloves, most fetching . . .

Huxley 788   but what he really needed, he told Aldous Huxley, was 'a reincarnation into a dashing body that doesn't cough'.

Tuesday, February 26, 1929.   THE EVENING STANDARD.   9

(LEFT TO RIGHT)
A "FRANK" WOMAN NOVELIST, SHAKESPERE, SHAW, WELLS, BENNETT, ALDOUS HUXLEY,
D.H. LAWRENCE, JAMES JOYCE. EACH IS ACCOMPANIED BY HIS LITERARY INSPIRATION; *except me, so I suppose I've got none!*
(AT BACK) DICKENS AND JANE AUSTEN

JIX, THE SELF-APPOINTED CHUCKER-OUT. *Bandol, where the Pansies were born. 2 March 19*

Lawrence arrived in Paris on 11 March and stayed there a month, with a week out at Suresnes at the home of the Huxleys. Though soon enfeebled by big-city 'grippe', Lawrence managed to conclude his business. His first approach had been to Sylvia Beach, publisher of Joyce's *Ulysses*, but she seemed content to rest on her laurels. The next approach was to Edward Titus, owner of a bookshop behind the Dome café, editor of *This Quarter*, and husband of the wealthy beauty-specialist Helena Rubinstein. Titus agreed to supervise the production of a cheap edition of 3,000 copies of *Lady C.*, henceforth to be referred to, in their correspondence, as Our Lady.

Frieda, who had been to Baden, joined Lawrence on the 25th. Davies had been troubled by the nightly coughing and restlessness of Lawrence in the next room, and was relieved at Frieda's return. He was out shopping the afternoon she arrived.

Davies 157   Returned, I knocked on Lawrence's door and was told to enter. The couple lay in bed under a tumbled counterpane of crimson velvet, Lawrence's bearded head nestling contentedly on a hearty bosom refreshed by a fortnight's breathing of its native air.

The following weekend the Lawrences spent with the Crosbys at the Moulin du Soleil, Ermenonville. Harry's diary entry for 29 March reads:

Crosby 244   He wanders in the field picking flowers. I pray from my sun-tower into the setting sun. Caresse plants tulips. Frieda walks in the wood. At supper-time in front of the fire I played the gramophone James Joyce reading aloud from *Ulysses* and after listening to it Lawrence said Yes I thought so a preacher a Jesuit preacher who believes in the cross upsidedown. And how he hated the Empty Bed Blues. And how he was shocked when I gave a dissertation in favour of la morsure in love-making.

Frieda listened so often that weekend to Bessie Smith singing the 'Empty Bed Blues' that Lawrence broke the record over her head. Harry bought another copy for Frieda, and a gramophone to play it on, much to Lawrence's disgust:

Moore 1213   The gramophone – 'Kiss your hand, Madame' – I only allow in the kitchen. I do mortally hate it.

On Easter Sunday Harry took Lawrence to see his racehorses:

Crosby 244   Easter, and Lawrence and I drove over in the car to Chantilly to look at Gin Cocktail and Sunstroke and at suppertime around the fire he began to talk of a new unpublished book of his called *The Escaped Cock* about the wanderings of Jesus after his resurrection and of how he met a priestess of Isis in a little temple on the coast of Phoenicia and how they lived together and how this is the missing link in the history of the Christ and C and I are excited and we offer to bring this book out at our Black Sun Press and all the candles burned low and guttered and went out and we looked into the redgold of the fire and it was like a conspiracy.

The Black Sun Press *Escaped Cock* was to be the most beautiful edition ever printed of a work of Lawrence's.

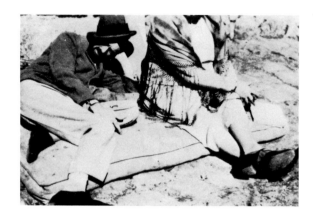

Le Moulin du Soleil

The Lawrences with Harry and Caresse Crosby.

'It was the season of daffodils and we went searching. Lawrence and I in the donkey cart, jogging down long aisle-like paths where no flowers grew. We hunted in the most unlikely places and with a shawl tucked round his knees, collar up and his soft hat pulled over his scorching eyes, we briefed each copse and sward, talking, talking, talking all the while.' (Caresse Crosby)

A few days later Lawrence was at the mill again, being sculpted by Caresse. Harry went off to meet Joyce to sign the contract for *Tales Told of Shem and Shaun*. Afterwards he offered to take Joyce to meet Lawrence, but Joyce was shy, and made the excuse that his eyes hurt.

It is difficult to imagine anyone more different from Lawrence than Harry Crosby, with his income of $12,000 a year, dogs, horses, servants, mistresses, gambling and flying, drinks and drugs. Since he could afford to satisfy his wildest desires, they soon evaporated and had to be replaced with still wilder ones, until he spiralled into insanity:

Crosby 241 I am a visionary I like to soar he is all engrossed in the body and in the mushroom quality of the earth and the body and in the complexities of psychology. He is indirect. I am direct. He admits of defeat. I do not. He is commonplace. I am not. He is unthoroughbred. I am thoroughbred. He was 'seedy' looking how I hate the word 'seedy'. I guess he is a sick man I forgive him a great deal because of *The Plumed Serpent* but I can see no excuse for writing *Lady Chatterley's Lover*. . . . Lawrence stayed until four attacking my visionary attitude but my fort withstood the bombardment and I marshalled my troops and sallied out to counter-attack all of which took time so that I was not able to go out to the opening of the flat races at Maison Lafitte where I wanted to see the Lady of the Gold Horse and watch The Arrow win at seven to one I had a thousand on her to win.

Phoenix 257 Lawrence found in his poems 'only a repetition of sun, sun, sun, not really as a glowing symbol, more as a bewilderment and a narcotic'. Crosby had a huge sun tattooed on his back; and a sun engraved on the automatic with which he shot his mistress and himself on 10 December 1929.

Ottoline 137 On 7 April the Lawrences left Paris for Spain – 'was so glad to leave that city of dreadful night'.

Lawrence refused to go into ecstasies over Majorca as Frieda did, castigated the Moore 1144 local wine as 'the sulphurous urination of some aged horse' and the local faces as 'Spanishy', and got malaria again so that his teeth 'chattered like castanets'. In spite of the sun, the sea and the flowers, he felt too 'peeved' to work or settle, though he stayed there for a month:

Huxley 806 This is a wonderful place for doing nothing – the time passes rapidly in a long stretch of nothingness – broken by someone fetching us out in a motor, or somebody else in a donkey-cart. It is very good for my health, I believe. This letter is my most serious contribution to literature these six weeks.

Lawrence had decided that his destiny would not let him return to the ranch, which might as well be sold to pay for the proposed new house. But Brett insisted on first refusal, and offered $5,000, though Lawrence knew she had no money at all. In fact he suspected her of secretly selling some of the manuscripts he had left at the ranch. To save Lawrence further bother, Frieda offered to let Brett live at the ranch

The Warren Gallery Exhibition. The paintings are, left to right, Flight Back into Paradise, Close-Up Kiss, Resurrection *and* Red Willow Trees.

Dorothy Warren and Philip Trotter.

for nothing if only she would hand over the remaining manuscripts, which she did. Most of the missing ones turned up elsewhere.

On 18 June the Lawrences left Majorca, Lawrence to stay with the Huxleys in Forte dei Marmi, Frieda to go to London to see the Warren Gallery exhibition, which had finally opened, to coincide with the publication of the Mandrake *Paintings*. She found a gay flag with Lawrence's name on it flying outside the gallery. The pictures themselves, so right for the big bare rooms at the Mirenda, seemed to her 'wild and overwhelming' in the elegant, delicate rooms of the galleries. Twenty-five paintings were exhibited, fifteen oils and ten watercolours.

Frieda 212

Most of the press notices were prurient, patronizing and facetious. The authorities made no move until a complaint was lodged by a common informer. It was 5 July when the police descended on the gallery. By that time more than 12,000 people had seen the paintings. Dorothy Warren and Philip Trotter refused to close the gallery while the raid took place. The police had just turned *Contadini* and *Dance Sketch* to the wall when the Aga Khan, resplendent from a Buckingham Palace garden party, entered. Philip Trotter has a beautiful account of what followed:

Nehls 3, 345

I begged to cut a passage through for him to *Boccaccio Story*, whose turn was now imminent and whose fate was inevitable; and there he and [Detective-Inspector] Hester met, and bowed, to the latter's embarrassment. On the Aga's heels came a shabby little man from Nottingham, to see his famous co-citizen's pictorial work. I expressed regret that he was too late for *Contadini*. He sidled towards it and began furtively revolving the frame as on an axis. Hester, glad to relinquish *Boccaccio Story* to the Aga Khan, muscled back to *Contadini*.

'Stand aside, please,' he said sternly. 'That picture is no longer on view.' The little man slunk away. But the Aga Khan had followed Hester. Pointing his splendid cane at the stretchers of *Contadini*:

'Will you turn that picture round, please? I should like to see it.' The police made easels of themselves. 'Light all right, your Highness?'

Then the Aga Khan signed the man from Nottingham to his side, and they enjoyed *Contadini* together.

Thirteen pictures were seized: *Boccaccio Story, Fight with an Amazon, Dance-Sketch, Family on a Verandah, Contadini, Accident in a Mine, North Sea, Spring, Singing of Swans, Leda, Yawning, Fire-Dance,* and *Under the Mango-Tree*. The police also seized copies of the Mandrake reproductions, George Grosz's *Ecce Homo*, and Blake's *Pencil Drawings*. It was Blake's Adam and Eve, newly created, who were deemed obscene by Mr Hester, whose rule-of-thumb equated obscenity with pubic hair. The exhibition remained open, the gaps filled with some of Lawrence's early paintings.

On the same day as the raid, Lawrence in Forte was taken violently ill with stomach pains. Nevertheless, he travelled to Florence the following day. There Orioli was so distressed by his appearance, his head and arms dangling limply over the sides of his bed like a descent from the Cross, that he had him brought by car to his own flat, and telegraphed Frieda to come at once. A few days later he was well enough to travel with her to Baden.

Lawrence was outraged when he heard about the raid:

Ada 194   The dirty swine would like to think they made you weep.

He instructed Dorothy Warren, who wanted to make a test case of it, to get his pictures back safely at all costs, especially his beloved *Boccaccio*:

Moore 1164   To admit that my pictures should be burned, in order to change an English law, would be to admit that sacrifice of life to circumstance which I most strongly disbelieve in. No, at all costs or any cost, I don't want my pictures burnt. No more crucifixions, no more martyrdoms, no more *autos-da-fé*, as long as time lasts, if I can prevent it.

The Trotters had until 8 August to organize their defence. They recruited an impressive array of artists and art experts willing to testify that Lawrence was a true artist: Augustus John, Colin Agnew, connoisseur and dealer of international standing, Dr Tancred Borenius, a famous art historian, Glyn Philpot and Sir William Orpen. Many more famous artists, writers and members of Parliament signed a petition, including those victims of Lawrence's scorn in his introduction to the *Paintings* – Clive Bell and Roger Fry, along with the rest of the Bloomsbury set.

Nehls 3, 382–4   In the event Mr Justice Mead refused to admit the evidence of experts on the grounds that 'the most splendidly painted picture in the Universe might be obscene.' At this point, Lady Ottoline Morrell rose at the back of the room, pointed a long finger at Mr Mead, and intoned: 'He ought to be burned.' Mr Herbert Muskett, who had also appeared for the police in the case against *The Rainbow*, submitted that 'these paintings are gross, coarse, hideous, and unlovely from any aesthetic or artistic point of view, and are in their nature obscene.' Mr St John Hutchinson, representing the Warren Gallery, argued strongly that the case created a precedent whereby police officers would be empowered to remove masterpieces from public galleries and destroy them if a single magistrate agreed that they were obscene. Nevertheless, in accordance with Lawrence's wishes, he submitted a compromise proposal undertaking that if the paintings were returned to their owners they would not be exhibited in England again. This proposal was accepted and the paintings saved. The four seized copies of the Mandrake reproductions were ordered to be destroyed. The Warren Gallery paid costs of £5. 5s.

Meanwhile Lawrence, at the Kurhaus Plättig, had recovered sufficiently to hit
Moore 1173   back with 'a few stinging *Pansies* which this time are *Nettles*':

Poems 680   Lately I saw a sight most quaint:
                             London's lily-like policemen faint
                             in virgin outrage as they viewed
                             the nudity of a Lawrence nude!

Moore 1180   What was the point of pouring one's dwindling energies into serious work for 'a nation of poltroons in the face of life ... bossed by the witless *canaille* and offsweepings of a dead nineteenth century'? Nevertheless, the trouble over *Lady C.* and the paintings generated three of Lawrence's finest essays, 'The Risen Lord', 'Pornography and Obscenity' and 'A Propos of Lady Chatterley's Lover'.

19 The Longest Journey

Lawrence was still thinking of a permanent home in Italy:

Moore 1174 It will be great fun if we can find a house and have ducks and goats. I've never tried my hand yet at pigs, but why not? They must be nicer than human ones. We might even make bacon, and hang a long flitch against the wall. My father always said that was the beautifullest picture on a wall – a flitch of bacon! and Boccaccio could hang opposite – all the carnal sins together.

For the first time in his life, Lawrence had no financial problems. His final settlement with Orioli revealed that *Lady C.* had made a profit of £1,616, of which only ten per cent went to Orioli. Lawrence was even able to refuse an offer of $3,000 for the manuscript.

Rumours were now circulating that Lawrence was dying, and some of them got back to him:

Moore 1178 They have determined I shall die. So of course I shall live a hundred years, and put wreaths on all their graves.

A doctor told Lawrence that his lung had healed, but that his bronchitis and asthma were worse, and he should go to the sea. Lawrence and Frieda descended again to the Hotel Löwen, where Frieda celebrated her fiftieth birthday. She had dislocated her ankle on the rocks in Majorca, and was still limping. Lawrence depended on her never to be ill, or even moody, but a steady fount of chirpiness.

At the end of August they left Baden for Bavaria, to be near Max Mohr in Rottach. Mohr was a dramatist, novelist and doctor, and a great admirer of Lawrence, whom he had visited at Irschenhausen in 1927 and Les Diablerets in 1928. In some ways – in his love of mountaineering and other outdoor pursuits, of youth activities and of folk-music – he resembled Rolf Gardiner. Most important, at this stage of his life, Lawrence found his company agreeable and undemanding.

In Rottach, for the first time, Lawrence confronted the probability that he was dying:

Frieda 213 My sister Else came to see him, and Alfred Weber. When he was alone with Alfred Weber, he said to him: 'Do you see those leaves falling from the apple tree? When the leaves want to fall you must let them fall.' Max Mohr had brought some doctors from Munich, but medicine did not help Lawrence. His organism was too frail and sensitive. I remember some autumn nights when the end seemed to have come. I listened for his breath through the open door, all night long, an owl hooting ominously from the walnut tree outside. In the dim dawn an enormous bunch of gentians I had put on the floor by his bed seemed the only living thing in the room.

The doctors put Lawrence on a diet, and prescribed arsenic, which made him much worse. 11 September was his forty-fourth birthday. He knew it might well be his last:

Poems 955

> What a journey for my soul
> in the dark blue gloom
> of gentians here in the sunny room!

Lawrence had asked Orioli to look out for a suitable house in the hills above Florence. But he decided he should return to Bandol, where he had been so cheerful and well the previous winter. He was delighted to be back on the Mediterranean:

Moore 1205

I still love the Mediterranean, it still seems young as Odysseus, in the morning.

Moore 1213

Frieda soon found a house – the Villa Beau Soleil, 'one of those chalet-bungalow affairs', rather like 'a little railway station', but with the much-desired central

Lacy 83

heating, and 'wonderfully in the air and light'.

In August Lawrence had re-established contact with Frederick Carter, and by October they were planning a joint project in which Lawrence would write a commentary on the Book of Revelation as an introduction to Carter's more esoteric and fragmented commentary. Lawrence sent off for several scholarly books on the subject. The following month Carter came to stay in Bandol, but Lawrence found him a 'Willy-wet-leg', the spark gone out of him. Nevertheless, he inspired Lawrence to write his last sustained work, *Apocalypse*:

I very much want to put into the world again the big old pagan vision.

Moore 1205

On 15 October the long-awaited Black Sun Press Edition of *The Escaped Cock* arrived. But in the same letter in which Lawrence expressed his thanks to Caresse Crosby, he revealed for the first time that he expected to have to go into a sanatorium

Lacy 89

'unless I pick up very soon'. He could not walk to the nearest corner. Also for the first time, he complains of the number of letters he has to write – 'I get tired to death of them.' The letters he does write are subdued, and full of complaints about his health and enforced inactivity. He would never have the shutters closed or curtains drawn, so that he could see the night sky from his bed as he lay coughing before dawn, wrestling with the demon in his chest:

Frieda 302

But then at dawn I believe he felt grateful that another day had been given him. 'Come when the sun rises,' he said, and when I came he was glad, so very glad, as if he would say: 'See, another day is given me.'

The sun rose magnificently opposite his bed in red and gold across the bay and the fishermen standing up in their boats looked like eternal mythological figures dark and alive against the lit-up splendour of the sea and sky.

His courage and unflinching spirit doing their level best to live as long as he possibly could in this world he loved so much, gave me courage too.

Apocalypse As his body failed, the life of the senses and the gifts of the natural world became more and more precious to him. His last poems celebrate 'the magnificent here and now of life in the flesh' with assurance, playfulness and joy. Even the poems about death, though poignant, never waver in their faith that death is only a part of life, the longest journey, perhaps the greatest adventure:

Poems 727   And if, in the changing phases of man's life
I fall in sickness and in misery
my wrists seem broken and my heart seems dead
and strength is gone, and my life
is only the leavings of a life:

and still, among it all, snatches of lovely oblivion, and snatches of renewal
odd, wintry flowers upon the withered stem, yet new strange flowers
such as my life has not brought forth before, new blossoms of me –

then I must know that still
I am in the hands of the unknown God,
he is breaking me down to his own oblivion
to send me forth on a new morning, a new man.

Max Mohr had stayed in Bandol to help look after Lawrence. Just as he was preparing to leave, the Brewsters arrived to spend the winter nearby:

Ada 199   I'm glad, it is good to have someone near.

Earl would come every day to massage Lawrence's wasted body with coconut oil. Lawrence improved towards the end of November and was able to take little walks. He had come to the conclusion that his sickness was 'a sort of rage' and wrote to Bynner that he could not digest his spleen in Europe, and would try with all his might to get back to New Mexico in the New Year. He was somewhat cheered by the huge sales of his pamphlet *Pornography and Obscenity* (1,200 a week), which Faber had *Moore* 1219 published, and by the review of it in the *New Statesman* ('standing up for me boldly') by R. A. Barclay:

Draper 314–7   It is a real masterpiece of fundamental analysis written by a man of genius from the very bottom of his heart. . . . It is one of the most powerful and sane and penetrating pieces of writing that we have read for very many years. His pamphlet is a pamphlet which, if it wins understanding, may well mark an epoch in the history not only of censorship but of the reasonable appreciation of the realities of sexual morality and sexual honesty and decency.

Lawrence heard that Murry had decided there was no God. 'Now I know there is,' said Lawrence. He was not merely being flippant, for he said to Earl Brewster:

Brewster 224   I intend to find God: I wish to realize my relation with Him. I do not any longer object to the word God. My attitude regarding this has changed. I must establish a conscious relation with God.

In November Kot wrote to Lawrence about a Dr Morland, resident physician at Mundesley sanatorium, where both Gertie Cooper and Mark Gertler had been treated with some success. He was passing through the south of France in January. Would Lawrence see him? Lawrence replied unenthusiastically; but Frieda wrote:

Frieda 239   Tell that doctor how glad I would be if he came to see Lawr.

Carter left Bandol at the beginning of December; but there were new visitors – Ida Rauh from Santa Fe, and the di Chiaras from Capri. For Christmas there were plum puddings and Christmas cakes from Lawrence's sisters. But Lawrence was in bed with linseed poultices – 'A real seasonal Christmas!'

At the New Year there were flying visits from Pino Orioli and Norman Douglas ('on Moore 1229 the holiday razzle'), and from the Brett Youngs ('How are the puny risen!'). Laurence Pollinger and Else came for a few days, then Barby. Lawrence was at the end of his Moore 1232 tether, trying to console himself by discussing with Ida Rauh his plans to return to New Mexico in the spring.

Dr Morland examined Lawrence on 20 January, and on the following day Lawrence wrote to Mabel Luhan:

Moore 1235   The doctor from England came on Monday – says the bronchitis is acute, and aggravated by the lung. I must lie still for two months. – Talks of my going into a sanatorium near Nice, but I don't know if it's suitable.

Mohr 540   He was not to attempt to work, or read, or see anyone. 'I get weary in my soul,' he wrote to Max Mohr. Ten days later Morland wrote from Vence, strongly recommending the sanatorium there. Lawrence was still reluctant, though his weight was down to six stone:

Moore 1238   If I make good progress as I am, I shan't go to Vence: if I don't I shall.

Three days later he had decided to go:

Moore 1239   Dr Morland assured me I should get better so much more quickly in a sanatorium, and be able to *walk* again – and that is what I want. I want my legs back again.

On 6 February Lawrence set out on his last journey, from the Villa Beau Soleil to the Ad Astra Sanatorium, from the sun to the stars.

Frieda 306   There he lay in a blue room with yellow curtains and great open windows and a balcony looking over the sea. When the doctors examined him and asked him questions about himself he told them: 'I have had bronchitis since I was a fortnight old.'

Two weeks later Lawrence wrote to Maria Huxley:

'It's no different from being in an hotel, not a bit – except that a nurse takes my temperature. I have the ordinary hotel food – and do just as I like – and am far less "looked after" than I was in the Beau Soleil. So much for a sanatorium.'

Moore 1245   I am rather worse here – such bad nights, and cough, and heart, and pain decidedly worse here – and miserable. Seems to me like *grippe*, but they say not. It's not a good place – shan't stay long – I'm better in a house – I'm miserable.

Frieda has Barbey with her – and Ida Rauh. When do you think of coming? P.S. This place no good.

Several nights he asked Frieda to stay with him, and she slept on the cane chair in his room. Dr Morland had failed to allow for the extent to which Lawrence's survival had been, for years already, a matter of will:

Morland 48   I wish now that I had never urged him to go to Vence as I am afraid my efforts only made his last weeks more unhappy.

Lawrence wrote only one thing at the Ad Astra, his review of Eric Gill's *Art Nonsense*. According to Frieda:

Powell 65   Lawrence wrote this unfinished review a few days before he died. The book interested him, and he agreed with much in it. Then he got tired of writing and I persuaded him not to go on. It is the last thing he wrote.

It was written, like his earliest writings, in a child's exercise book. Lawrence intended to write an essay when he had finished the review. Halfway through the book he wrote the title: 'God and Art'. The rest is blank.

On 24 February H. G. Wells visited Lawrence ('a common temporary soul'), and, three days later, the Aga Khan:

The last letter Lawrence wrote was to Earl Brewster on 24 February 1930. It ended: 'Jo Davidson came and made a clay head of me – made me tired – result in clay mediocre.'

Moore 1246

Today the Aga Khan came with his wife – I liked him – a bit of real religion in the middle of his fat face.

On 25 February Dr Morland wrote to Mark Gertler:

Morland 47

I have at last heard from Dr Medinier of Vence about Lawrence. I am afraid his report is none too good. Both lungs appear to be affected with moderate severity but it is his general condition which is causing the greatest amount of anxiety; his appetite is poor and he does not seem to be responding to treatment. It is obvious that his case is not suitable for any special treatment and that reliance will have to be placed on prolonged rest and good food. . . . I do not think much of French sanatoria and think that it would not be wise to urge him to stay on there very much longer.

In fact Lawrence had already decided to take a house in Vence, with an English nurse from Nice.

The move to the Villa Robermond took place on 1 March, in a shaking taxi. It was too much for Lawrence. That night Frieda sat by his bed singing to him the songs they had sung so many evenings in the past.

Frieda 308–9

The next day was a Sunday. 'Don't leave me,' he said, 'don't go away.' So I sat by his bed and read. He was reading the life of Columbus. After lunch he began to suffer very much and about tea-time he said: 'I must have a temperature, I am delirious. Give me the thermometer.' This is the only time, seeing his tortured face, that I cried, and he said: 'Don't cry,' in a quick, compelling voice. So I ceased to cry any more. He called Aldous and Maria Huxley who were there, and for the first time he cried out to them in his agony. 'I ought to have some morphine now,' he told me and my daughter, so Aldous went off to find a doctor to give him some. . . . Then he said: 'Hold me, hold me, I don't know where I am, I don't know where my hands are . . . where am I?' Then the doctor came and gave him a morphine injection. After a little while he said: 'I am better now, if I could only sweat I would be better . . .' and then again 'I am better now.' The minutes went by, Maria Huxley was in the room with me. I held his left ankle from time to time, it felt so full of life, all my days I shall hold his ankle in my hand.
He was breathing more peacefully, and then suddenly there were gaps in the breathing. The moment came when the thread of life tore in his heaving chest, his face changed, his cheeks and jaw sank, and death had taken hold of him . . .

✐

Phoenix 698

Do I fear the strange approach of the creative unknown to my door? I fear it only with pain and with unspeakable joy. And do I fear the invisible dark hand of death plucking me into the darkness, gathering me blossom by blossom from the stem of my life into the unknown of my afterwards? I fear it only in reverence and with strange satisfaction. For this is my final satisfaction, to be gathered blossom by blossom, all my life long, into the finality of the unknown which is my end.

✐

To E. M. Forster Frieda wrote:

Unpub.

Lawrence died so splendidly – inch by inch he fought and life with him never lost its glamour, not right to the end, when he asked for morphine and died without pain or struggle – He looked unconquered and fulfilled when he was dead, all the suffering smoothed out – If England ever produced a perfect rose, he was it, thorns and perfume and splendour – He has left me his love without a grudge, we had our grudges out; and from that other side, that I did not know before his death, he gives me his strength and his love for life – Don't feel sorry for me, it would be wrong, I am so rich, what woman has had what I have had? and now I have my grief – It's other people I pity, I can tell you, who never knew the glamour and wonder of things.

Frieda's was the finest epitaph:

Tedlock 106

What he had seen and felt and known he gave in his writing to his fellow men, the splendour of living, the hope of more and more life he had given them, a heroic and immeasurable gift.

Frieda 310

Then we buried him, very simply, like a bird we put him away, a few of us who loved him. We put flowers into his grave and all I said was: 'Goodbye Lorenzo' as his friends and I put lots and lots of mimosa on his coffin. Then he was covered over with earth while the sun came out on to his small grave in the little cemetery of Vence which looks over the Mediterranean that he cared for so much.

A local craftsman made a headstone with a phoenix in coloured pebbles.

Several months later Frieda returned to the ranch, accompanied by Angelo Ravagli, whom she later married. In 1934 Angie built a small white chapel on the hillside above the ranch, with a phoenix on top and windows like the sun. Brett decorated the interior. Lawrence's body was exhumed and cremated and his ashes brought there.

It is surely the right place, a spot which meant more to Lawrence than any other on earth.

References

Ada	*Young Lorenzo: Early Life of D. H. Lawrence*, Ada Lawrence and G. Stuart Gelder, Orioli, Florence, 1931.
Album	*Lady Ottoline's Album*, ed. Heilbrun, Knopf, New York, 1976.
Arnold	*The Symbolic Meaning*, ed. Arnold, Centaur, Arundel, 1962.
Asquith	*Diaries 1915–1918*, Lady Cynthia Asquith, Hutchinson, 1968.
Art	*The Art of D. H. Lawrence*, Keith Sagar, Cambridge, 1966.
Brett	*Lawrence and Brett: A Friendship*, Dorothy Brett, Santa Fe, 1974.
Brewster	*D. H. Lawrence: Reminiscences and Correspondence*, Earl and Achsah Brewster, Secker, 1934.
Bynner	*Journey with Genius*, Witter Bynner, Peter Nevill, 1953.
Carswell	*The Savage Pilgrimage*, Catherine Carswell, Chatto and Windus, 1932.
Centaur	*The Centaur Letters*, D. H. Lawrence, Texas, 1970.
Corke	*In Our Infancy*, Helen Corke, Cambridge, 1975.
Crosby	*Shadows of the Sun: The Diaries of Harry Crosby*, ed. Germain, Black Sparrow Press, Santa Barbara, 1977.
Davies	*Print of a Hare's Foot*, Rhys Davies, Heinemann, 1969.
Delany	*D. H. Lawrence's Nightmare*, Paul Delany, Harvester, 1979.
Delavenay 1	*D. H. Lawrence: L'Homme et la Genèse de son Oeuvre*, Emile Delavenay, Klicksieck, Paris, 1969.
Delavenay 2	*D. H. Lawrence: The Man and his Work*, Emile Delavenay, Heinemann, 1972.
Draper	*D. H. Lawrence: The Critical Heritage*, R. P. Draper, Routledge and Kegan Paul, 1970.
Eder	*David Eder: Memoirs of a Modern Pioneer*, ed. Hobman, Gollancz, 1945.
Frieda	*'Not I, But The Wind . . .'*, Frieda Lawrence, Santa Fe, 1934.
Gray	*Musical Chairs*, Cecil Gray, Home and Van Thal, 1948.
Huxley	*The Letters of D. H. Lawrence*, ed. Aldous Huxley, Heinemann, 1932.
Irvine	'D. H. Lawrence: Letters to Gordon and Beatrice Campbell', ed. Peter Irvine and Anne Kiley, *D. H. Lawrence Review*, Spring 1973.
Irvine 2	'D. H. Lawrence and Frieda Lawrence: Letters to Dorothy Brett', *D. H. Lawrence Review*, Spring 1976.
Jessie	*D. H. Lawrence: A Personal Record*, E. T. [Jessie Chambers], Cape, 1935; Cass, 1965.
Kot	*The Quest for Rananim: D. H. Lawrence's Letters to S. S. Koteliansky*, ed. Zytaruk, Montreal and London, 1970.

Lacy   *The Escaped Cock*, D. H. Lawrence, ed. Gerald M. Lacy, Black Sparrow Press, Los Angeles, 1973.

Letters 1   *The Letters of D. H. Lawrence*, Vol. 1, ed. James T. Boulton, Cambridge, 1979.

Look!   *Look! We Have Come Through!*, D. H. Lawrence, Ark Press, Marazion, 1958.

Lowell   *Amy Lowell: A Chronicle*, S. Foster Damon, Houghton Mifflin, Boston and New York, 1935.

Lucas   *Frieda Lawrence*, Robert Lucas, New York, 1973.

Luhan   *Lorenzo in Taos*, Mabel Dodge Luhan, Knopf, New York, 1932.

Mackenzie   *My Life and Times, Octave Five*, Compton Mackenzie, Chatto and Windus, 1966.

Mansfield   *Katherine Mansfield's Letters to John Middleton Murry*, Constable, 1951.

Marsh   *A Number of People*, Edward Marsh, Hamilton, 1939.

Merrild   *A Poet and Two Painters*, Knud Merrild, Routledge, 1938.

Miscellany   *A D. H. Lawrence Miscellany*, ed. Moore, Southern Illinois, 1959.

Mohr   'Briefe an Max Mohr', *Die Neue Rundschau* 44, April 1933.

Moore   *The Collected Letters of D. H. Lawrence*, ed. Harry T. Moore, Heinemann, 1962.

Morland   'The Last Days of D. H. Lawrence: Hitherto Unpublished Letters of Dr Andrew Morland', ed. Zytaruk, *D. H. Lawrence Review*, Spring 1968.

Murry 1   *Reminiscences of D. H. Lawrence*, John Middleton Murry, Cape, 1933.

Murry 2   *Between Two Worlds*, John Middleton Murry, Cape, 1935.

Nehls 1,2,&3   *D. H. Lawrence: A Composite Biography*, Edward Nehls, Wisconsin, 1957–1959. Three vols.

Ottoline   *Ottoline at Garsington*, ed. Robert Gathorne-Hardy, Faber and Faber, 1974.

Phoenix   *Phoenix: The Posthumous Papers of D. H. Lawrence*, ed. Edward McDonald, Heinemann, 1936.

Phoenix 2   *Phoenix II*, D. H. Lawrence, ed. Roberts and Moore, Heinemann, 1968.

Poems   *The Complete Poems of D. H. Lawrence*, ed. Pinto and Roberts, Heinemann, 1964.

Powell   *The Manuscripts of D. H. Lawrence*, Lawrence Clark Powell, Los Angeles, 1937.

Priest   *The Priest of Love*, Harry T. Moore, Heinemann, 1974.

Russell   *D. H. Lawrence's Letters to Bertrand Russell*, ed. Moore, Gotham Book Mart, New York, 1948.

Schorer   'I Will Send Address', Mark Schorer, *London Magazine*, February 1956.

Secker   *Letters from D. H. Lawrence to Martin Secker*, Secker, 1970.

Seltzer   *D. H. Lawrence Letters to Thomas and Adele Seltzer*, ed. Lacy, Black Sparrow Press, Santa Barbara, 1976.

Skinner   *The Fifth Sparrow*, M. L. Skinner, Angus and Robertson, 1973.

Tedlock   *Frieda Lawrence: The Memoirs and Correspondence*, ed. Tedlock, Heinemann, 1961.

Wilkinsons   'Lawrence and the Wilkinsons', Keith Sagar, *Review of English Literature*, October 1962.

Young   'Three Separate Ways: Unpublished D. H. Lawrence Letters to Francis Brett Young', Keith Sagar, *Review of English Literature*, July 1965.

Sources of Pictures

Index

WORKS OF
D. H. LAWRENCE

FICTION